A Case Study Approach to Educational Leadership

A Case Study Approach to Educational Leadership takes on six core areas of school leadership—organizational vision; curriculum, instruction, and assessment; school and external community; school climate and culture; equity; and improvement, innovation, and reform. Using a case learning approach, this volume introduces salient theoretical and empirical literature in each core area and provides illustrative cases designed for individual and group analysis. Written for aspiring educational leaders, this book facilitates the discussion and reflection of individual and collective professional judgment and helps developing leaders make sense of the challenges school leaders face today.

Special Features:

- **Featured Cases** direct readers toward the issues of practice embedded within the theoretical content area
- Linkage to relevant **Professional Standards for Educational Leaders (PSEL) standards** ground each chapter in the latest guidelines for the field
- **Discussion Questions** foster reflection of content and practical applications
- **Leadership Activities** and **Web-Based Resources** support leaders in making further connections to practice

Sharon D. Kruse is Academic Director and Professor of Educational Leadership at Washington State University Vancouver, USA.

Julie A. Gray is Assistant Professor of Educational Leadership at the University of West Florida, USA.

A Case Study Approach to Educational Leadership

Sharon D. Kruse and Julie A. Gray

Routledge
Taylor & Francis Group

NEW YORK AND LONDON

First published 2019
by Routledge
711 Third Avenue, New York, NY 10017

and by Routledge
2 Park Square, Milton Park, Abingdon, Oxon, OX14 4RN

Routledge is an imprint of the Taylor & Francis Group, an informa business

© 2019 Taylor & Francis

Library of Congress Cataloging-in-Publication Data
Names: Kruse, Sharon D., author. | Gray, Julie A., author.
Title: A case study approach to educational leadership / by Sharon D. Kruse and Julie A. Gray.
Description: New York : Routledge, 2018.
Identifiers: LCCN 2018006562| ISBN 9781138091061 (Hardback) |
ISBN 9781138091078 (Paperback) | ISBN 9781315108308 (eBook) |
ISBN 9781315108308 (Master) | ISBN 9781351609661 (Web PDF) |
ISBN 9781351609654 (ePub) | ISBN 9781351609647 (Mobi/Kindle)
Subjects: LCSH: Educational leadership—United States—Case studies. |
School management and organization—United States—Case studies.
Classification: LCC LB2805 .K69 2018 | DDC 371.2—dc23
LC record available at https://lccn.loc.gov/2018006562

ISBN: 978-1-138-09106-1 (hbk)
ISBN: 978-1-138-09107-8 (pbk)
ISBN: 978-1-315-10830-8 (ebk)

Typeset in Sabon and Helvetica
by Florence Production, Stoodleigh, Devon, UK

For Paul Karlin, for whose wisdom and respect I am eternally grateful.

(SDK)

To my parents, Bob and Maggie Gray, and Grandmother Josie Saxon, who taught me the value of hard work, dedication, persistence, and life-long learning. They were my first teachers and outstanding role models.

(JAG)

Contents

Detailed Contents

Preface

A Case Study Approach to Educational Leadership promotes three key theoretical ideals. First, the volume is rooted in a *social justice orientation* to school leadership. We have explicitly included a chapter on equity leadership. However, a social justice leadership orientation pervades each chapter of the volume. Our cases and examples purposefully address issues of gender, race, ethnicity, disability, and sexual orientation, highlighting the charged and critical issues school leaders face in today's schools. Second, we embrace the notion that *improvement*, at all levels of the school organization, is required for schools to be just, effective, and responsive to student growth. While we have included a chapter that specifically addresses improvement and change, we also feature improvement work prominently within each chapter of the book. This focus is purposeful because the landscape of school leaders' work is constantly changing and an improvement focus provides the foundations necessary for success. Finally, we take the stance that *leadership is communal work*. To this end, we stress distributed, shared, and intensified leadership models throughout our discussion of what it takes to lead today's schools.

This volume takes on six core areas of leadership practice—organizational vision; instruction, curriculum, and assessment; school and external community; school culture and internal community; equity; and improvement, innovation, and reform. Utilizing a case learning approach, this book introduces relevant theory and frames current, relevant problems of practice, allowing students to use their understanding of theory to analyze salient case data and detail. We have organized the book around cases because we believe that case learning creates opportunities for students to bring their collective experience to the table—reflecting on their individual and collective professional judgment and making decisions regarding how best to act.

INSTRUCTIONAL METHODOLOGY

We approached this work from the stance that developing professional judgment requires that students not only read theory but that they apply it. Our thinking is based on the argument that school leaders enter the profession with a great deal of *a priori* (i.e., knowing about) knowledge. Yet, this knowledge does not immediately translate into effective leadership (i.e., *knowing how* or *a posteriori* knowledge). We believe that leadership skills are honed as a student of school leadership reconciles the knowledge learned from engaging in leadership activity (*knowing how*) with the working knowledge used to inform this act (*knowing about*). We suggest that case learning bridges this gap. By creating learning experiences that link theory and practice, and new and prior knowledge by drawing on individual and collective understanding, leadership learning is enhanced. As leaders braid their 'knowing how' and 'knowing about' knowledge in effective ways, they are better prepared to make sense of and within their school organizations. Cases provide prospective leaders the opportunity to practice this skill set.

AUDIENCE

A Case Study Approach to Educational Leadership is appropriate for aspiring school leaders, students in leadership preparation programs, and teacher and administrative leadership Master's degree students. The volume is equally appropriate for introductory and capstone courses. Read as part of an introductory course, students will learn the breadth of theories that inform our field and the practice of school leadership. Read as a part of a capstone experience, students can revisit key themes of leadership practice and use the cases to reflect on their own leadership experiences. Likewise, the volume would be appropriate for use as part of mentoring and coaching academies for new principals and other school leaders.

BOOK FEATURES AND ORGANIZATION

The book includes several important features. Chapters include linkages to relevant Professional Standards for Educational Leaders (PSEL) standards, a feature case to focus the reader, an overview of theory, practice cases, resources, and activities. The goal is to provide the reader an opportunity to build professional leadership practice through explicitly presented content-driven and research-based knowledge.

After a brief introduction, a feature case is provided that directs the reader toward the issues of practice embedded within the theoretical content area addressed throughout the chapter. The IPLAN model is introduced in Chapter 1 and encourages students to attend to the issues of each case including the people explicitly and implicitly affected by the issues of the case, the ways theory is linked to problem solving and decision making, how subsequent decisions might be assessed and evaluated, and where next steps for action and planning might be developed. The IPLAN case learning model is designed so that students will learn a process by which they can approach their own leadership challenges.

Following the feature case, each chapter includes a synthesis of current theory and research, providing students with necessary content and theory to make sense of leadership practices in schools. Each chapter includes three shorter cases and discussion questions designed to foster individual and communal reflection concerning content learning and practical leadership applications. Finally, each chapter concludes with additional, related leadership activities and Web-based resources to support aspiring and practicing school leaders.

FINAL THOUGHTS

Our goal in writing this volume was to assist classroom instructors and leadership workshop providers toward developing leaders who can make sense of their schools today. *A Case Study Approach to Educational Leadership* is purposefully focused on current issues and challenges school leaders face. We have not shied away from confronting issues of social justice, equity and inclusion, and controversy. In fact, the cases we present were chosen because they reflect the complexity of school leadership in today's schools. They are all based on real school events and happenings. All have been written in ways that protect the schools, leaders, and teachers from whom we gathered our data. All the names we use are pseudonyms and quotes have been edited to remove identifying information and data. We still, however, have remained faithful to the core of these stories and are grateful to the many school leaders and teachers who took time to assist us in the preparation of case material.

Acknowledgments

Many thanks to the College of Education at Washington State University, my Dean Michael Trevisan, and my Vice Chancellor Renny Christopher. Their support for my work is invaluable. Thanks also to the many teachers, principals, and superintendents who contributed their stories to this volume. The work educators do matters to the children who attend the schools in which they work and to the communities in which we all live. My appreciation for them extends beyond what they contributed to this work.

Sharon D. Kruse

A million thanks to my mentors, colleagues, and students, all of whom I learned a great deal from over the years. I am forever indebted to and thankful for my mentors, C. John Tarter, Sharon D. Kruse, and Roxanne M. Mitchell. I am also grateful for their mentors, Wayne K. Hoy, Karen Seashore Louis, and Patrick B. Forsyth. All have taught me much in their examples of dedication, loyalty, integrity, and support.

Julie Anne Gray

CHAPTER 1

Learning via the Case Method

On any given day, in any given school or school district, hundreds, if not thousands, of large and small events occur. These events include people—students, teachers, parents, and support staff. They occur in specific places—classrooms, playgrounds, meetings, and within grade levels, departments, and schools. At other times the setting includes the district, the community, and perhaps the region or state. Plots unfold. He did what? Who knew? When did it occur? And then what happened? Eventually, resolution is achieved. Often those involved question the results, the process by which issues were resolved, the rewards conferred, and the consequences dealt. Adding to the complexity of a given event is the truism that each event is unavoidably experienced from multiple and differing viewpoints. Sometimes a practical lesson is learned. Often new issues arise because of unaddressed factors or unintended consequences.

Leadership choices and decisions impact those directly involved with the issue and others in the school who are aware of the incident. Each time an event occurs, no matter how small, it offers an opportunity to lead and to learn. Often, our responses become stories that are told and retold as part of the narrative of who we are. These stories help to shape the culture of our schools as well as the subcultures within them. Stories with positive endings contribute to healthy workplaces. Stories that surface conflict and disagreement, or betrayal and duplicity undermine our work.

Case learning is the purposeful study of these organizational stories—narratives, accounts, vignettes, explanations, tall tales, and rumors all contribute to case learning. By breaking our stories down, by studying the events, the people, their choices, and considering what knowledge and skills might be brought to bear on the situation, we can learn how to better lead our own schools.

KEY LEARNINGS

In this chapter, you will learn how to:

- apply the educational leadership knowledge-base and practical skill-set to real world problems of practice as presented in cases;
- frame primary and secondary issues, surfacing the complexity of leadership; and
- make practical and theory-based recommendations for leadership practice and examine those recommendations for utility in the world of leadership work.

HILLTOP PUBLIC SCHOOLS

As will be true in each chapter, we begin by offering a brief case to illustrate these important learning outcomes. A small suburban district located in the Midwest, the Hilltop Public Schools serve just over 5,000 students in grades K-12. Home to three elementary schools, two middle schools, and one comprehensive high school, Hilltop is located within a well-known tornado corridor. Generally speaking, the threat of a tornado varies by season and the presence of warm, humid air. In Hilltop, the risk seems greatest in the early spring.

So, when one March evening a storm warning went out, no one was surprised or alarmed. In the next few hours, gusting winds, heavy rains, and hail battered the community. Yet, the storm passed quickly and it appeared damage would be limited to downed trees and localized power outages. As district policy recommended, the superintendent's first call was to the police chief inquiring about potential damage to area schools and property. Expecting minor issues, Superintendent Nick Allyn jokingly began the call asking, "So you'll have us cleaned up and ready to go by morning, right?" The response, "Ah, no. I'll have a cruiser by in a bit."

Within the hour, Allyn learned that a middle school had lost over 65 percent of its roof structure and that the high school athletic fields, including the newly installed football field, had sustained significant damage. Schools were immediately cancelled for the next day. The administrative team was called to report to the district office first thing in the morning. When the team of principals, assistant superintendents, and support staff assembled, the boardroom had been transformed. A series of questions were displayed on poster boards. Each posed a question focused on a different stakeholder group: If I were a parent, what would I want to know? What would I care about? How is the best way to get information to this group? If I were a teacher, what would be important to me? If I were a bus driver, and so on. Over two dozen boards were ready for team problem solving.

The magnitude of the work facing the team was evident. What sobered the group even further was Allyn's announcement that the priority of this first day was to provide as much information to parents, teachers, and community members as they could within the first three hours. They would follow the initial announcement with hourly updates providing the community with additional information the administrative team believed would be accurate, reassuring, and explanatory. As we will see in the coming discussion, employing this inclusive and outward facing frame, set the stage for successful school reopening and rebuilding. Before looking into how Hilltop Schools resolved this dilemma, we will discuss how case learning is best used to enhance leadership learning.

CASE LEARNING

Case learning is an effective, but underutilized, pedagogical tool that allows learners to both apply theoretical understandings and transfer experiential knowledge to a problem of practice (Anderson & Schiano, 2014). In case learning, students are presented with a carefully crafted narrative that focuses attention on one or more organizational issues. As we do in this book, cases are often accompanied by salient research and theory to aid the learner in making sense of the issue or issues a case presents. Then learners are able to apply their new knowledge, in concert with their prior professional and personal experience, to the case at hand. The tandem application of theory and research, to practical problems derived from authentic settings and concerns, underscores case learning. Best known as a model of teaching in business and law schools across the nation, case learning makes the development of professional knowledge a collaborative and collegial venture (Ellet, 2007).

The educational leadership literature has long suggested that the days of a single, heroic, school leader are long past, and that effective leadership incorporates the knowledge and skills of teachers (Kruse & Louis, 2009; Stoll & Louis, 2007), parents (Bolivar & Chrispeels, 2011; Hamlin & Flessa, 2016), and the community (Ishimaru, 2012; Lopez, Kreider, & Coffman, 2005). High quality educational leadership must be intentionally and purposefully intensified and collaborative. Intensifying leadership acknowledges that there are already multiple leaders in any school setting, including formal leaders—elected union representatives, grade level and department chairs, assistant and associate principals, deans of students, club advisors, and athletic directors—and informal leaders—well-regarded teachers, influential parents, and long-standing veterans of the faculty. To intensify leadership suggests that teachers, parents, and influential members of the school community must work together to coordinate their efforts. Doing so creates an environment that fosters attention on the work that matters for school success. Not doing so creates disharmony and confusion.

Case learning is supported by research across a variety of fields. As is highlighted by the work of Green (2005), Hargreaves and Fink (2006), and Vogus and Sutcliffe (2012), the practice of leadership in schools and businesses alike capitalizes on the talents, skills, and knowledge of others to produce effective, high-quality results. In the classroom, learning is enhanced by discussion, reflection on one's prior understandings, and the experiences and thinking of others. Like the work of school principals and other school leaders, case learning makes public the problem-solving process, requiring the contributions of many voices to create meaningful and shared understandings.

This approach is well aligned with recent research in educational leadership. As Bryk, Sebring, Allensworth, Luppescu, and Easton (2009), Leithwood, Louis, Anderson, and Wahlstrom (2004), and Ray, Baker, and Plowman (2011) suggest, understanding the problems facing school leaders today is less about the use of precise diagnostic tools, and more about recognizing and responding to the patterns of activity that occur day-to-day within the school organization. Recognizing patterns and linking them to explanatory theory takes practice. Pattern recognition requires multiple exposures to organizational situations, as well as numerous opportunities to consider and plan a response or responses (Brown, Roediger, & McDaniel, 2014). Case learning provides such an opportunity.

Additionally, working collegially does not come naturally. Case learning creates opportunities for prospective and current school leaders to bring their collective experience to the table allowing each to test, through reflection and discussion, their individual and collective professional judgment regarding how best to act. Developing professional judgment requires that leaders not only read theory, but that they apply it. Case learning poses questions for the learner to consider. What do I know? How do I know it? In what contexts do these actions and practices have the greatest potential for success? What is my guiding rationale? What is the purpose of and for my decision-making? Who is affected? What are the potential consequences of my actions and for whom are these consequences greatest? Exploring these questions, and others like them, enhances leadership learning and practice.

HILLTOP SCHOOLS REVISITED

In many ways, Hilltop Schools, under the leadership of Allyn, took a case learning approach to problem resolution. By focusing on the questions of importance to others, district leaders were able to frame the issues in multiple ways and through multiple lenses. Clearly, the primary problem facing Hilltop was assessing the damage and determining when and how school can resume. Superintendent Allyn recognized he had options regarding how to frame this core issue. As Allyn shared,

> We had two choices—we could talk about this as an issue of reopening school or we could talk about it as an issue of finding a way to provide a quality learning environment for students. We chose the second. I think, in the long run we did it because it fit with our mission and vision around student learning. I also think we chose the second because, oddly, it was easier. When we started, we didn't know much about the building structures but we could talk about kids and learning. We knew how to do that. It made that first day less strange.

The leadership team proceeded from the assumption that the middle school building would be unusable for the foreseeable future. However, the district was already pressed for space, so simply moving classes to another site was not a possibility. Briefly, the team considered rescheduling options. Could the high school schedule be shifted to accommodate the middle school? Could the second middle school double shift? Could a split shift option be developed? Would co-teaching offer relief? One by one these options were dismissed. Using the high school—too difficult. Second shift at the middle school—a transportation nightmare. Split shifting—too disruptive for student learning. Co-teaching—a potential but not a robust enough solution to address the magnitude of the problem.

Finally, it was determined that the district's best option was to seek space outside of existing district buildings. As Deidre Betts, the business manager, described, "We could look to neighboring districts for space, but we knew that was unlikely to provide what we needed, or start asking at local churches, or approach area businesses to see what they might offer." None of these options felt perfect. Additionally, the group questioned how they might consider reorganizing the students. If they couldn't relocate the school in its entirely, how might they break it up? Would it make the most sense to keep the fifth and sixth grades in one location, the seventh and eighth in another? What about science labs? How would health, physical education, music, and foreign language instruction teachers who taught across multiple grades be best handled?

Additional issues faced the district, as well. Included in the list of questions the group generated were those related to students and their families. How might the district assure student safety once school reopened? How would health services, school breakfast and lunch, after-school tutoring, and special education be provided? What about school sports and other extra-curricular activities? The administrative team knew that teachers would be concerned about when and where they should report back to work. Safely removing personal and district teaching materials from the school was a pressing issue. The science teachers were worried about classroom pets and lab materials. The complexity of the situation was quickly becoming overwhelming.

COMPLEXITY AND CASE LEARNING

Leaders, whether in a school setting or elsewhere, are frequently faced with complex problems that are emotionally and cognitively demanding. For students in leadership programs, it is critical for them to learn how to engage with and competently face such situations. Consideration of a problem, within the setting of case-based learning, provides opportunities for students to engage with others in solving the types of multi-faceted problems commonly encountered by leaders in real work settings. Richards (2015) describes the problem-solving process as "inevitably a creative learning process" (p. 79). This process allows students to hone their reasoning, communication, and problem-solving skills while simultaneously developing deep content knowledge related to their future craft. Bridges and Hallinger (1996) also assert that through engagement in problem-based learning students will learn to build consensus, implement solutions, and face the emotional side of leadership. Such skills are critical for school leaders.

In their review of leadership development programs, Bridges and Hallinger (1996) share that traditional approaches have focused on the passive learning of theory without an emphasis on more active and realistic activities that allow learners to thrive.

Engagement in the active development of solutions to complex problems, rather than the passive listening often observed during lectures, are the times when students learn best. Shared and collaborative learning experiences increase student engagement (Gray & DiLoreto, 2016; Jennings & Angelo, 2006) as learning is socially constructed (Vygotsky, 1978). According to Bridges and Hallinger (1997), one critical benefit of this active-learning approach is that students are provided with a realistic preview of what it means to be a school leader. They further state that learners not only acquire relevant skills, they also experience "what a leader does and how a leader feels" (p. 137).

FEATURES OF PROBLEM-FOCUSED CASE-BASED LEARNING

To create an environment where students acquire leadership skills, problem-focused case-based learning adopts three primary features: a learner-centered approach, the instructor serving as a facilitator, and the centrality of ill-structured problems.

Learner-Centered Approaches

The learner-centered aspect of problem-based learning, according to Savery (2006), empowers participants to integrate theory and practice, as well as apply knowledge and skills while they engage in research focused on a problem of practice. When engaging with a shared problem, learners must be aware of both what they already know and what additional information they need to know about the problem as well as which strategies should be used to solve the problem. As learners work collaboratively with others, they are provided multiple opportunities to manage group dynamics (Jennings & Angelo, 2006) and practice key leadership skills. Furthermore, working in groups allows students to demonstrate understanding and respect for their peers and develop their communication and listening skills. Collaboration also provides students opportunities to reflect on their own development as leaders (de Graaff & Kolmos, 2003).

Facilitation of Learning

In contrast to traditional teaching methods, the instructor in problem-based learning activities plays the role of a facilitator for participants. Modeling inquiry strategies and guiding the learning process are two key functions of the instructor during problem-based learning (Savery, 2006). The instructor also provides scaffolds for students that allow them to develop a variety of skills such as problem-solving, self-directed learning, and collaboration. Bridges and Hallinger (1997) further suggest that an instructor should observe the active learning process and clarify issues as students engage in problem-solving opportunities. Debriefing with students throughout and at the end of each learning experience is also a key role of the instructor (Bridges & Hallinger, 1997; Savery, 2006). In other words, instructors do not provide answers in problem-focused case-based learning. Instead, they serve to guide students to unpack the issues that are proposed within the case, consider salient explanatory theory, and generate a myriad of potential responses and solutions to the issue at hand.

III-Structured Problems

Central to case learning are ill-structured problems. Complex and authentic, case learning poses problems that may be encountered in the world beyond the classroom, and problems for which there are no simple answers. Bridges and Hallinger (1996) describe an ill-structured problem as "a typically messy situation that students are likely to encounter in their future professional practice" (p. 55). The problems at the core of case-based learning are often interdisciplinary in that the problems, and their solutions, cut across many aspects of school leadership (Bridges & Hallinger, 1996; Savery, 2006). This multifaceted feature, according to Bridges and Hallinger (1996), reflects genuine situations that leaders face as they use knowledge from many domains to address problems.

Case learning that includes these three key features provides students with opportunities to take responsibility for their own learning and develop their leadership skills. Both de Graaff and Kolmos (2003) and Bridges and Hallinger (1997) assert that problem-based learning activities motivate learners through peer interaction, promote critical thinking skills, and simulate the job of a school leader. Richards (2015) states that "problem-based learning exemplifies as well as encourages the kind of approach needed to address the increasingly complex and diverse 'wicked' problems facing the world in every aspect of both the social and natural domains of human life and activity" (p. 94). For all of these reasons, case- and problem-based learning is a solid approach for developing a variety of skills and mindsets critical to competently face the complicated and complex issues frequently encountered by school leaders.

HILLTOP SCHOOLS REDUX

Clearly, Hilltop School personnel were facing a wicked problem. First theorized by Rittel and Webber (1973), a wicked problem is one that is difficult to solve for at least four reasons: incomplete or contradictory knowledge, the difficulty of measuring success, direct and indirect costs, and the interconnectedness of the current problem to other problems. Central to Hilltop's wicked problem was the district's concern for student learning. Yet, student learning is linked to student safety, safety is linked to personal and legal concerns, learning is linked to classroom materials and resources, and resources are linked to the district's ability to mobilize the means to respond. As Horst and Webber identified, wicked problems have no definitive formulation. The problem of re-creating an optimal environment for student learning is similar across grade levels, but is discretely different when individual need is considered, so no one solution could satisfy. Simply put, at this juncture, the team did not have enough knowledge to fully identify all the aspects of the problem they faced. Second, they knew that as they began to address initial issues, others would surface.

Furthermore, the team was aware that success is hard to measure when solving a wicked problem. In the case of Hilltop, success could be measured in any number of ways—relocating students and teachers, and reopening the middle school in a timely fashion were important measures. However, other measures were equally important. As the middle school principal Paula Oldham noted, "Getting kids into classrooms couldn't be enough, we needed to be sure they were learning in those classrooms, and that all kids were getting their needs met." Assistant Principal Thom Lee added,

> We also needed to be sure that we were creating a learning environment that feltgood. We needed a space that was quiet enough to learn, but also had spaces for kids to be kids. I didn't want our kids and families to feel like they couldn't be themselves.

Finally, Superintendent Allyn defined success as, "how the community thought we handled this, I didn't want the district's reputation to suffer."

As the leadership team moved through the first days of addressing the problems facing them, they continued to balance their attentions between locating a physical space where the middle school might open with attention to the needs of those impacted. In many ways, district officials attended to the work of leadership by concentrating on both tasks and relationships. By concentrating on the task of locating new school sites, analyzing damage, and developing new transportation and schooling plans, leadership prioritized those tasks that would assure a timely reopening of school. By focusing on interactions with the community, teachers, parents, and students, leadership emphasized the importance of relationships both internal and external. As Superintendent Allyn, noted:

> I didn't want to come out of this angering more folks than I needed to. I knew people were going to be inconvenienced; you can't move an entire school without disrupting people's lives. Routine matters to our families. The bus needs to get there at the same time each day. So that was important. But also important was getting everyone to the place where learning was happening again.

In the end, Hilltop managed to secure space in three separate locations. The fifth grade was relocated to classrooms in a local church basement. The sixth grade was housed in a second church nearby. It was decided that, although imperfect, a combination of double shifting and co-teaching larger classes at the still intact middle school provided the best learning environment for seventh and eighth graders. As principal Paula Oldham said, "We only needed to get to the end of the year. We adopted the 'we can do anything for four months' stance. And we did."

Over the summer the middle school was rerooftop and the school fully cleaned. The district used the opportunity to make a few updates to the building, modernizing classroom lighting, carpets, and paint. As the assistant superintendent remarked, "Would I wish this on anyone? No. Did we handle as well as we could? I believe we did."

ANALYZING CASES

We now turn to thinking about how a case such as this might be analyzed to create an optimum learning situation for prospective and current school leaders. We begin by discussing three forms of reasoning one might bring to bear on case learning. We argue here that cases can be approached from three general reasoning orientations—inductive, deductive, and abductive.

Inductive Reasoning

Inductive reasoning takes specific ideas and generalizes them to larger understandings. Inductively, one can make observations based on the data at hand, seek patterns within those data, generalize from those patterns to new situations, and infer an explanation or theory of action that may be employed elsewhere. Working from the inductive, students can draw from their own experiences in schools to develop theories about what has occurred and what might be a best response.

In this way, inductive reasoning favors tacit knowledge—commonly held truths that are often acquired through experience and practice. Tacit knowledge is hard to quantify or write down and extremely difficult to teach. Intuition, humor, emotional intelligence or one's ability to read body language are all examples of tacit knowledge in practice. Tacit knowledge is often expressed as "knowing just what to do" or the "secret sauce" of leadership.

Yet, reliance on inductive reasoning and tacit knowledge can fail us. Inductively we can draw incorrect conclusions—even when all the premises we are using are correct. For example, one could observe the following true statements about Maria. Maria's hair is gray. Maria is a grandmother. Maria likes to garden. To conclude that therefore all gray-haired women are grandmothers, or that all grandmothers like to garden would be false, but could be logically induced from the data provided. Our tacit knowledge might confirm that yes, my grandmother was gray-haired and she gardened. Yet, we could quickly test our theory concerning gray-haired, gardening grandmothers beyond our own experience and realize our folly.

As such, inductive reasoning alone is inadequate for substantive leadership decision making. However, inductive reasoning has its place in problem solving and decision making. It allows us to develop hypotheses and suppositions that test if what we know about the specific applies more generally. Where we run into problems is when we inductively rely on our tacit knowledge and fail to test our conclusions. For example, we may inductively conclude, based on our prior experience, any number of misconceptions about students and their families. When we fail to consider that our tacit knowledge may be faulty or that we have drawn an incorrect conclusion, as leaders, we compromise our ability to attain our goals.

Deductive Reasoning

Deductive reasoning is the opposite of inductive reasoning. Deductive thinking starts with the general and applies that understanding to the specific. In deductive reasoning, when something is true for a class of things in general, it is also true for all members of that class. For example, if we consider human beings to encompass the general class we are examining, we can deduce at least two shared truths about specific individuals or groups within that class—namely, all human beings experience birth and death. So, we can state with certainty that if Alice is a human being, she has experienced birth and will, ultimately, be mortal.

Deductive reasoning allows us to apply empirical theory and research to situations we encounter. Deductive knowledge relies on more than tacit knowledge; it requires that we are able to state what we know and prove that our understandings hold true under examination. Deductive reasoning allows us to ask how theory and research helps us to understand the issues and circumstance that we face. It allows us to unpack that which confronts us through theoretical and empirical lenses, creating opportunity for learning and deeper understanding.

When we consider leadership learning and practice, deductive reasoning holds that we acknowledge the patterns we observe and test our thinking for veracity. Yet, in leadership work generally, and in educational leadership specifically, there are few universal truths. Our world is not a clear-cut place and our ability to deduce how we should act is limited. Furthermore, when we use theory as the sole lens through which we analyze case material, we forgo opportunities for creative and novel framings and solutions.

Abductive Reasoning

Unlike deductive reasoning and inductive reasoning, abductive reasoning acknowledges that in any given situation we often have incomplete and imperfect information. Abductive reasoning acknowledges the wicked problem. Our knowledge base may be lacking, or, as in the case of Hilltop, we simply cannot know all that is yet to confront us. Abductive reasoning takes what we do know and asks that we proceed to the most likely explanation for what is occurring. It acknowledges that all schools are not alike, but that similarities can be identified. Furthermore, abductive reasoning suggests that where a critical mass of similarities exists, we can draw a reasonable conclusion that our situation is enough like another so that we might move forward in a similar fashion.

Doctors use abductive reasoning to make an initial and best-first diagnosis. Given a set of symptoms, doctors draw conclusions as to the most likely illness the patient is experiencing and offers treatment accordingly. It is possible that muscle stiffness and fatigue is a result of Lyme disease rather than a weekend marathon or that a sore wrist is really arthritis instead of computer over-use, but each is unlikely. Abductive reasoning suggests that we apply knowledge that we know to be true, articulated, and provable to the circumstances at hand and draw probable conclusion. It is the application of Occam's Razor—the simplest explanation is also most likely to be the correct explanation.

Abductive reasoning allows for multiple explanations and conclusions. For example, if we observe that our coffee is cold, we could explain this in several ways. We may have left it sitting too long, our coffee maker might be broken, or someone may have intentionally added ice. We would need further data to arrive at a correct conclusion. In this way, abductive reasoning also suggests that we hold our conclusions up for examination, accepting the fact that we may, just this once, be incorrect.

Finally, abductive reasoning allows for the creative solution. When we acknowledge that there are potentially multiple explanations and analyses of any given occurrence, we open ourselves to serendipity. We are better able to learn from the ideas of others and to accept that our knowledge is limited and bounded. By looking beyond the obvious, abductive reasoning can open the door to imaginative and elegant responses to the problems we face.

We argue that it is important to consider inductive, deductive, and abductive reasoning when analyzing cases. In this way, it is possible to fully investigate where ideas may become developed and how understandings might be tested. At its core, case learning allows students to practice thinking broadly and deeply, to apply theory and research to issues at hand, and to surface our tacit knowledge as part of the learning process. To do so, we suggest that students consider the following questions when approaching case analysis. We have artificially divided them into questions that address each form of analysis. However, we acknowledge that in each case some overlap may occur.

Inductive Considerations

We suggest here that readers focus on the specific details of each case, clearly responding to the following questions:

- Who are the key players within the case?
- What happened?
- What are the key elements within the plot line or case narrative?
- What is the organizational context?
- How is this school or district like others you have studied or worked in?

Deductive Considerations

We suggest here that readers focus on how theory might inform your thinking about the case, clearly responding to the following questions:

- Have you articulated the important and key variables of the case and phenomena within the case demonstrating a thoughtful analysis of the material at hand?
- Why did events happen as they did?
- What are the leadership and organizational actions that influenced the events?
- How might theory be applied to understanding these events?
- What are several ideas that might be considered to make sense of the issues at hand?
- Have you offered a reasoned, evidence-based argument for a particular line of thinking or problem solving?
- If the argument is based on personal learning can it be supported by theoretical understandings?

Abductive Considerations

We suggest here that readers focus on broad applications of theory and practice that inform your thinking about the case, clearly responding to the following questions:

- What can be learned from this situation?
- How might a similar decision be faced in the future?

- Are the solutions and recommendations innovative and/or alternative solutions are posed and critically considered?

EVALUATING CASE LEARNING: USING IPLAN

It is important that the learner be able to formatively evaluate the quality and comprehensiveness of their learning as they move throughout this process. Additionally, while it is possible for case learning to be a solitary activity, as we have stressed, case learning is most effective when it is employed in a small group or problem-solving team. When team members are aware of the criteria that comprise a quality response they are able to push each other intellectually to better, more detailed, and theoretically dense thinking. We caution here that case learning is designed to foster divergent thinking. In this way, there is no one correct answer. Yet, when considered holistically and when attention is paid to multiple forms of reasoning, a strong foundation for case learning and leadership problem solving can be built. Outlined below, these evaluative strategies can be easily remembered by the mnemonic IPLAN.

I—Identification of issues
P—Players, perspectives, and positionality
L—Links to theory and research
A—Assessment and evaluation
N—Next steps, including action planning and attention to consequences

Before we learn about the IPLAN strategies, a note about them. The strategies are iterative rather than sequential and you may find yourself spending more time on one as opposed to another. Similarly, by focusing on each as a separate concern, it is possible to draw upon the strengths of a team, a particular theoretical understanding or approach, or to highlight areas of concern within the case scenario. Finally, at least as a mnemonic, "IPLAN" links leadership learning to practice. This is appropriate because it reminds us that the reason for engaging in leadership study is to *learn* about our schools and ourselves and to *plan* our leadership choices and decisions. We address the qualities of accomplished IPLAN responses below.

Identification of the Issues

Broadly, the identification of the issues within a case should describe those aspects of the case that are problematic. These may include concerns that may be managerial, legal, ethical, instructional, organizational, or financial. A case may include many overlapping and mutually informing issues or contain a few clear-cut yet, complex concerns. In any case, it is important that issues be identified in ways that focus thinking on the diagnosis of important strategic concerns and key problems. Descriptions of the issues at hand should be insightful and demonstrate a deep perceptive understanding. For example, in the case of Hilltop Schools, as we have noted, on the surface the issue the district faces is re-opening the middle school. Yet, to suggest that this is the sole issue is to miss other equally concerning issues including faithfulness to shared values and beliefs, concern for student learning environment, and the reputation of district leadership within the community.

We stress the importance of deeply exploring cases for the myriad of issues contained within for two important reasons. The first obvious reason concerns learning all that can be gleaned from the example at hand. While it is unlikely that many school leaders will face the exact same situation as Allyn in Hilltop or perhaps any of the leaders in this book, cases are designed for the reader to identify similarities and transferable learning. At some time in their tenure, all leaders will face a crisis of one sort or another. Remembering that any crisis presents a threat to personal and/or physical safety and the reputation of the organization and its members allows the reader to take away a key leadership lesson.

Second, leaders often fail when they neglect the less obvious aspects of issues. Think of a time when you were part of a situation that, on the surface, appeared to be resolved yet, no one involved felt satisfied with the outcome. It is possible that there were simply no good choices to be made. More probably, the primary issues were resolved but in doing so key organizational values were compromised, people's feelings ignored, or trust was violated. Doing so risks long-term possible negative outcomes. Getting it right is the mark of savvy leadership.

Players, Perspectives, and Positionalities

In every case, there are key players. These include those people explicitly included in the case description. At Hilltop, the superintendent and leadership team are obvious players in the case. Yet, every case also includes stakeholders who are not explicitly included. Implicit within the Hilltop case are teachers, students, and community members. Identifying, in an unambiguous fashion, who is engaged in the situation is an important first step for understanding all the issues a case presents.

Once clarity concerning the players is achieved, the perspectives of each should be surfaced. Perspective is the vantage point from which one regards any given situation. It is the point of view from which we approach how we make meaning. Perspective can be thought of as the way we see things. Positionality is generally defined as relational in nature. That is, positionality takes into account aspects of identity such as race, class, gender, and sexuality that are markers of relational position. Positionality suggests that who you are influences how you see things.

Surfacing, describing, discussing, and making public those aspects that position stakeholders and key players within a case make evident that there is no objective reading of the instances we face. By intentionally considering positionality, we are able to probe aspects of the context that may differ. Doing so allows us to examine conflicts of interest, strategic tensions, and inherent differences stakeholders bring to sense making. Here too, we note the importance of examining perspective and positionality as a learning tool and a leadership tool. One's ability to understand that others experience the world differently is a first step in leading with compassion and empathy.

Links to Theory and Research

A hallmark of high quality leadership learning is one's ability to make appropriate, discerning, and persuasive connections between the issues and problems within the case and relevant theory and research. Connecting our reading and thinking to the case at hand in a well-supported and well-justified argument enhances our ability to remember what we have learned and incorporate it into our leadership knowledge. Furthermore, a reader's ability to effectively integrate multiple sources of knowledge enhances long-term learning outcomes. In this way, transfer of new knowledge is enhanced.

Transfer is generally thought the ability to obtain knowledge and skills in one setting and apply them in another. Facilitated when new ideas are connected to older knowledge and skills, transfer is reinforced through application, reflection, and use. Yet, we know that transfer is hard. Situations do not always present themselves in ways that readily suggest what knowledge is needed. As time between the learning event and its application lengthens, understanding fades. We have all experienced being in a class, a workshop, or lecture and as we are listening to the speaker we feel we are gaining important new insights. Yet, when called upon, even a few hours later, our ability to remember even the most basic broad outlines of those ideas has begun to diminish. We may still be motivated by what we have heard, but we are hard pressed to recall it, let alone employ it.

By immediately and directly working to link our case analysis to theoretical knowledge we cement those understandings into a context that enhances our ability to recall them later. Moreover, doing so makes those ideas our own. The ability to present a balanced, in-depth, critical assessment of the facts of the case in light of relevant theoretical and empirical research helps us to develop insights and make reasoned, sound, and informed judgments. Theory offers a useful tool for understanding our work and practice, as well as the work and practice of others. As a leadership practice, employing sound theory and being able to justify your practice based on a solid theoretical foundation enhances your ability to feel confident in your choices and decisions.

Assessment and Evaluation

Tightly linked to connecting theory and research to our case thinking are the ways in which we go about assessing and evaluating the case presentation. This thinking is, intentionally, critical thinking. Whereas, identifying key players, plot lines, and central issues involves some employment of a critical lens, assessing and evaluating where significant decision points and actions calls upon your ability to think beyond what is presented within the case.

Critical thinking requires precision. Precision in one's thinking suggests that ideas are formulated using clarifying details, examples, and illustrations. Vital questions are raised and examined for their utility to enhance understanding. Relevant information is brought to bear on the issues at hand, and conclusions are tested against salient criteria and standards. One's assumptions are surfaced and examined, while intuition is rejected in favor of reason. Critical thinking asks that the thinker approach problems with curiosity, expressing a desire to learn something new and perhaps surprising. Critical thinkers are in many ways skeptical, uncertain, and doubting of the easy answer and unconvinced by attractive, but incomplete, solutions.

In short, when assessing and evaluating a case problem, critical thinkers take the long view, open-mindedly considering assumptions, implications, and practical consequences to arrive at conclusions that have logical consistence and theoretical support. Just as we strive to link assessment of learning to instruction in classrooms, we want to link the assessment of case data and evaluation of case issues and problems to the understandings we articulate and the solutions we pose. In the same way that evidence of student learning improves the instructional choices good teachers make, the provision of solid accurate and compelling evidence fosters the ability to learn from cases and to transfer that learning to leadership practice.

Next Steps

At times, it is enough to analyze a case for what it can teach us. In fact, purposely avoiding premature solution generation can deliberately focus learners and help them avoid the illusion that they already know the answer. It allows students the opportunity to practice intellectual discernment and see new situations in new ways.

Yet, there are times when it makes good sense for students to move forward with action planning and answer questions such as "What should be done?," "Who should do it?," "Who might be called upon to assist?," and "What is needed to make it happen?" High quality action plans identify a variety of alternative actions and identifies the benefits and limitations of each. By generating a variety of responses, students are able to effectively weigh choices and determine a best response solution. Posing a variety of responses allows students to weigh solutions against stated criteria and evaluate actions for their utility to address the central and secondary features of the case.

High quality action planning is detailed and realistic. That is, action plans attend to the ways in which recommendations can be implemented, potential costs of implementation, and where benefit is located and where limitations are present.

It poses the question, "What could possibly go wrong?" and seeks to explore how a leader would mitigate any negative consequences. Finally, the presentation of an action plan should include a well-reasoned justification as to why a particular course of action was recommended and the thinking on which the recommendation rests. Doing so brings the work full circle, attending to the issues the case raises as well as the theory and research that underscores exemplary leadership practice.

We would be remiss if we did not caution that every case need not include all of the above evaluative criteria and foci. For example, it may not be important that learners offer a plan of action in any given situation. It may be enough for readers to identify issues and salient theory for learning targets to be met. Additionally, we acknowledge that instructors might also wish to evaluate students on written and oral presentation of case learning, communication skills, linkage of key ideas to other course outcomes, and integration of learning into a comprehensive philosophy of leadership. Here we have chosen to stress criteria designed to direct the learner in ways that make the most out of their own efforts. At the conclusion of this chapter, we provide several rubrics that students and instructors could employ to formally evaluate learning.

CASES FOR ANALYSIS

Throughout the volume, we offer cases designed to build on the knowledge and skill set discussed in the chapter. We suggest that these initial cases be used as case learning practice, focusing on the process rather than the product of discussion.

CASE 1.1

To Spend or Not to Spend

As the end of the school year nears you discover that a significant amount of money, $25,000, is sitting in a grant account. The money must be spent within the next six months or be returned to the granting agency. Luckily, the granting agency has agreed that the money could be spent on professional development, classroom materials, or stipends for teachers to design new curriculum during the summer. To expedite matters, you decide to ask a few hand-selected faculty to design two or three choices concerning how to spend the money.

The small group of faculty meets several times and comes back with a single offering—a full faculty in-service offered by a national expert during the first week of July. You know from past experience that many teachers will not want to attend meetings during the summer months. On the other hand, you rationalize that those who do attend might benefit. Additionally, you see a potential benefit of having a group of well-educated faculty to lead in-house activity going forward. You begin to wonder if you should present this idea to the full staff and faculty, and perhaps even ask more teachers how they think the money could be spent. However, you are concerned that asking more opinions would further muddy the waters. How could something that seemed like such a great opportunity have become such a problem?

Discussing the Case

- Employ the inductive, deductive, and abductive question strategy to identify the key features, players, and issues in this scenario.
- Evaluate your thinking using the IPLAN model. Where did you excel? Where did you find your thinking lacking? In what ways might you approach future case learning differently?

CASE 1.2

___

How Much Is Too Much?

Stephanie Able, Superintendent of Midwinters Schools, describes herself as an engaged leader. She regularly attends school concerts, football and basketball games, and other district events. She makes it a practice to visit schools, in announced and unannounced visits, dropping in on classrooms, attending faculty meetings, and sitting in with the PTA. Following every visit she tweets a selfie, captioned with an upbeat comment.

She is proud that her Twitter account @MidwintersEdu has over one thousand followers and prides herself on her multiple daily postings. However, union leadership is less excited about her social media presence and her unannounced visits to schools. Citing the contract, the union president noted that classroom observations were to be scheduled and teachers were to have at least 24 hours' notice prior to an administrative visit. In an interview with the local paper he stated that he found the Twitter feed "unprofessional" and wondered "if, perhaps, she didn't have enough to do."

In response, Able dismissed his concerns suggesting that he simply doesn't understand "how schools operate today" and that her account had "raised awareness of all the great things we do here at Midwinters." Furthermore, she stated that her classroom visits were not evaluative and she only wanted to "be connected to the primary mission of the schools—student learning."

Still, the public nature of the dispute has concerned several board members. Citing the upcoming contract negotiation, they asked Able to limit her social media activity to a single daily tweet and to curtail her school visits "for the time being." Reluctantly and publicly, Able agreed. Yet, privately, she has begun to worry that maybe Midwinters Schools "isn't such a good fit."

Discussing the Case

- On the surface, what is the case about?
- What are the underlying issues?
- How significant are the union leader's charges?
- How significant are Able's concerns?
- If you were called in to make a recommendation to the union leader, Able, or the board what might it be?

CASE 1.3

___

They're Only Kids

Maintaining a safe learning environment for students in schools is among the most important roles of school leadership. To assure school safety, schools across the nation have crafted policy to address student behavior infractions ranging from dress code violations to the possession of drugs and weapons. In response to community pressure, in the mid-2000s Hazel Township Schools adopted a zero-tolerance policy regarding student behavior infractions. However, a recent internal review of a decade of discipline data suggested that the policy had little to no influence on student choices regarding their behavior. Furthermore, analysis suggested troubling disparities regarding which children were disciplined and the punishments they received for those infractions. The data suggested that even within the rules of "zero" tolerance, suspension rates among children of color were higher than those of their white counterparts.

Hazel Township leaders knew they were not alone in uncovering these findings. Furthermore, they were well aware that other neighboring schools had been publicly embarrassed by news reporting that exposed the suspension of an elementary school student for having a plastic knife in her lunch and a middle school student who had a water pistol in his backpack. Anxious to get ahead of the issue and to respond to the disparity data, the superintendent formed a task force to draft a new school discipline policy.

Included in the taskforce were an elementary principal, a high school assistant principal, several teachers, a school safety officer, a member of the local faith community, and a teacher's union representative. The team was asked to present a first draft within six weeks and to have their work completed within three months. Excited to participate, the elementary principal arrived at the first meeting with examples of policy he had downloaded off the Internet. Breathless, the assistant principal arrived late to the meeting, apologizing by saying, "I got tied up in a parent call, I certainly hope whatever we draft makes my job easier."

A teacher added, "As long as I can still kick kids out that are misbehaving, I'm good." The union representative nodded in agreement. At the same time Pastor Wilson, implored, "Let's remember they're only kids." The school safety officer remained silent.

Discussing the Case

- What are the issues of consequence in this case?
- What are the issues of lesser import?
- What perspectives might each member of the team approach revising the discipline policy?
- What additional concerns does drafting school discipline policy present?

ACTIVITIES

The following activities will further expand your case learning strategies, skills, and approaches.

ACTIVITY 1.1

Writing Your School Case

Consider your school or district as fodder for a case. Write your case focusing on telling a story that features an important leadership lesson. Pay attention to addressing the following details and issues.

- Who are the key decision makers in your organization?
- What are the key issues leadership is facing?
- Where are the points of disagreement and pressure?
- In what ways are stories about your school and district told and to whom?
- Which aspects of school leadership are most challenging?
- What do you know about those issues?
- Where do you need to learn more?
- If you were to write a case about your school or an event in your school what would you feature?
- How might others tell that same story?
- What are the key messages that get told about "who we are" from the stories about your school?

ACTIVITY 1.2

Thinking About Challenges in Your School

Case learning requires that the learner is able to temper one's natural instinct to immediately recommend an answer or solution to the concern presented. Case learning focuses on first framing the issue(s) and viewing the situation from a variety of frames, lenses, and/or viewpoints. It requires that you step back before making judgment. To practice this approach, choose one vexing issue you are grappling with at the moment. It might be professional or personal, urgent or trivial. Using IPLAN, evaluate the factors at play and the criteria for a good resolution. List the ways in which someone else might view this situation. Are there views you are missing? How might you collect more information so that you are better informed?

Consider a best-case resolution, a good-enough resolution, and a worst case scenario from your viewpoint. Would others characterize those solutions in the same way? How might others see them differently? Where might conflict arise if not everyone agrees on a best case answer? What work would you need to accomplish so that a best case solution might be achieved that could be welcomed by several parties? What do you need to know that you do not know at this moment? What can you control? Where might compromise need to be sought? What could possibly go wrong? How might you prevent that?

ACTIVITY 1.3

Learning by Observation

Cases present themselves in many ways. By observing the places where we work, our daily interactions, the ways others characterize situations, we can learn to take our day-to-day exchanges and turn them into opportunities for leadership growth. In part, learning in this fashion requires that we question our assumptions about what we think we know about any given situation. One way to practice thinking about learning from the things that happen around you and to you is to approach each by asking the following questions. What do I see? What do I think about it? What do I wonder about? Make an effort to find at least one event or issue you confront this week and pose those questions. Where do you see patterns? What surprises you? How did your thinking change as a result of taking a moment to wonder?

RESOURCES

Because this book is about learning how to lead and how to lead well, we strongly recommend that you familiarize yourself with the following resources. We choose to highlight these enduring associations because they present consistently thoughtful work that frames the wider discussion regarding how leadership is best understood and enacted.

Council of Chief State School Officers: www.ccsso.org/
The Council of Chief State School Officers (CCSSO) leads work designed to transform the public education system in the United States. Best known for its support in the development of leadership standards, the CCSSO has been instrumental in driving an innovation, legislation, and advocacy agenda designed to support school and district transformation. Available at their webpage are numerous leadership resources.

Learning Forward: https://learningforward.org/
Formerly the National Staff Development Council (NSDC), Learning Forward promotes the inclusion of high-quality professional learning at all levels of the school organization. Home of the *Journal of Staff Development*, *The Learning Principal*, and the digital quarterly *Knowledge Briefs*, Learning Forward enhances the practice of leadership in schools by linking leaders to professional learning opportunities and disseminates research findings and reports of interest to school leaders.

continued . . .

National Association of Elementary School Principals: www.naesp.org/
National Association of Secondary School Principals: www.nassp.org/
 ?SSO=true
NAESP and NASSP are national organizations dedicated to supporting practicing and aspiring school leaders. Focused on professional learning and advocacy, these organizations seek to support schools by providing a national voice for school leaders, build public confidence in education, and to strengthen the role of the principal as instructional leader. Publications include *Principal Leadership*, the *NASSP Bulletin*, and *Breaking Ranks*, a series of field guides for practice.

The Wallace Foundation: www.wallacefoundation.org/pages/default.aspx
The Wallace Foundation is a philanthropic organization that works nationally to fund research that strives to address the enduring dilemmas of society. Their work in education includes research grant funding designed to strengthen leadership practices and policies. At their Knowledge Center readers can find hundreds of publications, free reports, videos, and tools in areas of school leadership, afterschool programs, arts education, and expanded learning.

University Council for Educational Administration: www.ucea.org
Founded in 1954, the University Council for Educational Administration is a consortium of member higher education institutions committed to advancing the preparation and practice of educational leaders. Primarily an association focused on the promotion and dissemination of research on problems of schooling and leadership practice, UCEA partners with SAGE education publishing and hosts *Educational Administration Quarterly* (EAQ), the *Journal of Cases in Educational Leadership* (JCEL), and the *Journal of Research on Leadership Education* (JRLE).

IPLAN RUBRIC

Please see Table 1.1.

GENERAL CASE SCORING RUBRIC

Please see Table 1.2.

TABLE 1.1 Iplan Rubric

	Exemplary	Proficient	Developing
Identification of issues	Provides facts, details, and accurate descriptions of central issues and/or problems Utilizes case data in a compelling fashion to support issue and problem identification Descriptions are insightful and complete	Recognizes the primary issues and/or problems Case data is employed to support issue and problem identification Summary provides an adequate overview of issues and/or problems	Fails to recognize key issues and/or problems Identifies issues and/or problems unsupported by case data Displays little understanding or depth as related to issues and/or problems
Players, perspectives, and positionality	Descriptions of the variety of perspectives and positionalities of key players are developed and insightful Key tensions and conflicts between players are clearly presented and explained	Multiple perspectives are summarized With minor exceptions, potential conflicts are surfaced	Explanations of the perspectives of players are flawed or incorrect Differences in perspective or positionality are not accounted for
Links to theory and research	Theory and research is applied in an accurate and insightful fashion, accounting for case data and expertise derived from practice Multiple sources of theoretical and/or empirical understanding are applied to analysis Attribution to multiple appropriate sources is provided and correct	Theory or research is applied to case learning. The substance of explanation relies on conjecture or speculation Analysis relies on too few sources of theory and/or research to fully explore key learnings Attribution is limited and/or inappropriate as used	Connections to theory are undeveloped, inaccurate, or irrelevant Sources are inappropriate and/or misused Attribution is absent or incorrect

Assessment and evaluation	Assessment is impartial, unbiased, critical, and comprehensive attending to multiple issues and/or problems	Assessment provides an adequate analysis of some of the issues and/or problems	Assessment relies on personal experiences and/or unsupported claims and material unrelated to case data, issues and/or problems
logical consistency or clear	Conclusions are well-supported by sound judgment and reasoned, logical argument Results and outcomes are clearly linked to case data, key issues and problems	Connections are clear but lack consistent and thorough logic and reasoning Results and outcomes are tied to some features of the case	Connections are weak and lack reasoning Results and outcomes are not linked to case data, issues, and problems
Next steps—action planning and alternatives	Detailed plans of feasible action are presented and are responsive to multiple issues and/or problems Action plans recognize and are responsive to multiple players and interests Consequences of potential actions are developed and critiqued for viability, implications are identified Action planning is logical, clear, and coherent	Most of the issues and/or problems are addressed yet detail may be lacking or infeasible Action plans are responsive to most players and/or interests Consequences of potential actions are present and implications are identified Action plans are understandable and sound	A single course of action is presented and is unresponsive to key issues and/or problems Action plans are unresponsive to key players and/or interests Consequences of plans are not considered or identified actions are unlinked to case data Action plans lack logical consistency

TABLE 1.2 General Case Scoring Rubric

	Exemplary	Proficient	Developing
Understanding of the case and questions posed	Articulates important/key variables of the case and phenomena within the case demonstrating a thoughtful analysis of the material at hand.	Attention to key variables is inconsistent. Some are well developed and others lacking.	Key variables of the case are neglected. Analysis of the material is incomplete and/or unfocused.
Integration with leadership concepts, readings, theories, and key ideas	The case is analyzed using appropriate theories. Several ideas/constructs are considered to make sense of the issues at hand.	The case is analyzed using appropriate theory yet analysis lacks depth and/or clarity.	The response does not employ theory appropriate to the issues at hand. Theory is not fully developed and application to the case at hand is difficult to discern.
Reasoning and articulation within analysis	Offers a reasoned argument for a particular line of thinking or problem solving. Argument is based on personal or practice-based learning and supported by theoretical analysis.	Argument is inconsistent. Some areas well developed and others lacking. A majority of analysis relies on sources other than leadership theory.	Offers a thin argument relying solely on personal experience and/or conjecture rather than content knowledge.
Thoroughness and depth of analysis	Analysis goes beyond the use of theory as a checklist incorporating nuanced applications of ideas to the problems at hand. Innovative and/or alternative solutions are posed and critically considered.	Theory is used as a checklist rather than to provide a method for analysis, evaluation and creative problem solving. Innovative and/or alternative solutions may be posed but are not critically considered.	Argument is inconsistent. Some areas well developed and others lacking. A majority of analysis relies on sources other than leadership theory.
Writing quality and logical flow of the analysis	Well written, offers insights that bring the reader forward and engage him/her in the application of theory to practice.	Writing is inconsistent; in places the logic is clear yet in others analysis lacks coherence and/or application of theory to practice.	Poorly written, difficult to follow logic or argument.

REFERENCES

Andersen, E., & Schiano, B. (2014). *Teaching with cases: A practical guide.* Boston, MA: Harvard Business School Publishing.

Bolivar, J.M., & Chrispeels, J.H. (2011). Enhancing parent leadership through building social and intellectual capital. *American Educational Research Journal, 48*(1), 4–38.

Bridges, E.M., & Hallinger, P. (1996). Problem-based learning in leadership education. In Wilkerson, L. & Gijselaars, W.H. (Eds.) *New directions for teaching and learning* (pp. 53–61). San Francisco, CA: Jossey-Bass.

Bridges, E.M., & Hallinger, P. (1997). Using problem-based learning to prepare educational leaders. *Peabody Journal of Education, 72*(2), 131–146.

Brown, P.C., Roediger, H.L., & McDaniel, M.A. (2014). *The science of successful learning.* Cambridge, MA: Belknap Press.

Bryk, A., Sebring, P.B., Allensworth, E. Luppescu, S., & Easton, J.Q. (2009). *Organizing schools for improvement.* Chicago: University of Chicago Press.

de Graaff, E., & Kolmos, A. (2003). Characteristics of problem-based learning. *International Journal of Engineering Education, 19*(5), 657–662.

Ellet, W. (2007). *The case study handbook: How to read, discuss, and write persuasively about cases.* Boston, MA: Harvard Business Review Press.

Gray, J., & DiLoreto, M. (2016). The effects of student engagement, student satisfaction, and perceived learning in online learning environments. *International Journal of Educational Leadership Preparation, 11*(1), 98–119.

Green, R.L. (2005). *Practicing the art of leadership: A problem-based approach to implementing the ISLLC standards.* Upper Saddle River, NJ: Pearson.

Hamlin, D., & Flessa, J. (2016). Parental involvement initiatives: An analysis. *Educational Policy,* 1–31.

Hargreaves, A., & Fink, D. (2006). *Sustainable leadership.* New York: Wiley & Sons.

Ishimaru, A. (2012). From heroes to organizers: Principals and education organizing in urban school reform. *Educational Administration Quarterly, 49*(1), 3–51.

Jennings, J.M., & Angelo, T. (Eds.) (2006). *Student engagement: Measuring and enhancing engagement with learning.* Proceedings of the Universities Academic Audit Unit, New Zealand.

Kruse, S.D., & Louis, K.S. (2009). *Building strong school cultures: A guide to leading change.* Thousand Oaks, CA: Corwin Press.

Leithwood, K., Louis, K.S., Anderson, S., & Wahlstrom, K. (2004). *How leadership influences student learning: A review of research for the Learning for Leadership Project.* New York: The Wallace Foundation.

Lopez, M.E., Kreider H., & Coffman J. (2005). Intermediary organizations as capacity builders in family education involvement. *Urban Education, 40*(1), 78–105.

Ray, J.L., Baker, L.T., & Plowman, D.A. (2011). Organizational mindfulness in business schools. *Academy of Management Learning & Education, 10,* 188–203.

Richards, C. (2015). Outcomes-based authentic learning, portfolio assessment, and a systems approach to 'Complex Problem-Solving': Related pillars for enhancing the innovative role of PBL in future higher education. *Journal of Problem Based Learning in Higher Education, 3*(1), 78–95.

Rittel, H.W., & Webber, M.M. (1973). Dilemmas in a general theory of planning. *Policy Sciences, 4,* 155–169.

Savery, J.R. (2006). Overview of problem-based learning: Definitions and distinctions. *Interdisciplinary Journal of Problem-based Learning, 1*(1), 9–20.

Stoll, L., & Louis, K.S. (2007). *Professional learning communities: Divergence, detail and difficulties*. London: Swets & Zeitlinger.

Vogus, T., & Sutcliffe, K. (2012). Organizational mindfulness and mindful organization: A reconciliation and path forward. *Academy of Management Learning and Education, 11*(4), 722–735.

Vygotsky, L.S. (1978). *Mind and society: The development of higher psychological processes*. Cambridge, MA: Harvard University Press.

CHAPTER **2**

Organizational Vision

Vision matters to successful leadership. Functioning much like an organizational compass or North Star, an inspirational and unambiguous vision sets the direction for organizational goals, objectives, and decision making. Simply put, leaders who know where they are going are better able to get there. They are also better able to motivate others to join them on their journey. Furthermore, when pursuing a relevant and significant vision is a core feature of a leader's work, vision can act as a litmus test of sorts, providing guidance as to whether or not a decision is in the best interest of the school, its students, and the families it serves. Yet, visions rarely function alone. In schools and other organizations where vision is a powerful leadership tool, a vision is supported by a mission statement and clearly articulated, foundational, core values. We begin by drawing a distinction between vision and mission, and defining how the development and adoption of shared core values can enhance school success.

Vision and mission are two distinct, but complementary, concepts. In practice, a vision statement provides organizational direction for future work; it sets a purpose for the work of the organization. Vision statements also set forth an aspirational future direction for an organization. As such, visions tell the world who you wish to be and set out a clear and inspirational future (Gill, 2011; Murphy & Torre, 2015). In schools, vision statements tend to emphasize student learning and student well-being. They may also speak to how school climate and culture may be developed and enhance student learning. However, vision cannot be understood in isolation; in particular, it has to be connected to the mission and the core values of the organization's members.

Mission reflects the ways the vision can be tangibly achieved. Whereas vision is a principled direction for the future of the school, the mission answers questions such as: who will assist in achieving the vision, what is to be created or further developed, what the school values, and why members of the school organization should be engaged with this work (Collins & Porras, 1996; Gioia, Nag, & Corley, 2012; Haque, Titi Amayah, & Liu, 2016). Mission reflects the way in which vision can be transformed into tangible outcomes for the school. A good mission statement incorporates the concept of shared (Printy & Marks, 2006), distributed (Timperley, 2005), or intensified leadership (Kruse & Louis, 2009), where all members of the school are engaged in meaningful work, designed to achieve valued goals and outcomes.

An inspiring mission statement integrates organizational intellectual capital (Bratianu, Jianu, & Vasilache, 2007) with problem-specific and user-centered disciplined inquiry intended to drive growth and improvement (Bryk, Gomez, Grunow, & LeMahieu, 2015; DiPaola & Hoy, 2008). In this way, the mission statement provides the necessary guidance for developing instructional strategies, defining critical student learning and well-being success factors, searching out key opportunities for engagement and support, making resource allocation choices, and motivating key stakeholders (DiPaola & Hoy, 2008; Gill, 2011; Hallinger & Murphy, 1985; Murphy, 1990). Additionally, a strong mission statement should be reflective of a school's vision, as well as relevant to the community the school serves (Gill, 2011).

Importantly, vision and mission statements should be supported by a set of core values that represent the beliefs of school leaders, teachers, instructional support faculty, and professional staff. These values should be student-centered and based upon what the faculty believe to be true for themselves and their students. Inasmuch as core values form the foundation for how principals, teachers, staff, and students, should act as members of the school community, Murphy and Torre (2015), suggest that core values must support a sense of hope, norms of commitment, continuous improvement, and collective responsibility, as well as convey an assets-based approach to working with students and their families. Before further developing these ideas, we begin by exploring the role of vision, mission, and core values at Fort Du Marche High School.

KEY LEARNINGS

In this chapter, you will learn how to:

- review the mission and vision of the school to promote student achievement and academic success;
- strategically revise and develop the mission and vision to meet the changing needs and expectations of the school; and
- promote, articulate, and cultivate shared values among stakeholders that focus on student-centered education and continuous improvement.

FEATURED CASE

Taking Stock: Rooting a New Vision in a Strong Past

To say that being the principal at Fort du Marche High School (FMHS) has been a challenge for James Beene is a bit of an understatement. When he entered the position three years ago, Beene was tasked with "cleaning house." Located in a suburban working-class community, FMHS served a solid long-standing core of families. Most have lived in the community for decades. The majority of the 1,500 students are eligible for free and reduced breakfast and lunch services, and are categorized by the state as economically disadvantaged. Over 60 percent of the student body is African American, while 20 percent are Caucasian and the remaining 10 percent are Hispanic, Asian, or multiracial. Like many schools in the state, FMHS had struggled. Prior to Beene's tenure, the school's accountability rating had never risen beyond that of a C and improvement efforts would be adopted with great excitement only to falter within months.

When he accepted the position, Beene knew that if he were to turn things around, the school would need to drastically change. The superintendent who hired him was new to the district himself and had already developed a reputation for "brusqueness" although he saw himself as "a straight-shooter." He did not mince words during Beene's interview process, describing the school as staffed by "unmotivated" teachers and attended by "uninterested" students. Furthermore, he made it clear that he expected Beene to be able to either "help these folks to understand they need to improve or to leave." He was equally clear about his expectations for student behavior and achievement, stating, "Do what you need to but get the place under control and get those kids in class and learning."

Beene appreciated that the superintendent was signaling his support for Beene's work. He believed that beyond the sharp words, the superintendent wanted what was best for the school. Additionally, Beene was not new to the Fort du Marche community and he knew that the school had once been a place of pride. Beene believed that extensive administrative turnover—four principals in ten years—had eroded what had been, at one time, a strong school vision and mission. He hoped that by committing to the school he might make a difference in the lives of the students who learned there and the teachers who worked there. Beene began his work early, taking the summer prior to his official start to review the recent test and student achievement data, as well as graduation, end-of-course, and Advanced Placement exam results. He had hoped that he would find some successes upon which he might build a solid start.

Instead, what he found confused him. He realized that the data alone wasn't providing the kind of detail he needed to understand what had happened to FMHS. He knew that, in part, the superintendent was correct—some of the staff needed to go and student discipline needed attention. However, he also knew that the school was home to some excellent teachers. Despite the turnover and seeming lack of direction, many students had done well and graduated. In fact, the graduation rate had increased by 12 percent over the last eight years. Someone, he thought, had been doing something right. He just had to figure out who and what that was.

Taking Stock

When the staff came back in the fall for teacher preparation days, Beene welcomed the faculty to FMHS with a breakfast and a plan. He shared with the assembled teachers,

> I need to learn who you are and what you've been through. I know that when principals keep changing the thing you want to do is close your door and just do your job. I get it. But if we're going to make this school all it can be, I need you to do more than that. But I don't want to just skip over these past years, I need to know what happened and what mattered at FMHS during this time.

Beene asked that the faculty and staff break into teams of six and assigned each team a decade. Two teams were assigned 1970–1979, two 1980–1989, two 1990–1999, and two the first part of this century, 2000–2010. A final two groups were asked to take 2010 to the present. He asked that each team discuss and record on large poster paper the significant national, regional, and FMHS events that marked their decade. His plan, as he shared it with the faculty and staff, was to share who Fort du Marche had been so that they might plan for who they could become. A new vision would follow this work.

The teams worked thoughtfully for the next 45 minutes. When the posters were hung around the room and presentations began, it was clear that FMHS had a rich tradition in the community and that recent events had proven undermining and discouraging. The exercise surfaced the numerous programs the school had adopted over those years and they ways in which those adoptions were often inconsistent with each other and unaligned with school needs and goals. The exercise also evidenced how many veteran teachers had been the backbone of the school, helping students to succeed by supporting their learning. It also exposed the ways many teachers had felt district leadership had failed them and the amount of trust that needed to be rebuilt. The morning concluded with Beene noting several themes he saw across the stories that had been shared. He acknowledged FMHA had faced challenges. Yet, he chose to focus on the positive identifying, "academic effort," "student success," "community change," and "values and beliefs" as key themes of the school's past. He shared with the assembled faculty and staff that he saw in these words the, "raw material we need to create a new vision."

Listening

As the faculty and staff broke for lunch many noted, "this was the best back to school" they had enjoyed in a long time. Following lunch, Beene asked that the teachers, "now take a moment to listen." Joining him at the front of the room was a student panel of a dozen current and recently graduated students. He asked that they "answer his questions honestly and respectfully," stating that the panel would last "less than an hour," and he would be looking for students to answer only "two questions—what are the ways you learn best and what do you wish could be different at Fort du Marche?"

Passing the microphone up and down the row the students answered. To any educator what they shared was unsurprising: they liked classes that engaged and challenged them, teachers who cared about them, and instruction that they found relevant and relatable. They also stressed that they "got tired of looking at PowerPoints, slide shows, and screens." There were several poignant moments as well. One young woman shared that during her four years at Fort du Marche she had lived in five foster homes and added that the teachers at FMHS were more like her parents than any of her foster families.

Recommitting

After a standing ovation, the students filed out. Beene asked that "We all should sit with what we heard for a moment." He held the silence for several minutes. Finally, he broke the growing tension in the room by asking that each teacher write down three core professional values they held for themselves and could commit to supporting in the coming year. He promised that he would be working with them to "craft a clear direction for FMHS" and was looking to the faculty and staff to participate in a "yearlong visioning effort." He continued, "We learned where we've been today, I more so than many of you. Now I want us all to figure out who we want to be and then how we're going to get there together. I look forward to our first of many years together." As the faculty and staff filed out, Beene reflected on the day. He hoped that he had done a good job of messaging that while he expected changes at FMHS, he was also willing to work with and support the faculty. For Beene, the core of his vision work was collaborative effort, but he knew that first, trust needed to be established. He wanted to believe he had begun that process.

MISSION, VISION, AND CORE VALUES: ESSENTIAL ORGANIZATIONAL PRACTICES

Inasmuch that the purpose of a vision is to inspire and direct organizational members toward improvement efforts, it is important that organizational members—school leaders, teachers, staff and faculty—share clear understandings concerning how the vision and mission was developed and the values upon which they rest. Recent research (Bryk, Gomez, Grunow, & LeMahieu, 2015; Glatthorn, Jailall, & Jailall, 2017; Murphy & Torre, 2015) suggests that successful school leaders tailor their work by including three essential elements of organizational practice as they engage in visioning efforts—developing *consensus*, fostering *commitment*, and broadening *communication*. Ideally, the three work together, creating a supportive foundation for leadership efforts in the school.

Developing Consensus

Consensus that "yes, this is the direction we want for our school," is a critical indicator of a successful vision. As we saw in the example of Fort du Marche High School, it is important that the principal involves the entire faculty and staff in the development of the mission, vision, and core values of the school. A vision that inspires and serves the school—as opposed to one that merely hangs on the wall—must emerge from the collective values held by the members of the organization (Glatthorn, Jailall, & Jailall, 2017). A vision that truly serves the whole must be meaningful to the whole.

Furthermore, research (Bryk, Gomez, Grunow, & LeMahieu, 2015; Murphy & Torre, 2015) suggests that when school leaders frame vision and mission with the help and investment of others, rather than impose their own ideas, better outcomes for the school are realized. These outcomes include clarity and agreement concerning organizational *purpose* (Collins & Porras, 1996), how and which *functions* organizational members perform which tasks (Gill, 2011; Kruse & Louis, 2009), formation of *relationships* and the processes by which those relationships are maintained (Hord, 1997, 2008; Haque, Titi Amayah, & Liu, 2016), and the operational *structures* designed to support the work of the school (Murphy, 1990; Timperley, 2005). In this way, consensus around what the vision says, as well as the values upon which it rests, is necessary if the vision is to have long-term utility and act to support other important work.

Fostering Commitment

Yet, for a vision to have the kinds of positive impacts suggested above, it takes more than simply writing a vision. No matter how collaborative the effort, if the vision is not used to guide day-to-day decision making and leadership efforts, it will not have impact. Commitment is needed. All too often, visioning is treated as a bureaucratic task. Schools and other organizations write visions and missions because they know they should, only to abandon them once the work of crafting the statement is completed (Heck & Hallinger, 2010). We have visited many a school where the vision is prominently displayed or, as in some, recited at the start of each school day, and then ignored as problem situations arise. In these cases, we argue that commitment to the values and aspirations the vision was meant to embody is lacking.

We realize that it is hard to keep vision "in a starring role" (Murphy & Torre, 2015, p. 184) yet, absent its use as a directive tool for problem resolving and leadership effort, it is little more than symbolic. Commitment to acting in ways the vision suggests engenders trust among faculty and staff (Hoy & Miskel, 2008), centers teachers and support staff on key efforts toward school improvement (Hall & Hord, 2016), and communicates behavioral expectations (Kruse, Louis, & Bryk, 1995) concerning how members of the school community should act. Simply put, commitment to the vision requires that leaders use it for the purposes it was created.

Broadening Communication

As Murphy and Torre (2015) note, high-performing schools tend to have regular, ongoing communication with stakeholders about the mission, vision, and core values. Inasmuch as the principal is responsible for communicating the mission, vision, and core values to the community, these elements should be visible throughout the school and readily available to the public (e.g., prominently displayed on the website, and included in newsletters and other correspondence). Yet, as with commitment, it is not enough to share the vision in word alone. Broad communication regarding the vision and mission needs to encompass leadership efforts in tangible and symbolic ways.

Tangible communication of vision and mission can be found when leaders commit budget and other resources to efforts linked to vision attainment and support of the school goals (Fullan, 2014; Murphy, Elliot, Goldring, & Porter, 2006). If, for example, a school's vision states that "student well-being and success" matter, then resources should be directed to activities such as after-school programs, tutoring and mentoring, school-based health clinics, and instructional resources to support classroom learning. In turn, when school practices or policies are present that undermine a student's well-being or success (e.g., exclusionary discipline or academic tracking), they should be actively examined and reformed.

Symbolic communication of the vision and mission occurs through the use of stories, rituals, ceremonies, and traditions (Deal & Peterson, 2016; Kruse & Louis, 2009). The development of meaningful activities, purposefully linked to vision work, progress, and success toward those goals, fosters a school culture where the vision and its central role in the work of the school is articulated and encouraged. What is important, from a leadership sense, is that school activity is communicated as vision-driven and linked to who we communally wish to become. When Principal Beene asked that the faculty and staff recall and share the history of FMHS, he was asking them to engage in a tangible activity with symbolic purpose. When, in subsequent years he asks that the school's story be retold each fall, he roots current effort in the school's shared past. Beene's symbolic communication regarding the vision resonates with faculty and staff because it reinforces who FMHS is today and how far they have come to get there.

LEADERSHIP FOR MISSION, VISION, AND CORE VALUES

Principals and teachers are busy people. All too often they find themselves overwhelmed by the myriad of details that fill their days. As they move from task to task there is often little that links, for example, the parent meeting at nine with a class or teacher evaluation at ten. Shifting from activity to activity is exhausting and disorienting. If our day is filled with tasks that we cannot quite link to one another, if each event we attend seems unrelated to other aspects of our work, and if the work in which we are engaged is inconsistent with what we value, we cannot make sense of the reason why we are doing these things. Consequently, we respond by going through the motions, by attending the meetings but not paying attention, by talking but not listening. Our work becomes unimaginative and rote. We become stressed and isolated. What we lose as we run from thing to thing is the meaning behind what we are doing.

Purpose

Purpose helps us to identify what we value, and in turn, define what we find meaningful. At the school level, organizational purpose can direct us toward identifying our shared communal values and find ways to incorporate those understandings into our vision-guided decision making and shared work. Purpose underscores why we have chosen the vision we have and the reasons we believe it matters. Additionally, research suggests that purpose advances collegial collaboration and imagination (Vaill, 1984; Printy &

Marks, 2006), and individual morale and achievement within the school (McLaughlin & Talbert, 2001; Murphy, 1990). Furthermore, purpose-driven vision and mission statements offer leaders a compelling reason for making the choices they do and a vocabulary for talking about those choices. Purpose answers the question, "What should we do and how will it help us achieve what we value?"

When schools lack shared values related to communal purpose, instructional practices, and expected professional behavior, schools struggle to achieve goals and improve over time (Kruse & Louis, 2009). Furthermore, the articulation of a school's shared values surface the fundamental character of the school and sense of identity (Hoy & Miskel, 2008). In this way, shared values communicate the expectations of the school to the community, district, parents, students, and other stakeholders. However, these statements are meaningless if they are not supported by principals' and teachers' actions, behaviors, decisions, and their approach to interpersonal relationships (Murphy & Torre, 2015).

For this reason, statements of shared values usually include working norms for the school organization. These norms represent how things are done, the structure of cooperative work, and what members believe can be achieved by working together. In turn, as educators understand what the school believes in and stands for, they are more likely to take actions and make decisions that support shared values (Hoy & Miskel, 2008). Yet, identifying shared values is difficult. On one hand, it is easy to suggest that a school might value excellence, creative work, high standards, and innovation. It is harder to define what those ideals mean in practice or how we might, as a school community, enact them over time and in the variety of classrooms that comprise the school. Yet, doing so is impactful for communicating and stewarding a vision. It is worth the time it takes to have rich thoughtful dialogue about what the words we choose to represent our values mean and how they are evidenced in practice.

Some schools and districts choose to carefully define what words like excellence, innovation, creativity, and high standards mean. They do so in ways that articulate how every student can achieve what is expected of them, and how faculty and staff will be supported in helping students succeed. The very act of defining and then articulating for themselves and others, what these words and ideals mean, helps school leadership, faculty, and staff understand what is expected of them and their practice. In turn, actions become more purposeful and intentions clearer. As the intended purpose for doing what we do is clarified as a community we better understand, and are willing to live with, the consequences of our actions; and the importance of and the value we place on the work we do are evident (Kruse, 2009; Mendels, 2012). Furthermore, when leadership actions are purposeful, it is easier to build trust and respect (Tschannen-Moran, 2014).

Employing Soft Systems

As a process for identifying shared values and then turning those into collective vision and mission, we suggest that schools adopt a soft systems orientation to this work. Originating decades ago (Checkland, 1981) and developed as a problem-solving model for a broad range of organizations, soft systems thinking was designed to purposefully include the ideas, experiences, and perceptions of members of the organization in organizational change efforts. It stands as a counter-point to hard systems approaches that privilege situations where data is knowable and easily understood and options are relatively straightforward.

Said another way, hard systems thinking looks toward "how to do it" when "what to do" is already well defined. Hard systems analysis is less effective at answering questions that begin with "why" or 'what." Soft systems thinking addresses "why" questions. In this way, soft systems thinking is particularly well suited to visioning efforts because a well-crafted vision directs faculty and staff toward future work, providing an inspiring "why" for staff and faculty effort.

More recently, researchers (Heifetz, 1994; Heiftez, Grashaw, & Linsky, 2009) have written about the distinction between hard and soft problems, referring to them as technical or adaptive. In Heifetz's discussion, technical or hard problems require less learning—both for individuals and the organization as a whole—than adaptive or soft issues. Furthermore, in describing adaptive problems, Heifetz and his colleagues distinguish between problems and issues where the question (e.g., what issues are we facing?) is clear but the solutions (e.g., how do we address them?) are unknown and problems and issues where both the question and solution require new learning. A hallmark of addressing an adaptive problem is learning.

As Murphy and Torre (2015) suggest, shaping vision work is an adaptive problem. Visioning requires that the school community learn its way into becoming something new. In some schools, knowing where they wish to go is clear, in others less so. But as we have already suggested, even in schools where faculty and staff can agree that, for example, "assuring a high-quality and challenging learning environment" is a shared value, what those words mean for each member of the school community may differ.

In traditional visioning models, either the principal or a small team of teachers and staff work to craft a vision statement. This statement may be based on wide-ranging input or not. In any case, most typically, the statement is brought to the whole and after some wordsmithing and edits, the statement is voted on and adopted. It then rests on the principal's shoulders to secure "buy-in" for the vision and mission. The issue of visioning has been treated as if it were a hard, technical problem. And for those reasons, the exercise falls flat and the vision and mission fail to deliver on their promise (Bryk, Gomez, Grunow, & LeMahieu, 2015; Heck & Hallinger, 2010).

As applied to schools, soft systems work suggests that the interpretations faculty and staff have concerning their beliefs and professional experiences—both positive and challenging—are an integral part of understanding the school itself. Soft systems thinking also suggests that how one experiences the world around them and the belief structures that arise out of those experiences influences how day-to-day work is approached. In other words, absent real and tangible work that engages members of the school community in discussing and deeply understanding the core values that underscore a vision and mission, these efforts are unlikely to have impact (Bryman, 2004; Heiftez, Grashaw, & Linsky, 2009). In this way, soft systems thinking suggests that surfacing, and in turn, understanding, the deeply held beliefs of faculty and staff, students and their families, matter for the school to move forward.

Soft Systems in Practice

In practice, soft systems work is designed to surface diverse worldviews. It unfolds as part of an inquiry process. First, faculty and staff are asked to identify a topic, (e.g., "What does the word equity mean to you?" Or "What does engaging work look like in your class?"). The goal of this initial stage of thinking is to develop rich images of the meaning that people hold when significant words or phrases are used. The idea in this first phase is to broadly obtain as many perspectives as possible. The focus on including a variety of organizational members (e.g., faculty, staff, parents, students, and community members) is designed to establish mutual trust and cooperation as the school works to articulate and adopt a vision (Checkland & Poulter, 2006; Checkland & Scholes, 1999; Jackson, 2003). As such, interviews, focus groups, and internal and external community meetings may be venues for collecting this data. Once assembled, the rich images that arise from multiple descriptions and definitions can then be examined in relation to each other.

As a faculty and staff, members can then probe these descriptions as communal data, at once surfacing the variety of meanings any one word or phrase might evoke, while protecting and respecting the individuals who offered them. When school leaders, faculty, and staff take the time to probe the shared values that underscore vision work, they set the stage for creating a vision with longevity and purpose. Furthermore, when care is taken to listen to the thoughts of the school community in this fashion, it is easier to approach the task from a stance of learning. Tempers are less likely to flare and understanding is more likely to surface. The richness of this process lies in the discussion that follows. In this way, consensus and commitment are built into the work of creating the vision rather than by "selling" the vision once it has been written.

Soft systems work builds on the interplay of "doing in order to think" and "thinking in order to do" (Mintzberg, 2009), focusing attention on the individual dynamics that are unavoidably present in this work and fostering deep organizational learning designed to move the school forward. In turn, attention is directed toward the development of vision and mission that have been truly communally developed and vetted. As Mintzberg (2013) notes, when people understand what is broadly expected (e.g., treating each other with respect), they are better able to maintain commitment to the common good as well as deepen their own sense of contribution toward communal efforts. In this way, community members can learn their way into new ways of organizing and being. As a result, meaningful changes in a school's organizational culture can emerge (Kruse & Louis, 2009; Kruse & Johnson, 2017) and the school can be better prepared for the implementation of a new vision and mission.

SUSTAINING VISION EFFORT: HIGH-IMPACT PRACTICES

Creating and implementing vision and mission statements is only the beginning of this work. In fact, as we have suggested, unless the vision is used, it is unlikely to have its intended results. At best, it simply becomes something the school "did" and at worst a bureaucratic exercise that undermined school community and trust. As such, attention to sustaining the school vision counts. Sustaining the vision requires more than its regular communication. It requires the employment of the ideals and aspirations in the daily work of the full school community. It also requires that leadership actions and decisions are congruent with stated directions and goals. In short, it requires that the vision become an active, guiding force for not only what leaders do but, also, how they do it. The arenas of instructional leadership, school environment and management, and parent and community partnerships provide important opportunities for high-impact, vision sustaining, leadership practice. Although we discuss each in more detail in future chapters, we highlight here how work within each can evidence and sustain the vision. Finally, we conclude with a discussion about revisioning and introduce ideas designed to assist school leaders in cases where change is required and a vision already exists.

Instructional Leadership

Instructional leaders help teachers translate the big ideas included in the vision and mission statements into day-to-day instructional practice. By focusing on those aspects of the vision that directly relate to the classroom (e.g., high quality instruction, creativity and challenge, student progress and growth) principals who lead from the vision do so by being a visible presence in classrooms (Johnson, 2007). They practice vision-in-action by evidencing an up-to-date knowledge and skill set, including different models of teaching, differentiation of instruction, the use of technology, and formative and summative assessment techniques. Clearly, principals cannot be subject area experts in all content. While this is particularly true in high schools where upper level courses often include highly technical knowledge, effective principals seek teacher leaders, build consensus, and share decision making to invest others in the decisions made that affect and influence instructional practices (Mendels, 2012). In this way, they intensify their own knowledge and skill set and reinforce the values that underscore vision work by honoring what teachers—as classroom professionals—bring to the effort.

School Environment and Management

Similarly, how the school environment is managed matters if vision-in-action leadership is to be experienced as trustworthy and dependable. Often vision statements include some attention to student well-being or a statement that suggests each child's talents and skills will be honored and nurtured. Yet, just as often, we find ourselves in schools where individuality is not celebrated, where students' dignity is regularly compromised, and the capacity of forgiveness is sorely lacking. Make no mistake, we are not advocating for schools without attention to student safety or well-established policy and procedure.

We know many schools that are deeply challenging places. However, we are suggesting that if a school's vision suggests that a school is focused on "challenging each student within a respectful environment for learning" or that the school be a place for "inclusion and diversity," school leaders intentionally determine what that looks like in practice. This includes, but is not limited to, a reconsideration of classroom and school discipline policy and practice, the development of spaces that welcome and keep every student safe, and a review of instructional and curricular materials for bias and partiality. Doing so fosters a vision-centered school environment and assures the community that the school is serious about sustaining the work.

Parent and Community Partnerships

Interactions with external partners provide school leaders valuable opportunities to sustain vision work. Starting with the choice of what area organizations and companies are invited into the school and extending into determining the roles they play in school community partnerships, a focus on the vision-in-action can help sustain progress as well as broadly publicize the vision. If a school vision suggests that students are to "become engaged citizens with a global understanding" or "twenty-first century learners prepared to compete on a world stage" activities with parents and community partners should evidence those foci. Doing so requires that school leaders seek out partnerships that support the aspirations of the school. It is critical to understand that each prospective school partner has their own reasons for participating. Rooting participation in the vision sets forth, from the beginning of the partnership, the expectations for inclusion and intended outcomes for students.

Revisioning

A vision is not static. On occasion, it will need to be refreshed or renewed, and in some cases, replaced. There are several circumstances many school leaders face that call for revisioning of the school's goals and vision. If a school has experienced significant demographic, enrollment, or zoning changes, then revisioning may be needed. Whenever a school is restructured or reorganized as a magnet school, academy, or other specialized setting, revisioning and rebranding should be considered. Finally, if a new principal inherits the vision of a previous leader, revisioning can allow for a fresh perspective under a different leader (Bryman, 2004; Sun & Leithwood, 2012). Yet, the process of revisioning is as important as the development of a new vision statement. Even in cases where the existing vision has "gone missing," faculty and staff, community and parents, will have an investment in how the school operates and in maintaining the status quo. All too often, new principals fail to develop trust and respect because they have handled their entry into a new situation poorly. Remembering that schools, and the people who work and live in them, have a past matters when revisioning is needed. As Deal and Peterson (2016) suggest, even as leaders work toward change, honoring what has come before is necessary, vision-related culture work.

Whether newly constructed or recently revised, a strong and inspiring vision and mission statement sets the stage for moving any school toward better outcomes for students. However, effective vision and mission leadership requires more than words on a page. It requires that clearly understood and shared values be articulated and that those understandings of "who we want to be" become part of our daily work. As such, once written, a vision should be lived, acted upon, and ultimately realized by our successes with students in our classrooms and schools.

CASES FOR ANALYSIS

CASE 2.1

Do We Have a Vision?

Rotheville Middle School (RMS), built in 2004, serves about 750 students in grades five through eight. RMS was built because district growth required an additional school for middle level students and teachers applied to transfer to the new school from within the district. Additional teachers were hired in 2004 and some, but not all, were assigned to RMS. Each grade level is home to two teaching teams of faculty with primary responsibility for 70 to 80 students who attend classes in educational pods designed for large group and small group instruction. Movable walls separate classroom spaces and most furniture is on wheels, allowing for easy and quick changes to fit a variety of instructional modes. The school also has dedicated science lab spaces, an auditorium, a large multipurpose room, a library, and several art rooms.

When RMS opened, much was made about its innovative structure. The intention was that by providing "mobile and mutable" space, the school would be "better able to meet the needs of all learners." Upon opening, the RMS faculty and staff came together to formalize a new vision for the school. Time was set aside during August professional learning days for the faculty to meet, discuss core values, draft statements, and ultimately decide on the school's new vision and mission. To facilitate the process, the district hired the services of Dr. Fay Proper, a superintendent who had recently retired from a neighboring district. One veteran teacher remembers the effort in this way:

> It was kind of great. Opening a new school was exciting and Fay was really helpful. She worked with us to brainstorm what we wanted to say about our wishes for RMS and she was really good at putting words to our ideas. She also worked really hard to help us write something we could all agree on. We took a few days, wrote some ideas out, and then we voted on what our three favorites were. We then took those to the students and their families to read, and vote on also. The one that had the most votes in the end won. We then had it painted on the wall in the multipurpose room. I think it's still there.

When pressed to remember what happened next the teacher falters:

> I guess, I mean we had the vision. We did it. For a while students recited each day after the pledge but when Ms. Rogers, the first principal, left we stopped doing that. We still had the same vision but it just seemed like less of a focus. We moved on to other things. We had a new reading program and then we really worked on our school discipline policy. It just didn't matter as much. It got us started and then we just went.

Another teacher adds to the story:

> We did the vision really hard for the first bit. There was a lot about collaborative learning and being focused on the whole student. We worked in our teams to really make sure each kid had a great day, every day. For those first years, Ms. Rogers really talked a lot about leading with the vision in mind. She kept sending us back to our main goals.

When Maria Rogers retired in 2008, she was replaced by Tim Yoder. Yoder was no stranger to RMS. He had been a founding teacher and had left to pursue his first principalship in a nearby school. He still counted many RMS teachers as his close friends and looked forward to "coming home." His intention was to "continue the great work Maria had started." Yet, almost from his first day, he began making subtle changes in the way the school was run. Maria Rogers had led by walking the building. She could often be seen in classrooms and in the halls. It was rare that she missed a lunch duty or dismissal and made a point to be part of team meetings as often as she could.

Yoder spent more time in his office. He prided himself on being a data-driven leader and invested hours in unpacking the school's test data. When he did meet with teachers he often had his laptop or iPad at the ready to call up a pie-chart or data display to make his point. As he put it, "I wanted everyone to know I was serious about student learning." He added, "For me, the best way we could serve our kids was to be sure the decisions we were making were informed."

Yoder also immediately rewrote the student and parent handbook. His intention was to "streamline" the volume and make its contents fully searchable from its Web location. He removed much of Rogers's material concerning the school vision and replaced it with the motto, "Every student, every day, in every way." The handbook outlined RMS's procedures for reporting absences, homework and grading, dress code, and other procedural matters. Prior to its final posting, a small group of teachers reviewed the product and approved the changes. As a music teacher stated, "No one thought it was a bad thing. We were super excited that it was easier to use and would be better for parents. Kind of honestly, we didn't notice the vision was not there anymore."

After Yoder settled into his new role, teachers found him easy to work with. Many liked the autonomy they now enjoyed and as a fourth-grade teacher said, "It was sort of nice no one was looking over my shoulder all the time. I mean, the data stuff was hard at first but once I got the fact that all I had to do was talk numbers with Tim, it made sense." RMS settled into a steady and predictable rhythm of activity. Student achievement remained consistent, the school was "good" and parents were happy to have their children attend RMS. Faculty and staff turnover was low. It was understood that "not much changes at RMS."

In 2014, a new superintendent joined the district. Hired with the agenda to take the schools from "good to exceptional" Carole Reck started her work by establishing committees of faculty, staff, parents, and community members to examine district and school mission and vision. Yoder was confident that RMS would pass with flying colors and at a full staff meeting, proudly pointed to the school's Web page and statement of commitment to every student. After reviewing the pages, Reck looked to

Yoder and the assembled teachers and said, "Yes, it's a great motto, I can see that, but what's your vision?" Flustered, Yoder repeated the motto. A few teachers offered support mentioning the school's focus on data-driven decision making. Others talked about curriculum initiatives and school discipline plans. Reck was patient and positive, saying, "I know RMS is a good school, I know you work hard here, but I still need to know, what's your vision?"

Discussing the Case

Review the key players, the timeline of activity, and the ways theory can help you to make sense of the case as presented. Consider the following questions:

- Does RMS have a vision?
- Does RMS need a vision?
- If you were Yoder, how might you respond to Reck's question?
- What work might the faculty and staff at RMS need to complete?
- What aspects of the school might need to change?
- What aspects of the school could serve to inform new visioning work?
- How might a new vision change RMS?

CASE 2.2

How Much Does Teacher Buy-In Cost?

Intracoastal Elementary School (IES) is located close to the coastline and in a well-established, suburban community within Southeastern School District (SSD). As one of the 30 largest districts in the United States, SSD divides its many elementary, middle, high, and alternative schools into several regions. Intracoastal Elementary School serves over 650 students. Over 90 percent of the students qualify for free or reduced lunch services, indicating low socioeconomic status. Following the retirement of Kathy Rutherford, who has led IES for the last 15 years, Mary Elizabeth Johnson was hired as principal of IES. When Johnson was announced as the new principal for IES, many teachers were still mourning the retirement of Rutherford. Yet, Johnson was not without prior administrative experience. In the past 10 years, she had worked in two secondary schools in another region of the district. In her previous positions, she oversaw curriculum in a magnet middle school and most recently in a large, International Baccalaureate high school. She believed she could work well with the faculty and staff at IES.

As one of her first tasks as the new principal, Johnson proposed reviewing the school vision and mission, which had not been updated since Rutherford joined the school. Johnson's sense was that the teachers were resistant to change, yet, she forged ahead hoping she might energize interest in the effort. Johnson planned to survey the teachers and staff prior to the end of school and the beginning of summer break so that she might get to know them and the school a bit better before she began in the fall. Knowing that her efforts were potentially unwelcome, she chose to keep the anonymous questionnaire upbeat and positive, and decided to ask the following questions:

- What do you love about our school?
- Which words come to mind to best describe our school?
- What values best represent our faculty?
- Which traditions do you value the most at our school?
- How can we improve Intracoastal Elementary School?
- What type of support do you need most from your principal?

In addition to the survey, Johnson also hoped to develop a work group to meet over the summer months. Johnson hoped that by supporting this group's efforts and providing any needed resources requested, she might secure their buy-in and support for a new vision and mission. To encourage participation, Johnson offered the teacher volunteers a stipend for the days they worked over the summer and promised to provide lunch when they met at the school. She was pleased when several teachers stepped up and agreed to become part of the new workgroup.

In the end, the team was staffed by a grade level representative from each grade at IES and members of the special education staff. Johnson tasked the teachers to begin with reviewing the results of the survey questions and to consider how they might lead a session to review and revise the school's vision and mission during teacher preparation days in August.

While most teachers' responses to the questionnaire were positive and encouraging, the group was surprised by the negative responses of some of their colleagues. One respondent wrote, "I don't know why we need to change anything at all. If it ain't broke, don't fix it." Another teacher wrote, "What do I need? I need you to leave me alone to do my job and quit having meetings. Let me close my door and teach my kids." A third colleague quipped, "What do I love about our school? I loved Mrs. Rutherford. Why did she have to retire?"

Johnson's original plan included sharing the survey results as a part of the revision of the vision, mission, and school improvement plan writing. Ideally, the responses would inform and guide the revision process and discussion. The teacher team knew that ignoring the negative comments would not serve the school well. Yet, they worried that by including these voices the effort would become hijacked by negativity and Johnson's efforts toward establishing a new vision and mission would be derailed. The teacher group was divided concerning what they should do and where they might go now that they had the survey information. They approached Johnson, hoping she could offer some direction and support. Instead, she suggested, "I really want this to be a teacher-led effort. I know you'll reach a decision that is best for all of us."

Discussing the Case

- How effective was Johnson's approach?
- Were the survey questions effective in gathering the information needed?
- Was Johnson right to delegate this task to teachers? Should Johnson have been more involved in the process?
- Do you think she gained teacher investment in the visioning process by forming the team?

- As a member of the teacher team, what would you do in this case?
- How else could a principal gain teacher support for a new program, initiative, or change?
- When introducing a new initiative, what is the best pace for a new principal to proceed?

CASE 2.3

What's to Fix?

Mateo Diego had been Associate Principal for Learning (APL) at Rhoades High for over eight years when he was tapped to become Rhoades's next principal. A Title I School, Diego believed he knew the Rhoades community and knew how he could contribute to the school's ongoing success. During the time Diego had been at Rhoades, the school had moved from being rated unsatisfactory to maintaining and then to commendable. Diego credited the exiting principal Jamie Duncan with much of the school's success. Duncan's leadership style was open and supportive. He had worked closely with the staff to develop a clear vision for school success and had been instrumental in fostering a culture of improvement.

Recently, those efforts had paid off and the school had received national recognition as a Blue Ribbon School. Deservedly proud, Diego believed that Duncan's leadership regarding the school's vision had played a crucial role in focusing the school in a positive direction. Simple and direct, the vision stated:

> Rhoades High School is a community of high expectations, academic and otherwise. We believe that we should provide opportunities for all learners, helping students to develop their intellectual, athletic, artistic, and personal interests so that they will be well positioned for a lifetime of well-being and success.

Diego had served on the leadership committee that crafted the vision. The committee had included broad participation of the school community including teacher, parents, the community advisory board, and student government representatives. Although many of the members of the committee had moved on to other positions, each fall Duncan reintroduced the vision to the faculty and staff and retold the story of its crafting. He made certain to acknowledge by name each and every member that had worked on the initial team. He also took pride in recounting the successes the student members had enjoyed since graduation.

Each year he offered the assembled faculty and staff the option of reworking the vision. To date, no one had thought a revision was necessary. Yet, changes had been made to the supporting core values. Originally, the document had included two underlying values—responsibility and respect. The values were defined as:

- Responsibility—Faculty, staff, and students will take ownership of our behavior as individuals, thinking and acting in ways that demonstrate our commitment to solving the problems that face us and supporting others in their efforts to succeed.

- Respect—Faculty, staff, and students believe in the inherent dignity of all people. We shall celebrate individuality by honoring others through our words and actions.

Over time, the faculty and staff had added a third core value: that of integrity. The school defined integrity as, "Standing up for what we believe, being fair in our judgments and actions, and fulfilling our commitments and promises to ourselves and each other to promote a compassionate and safe community." As Diego stated, "As the world has changed we thought we needed to stand up for integrity in our community. There were some of us that thought it was implied by the two Rs, but it was still important to say this part out loud. So we added it."

The vision and core values were supported by goals written by the team, including the development of:

- challenging standards and curriculum;
- active teaching and learning;
- technology integration in the support of student learning, and
- data systems and structures to evaluate progress toward outcomes.

As Diego stated: "We wanted to keep things clean. Flowery language that people didn't understand wasn't what we wanted. Were there fancier ways to say these things, sure. But this worked for us." He went on to note that "Where we really focused our efforts was on those goals. What did we need to make that happen? What did we need to change? Who could we learn from? So, the goals don't change. What changes is our work toward making them happen."

By all accounts, one of the reasons Mateo Diego was tapped to be Rhoades's next principal was his involvement with the school's recent success. As the associate principal for learning, Diego had managed and led many of the initiatives that had contributed to the school's progress. He had also been responsible for supporting mentoring for new teachers and had worked closely with the assistant principal, Karin Lopez, who had handled teaching evaluations. He was confident he would be able to promote Lopez into his old role once he took over as principal and that the school would continue to excel.

What troubled Diego were the words of the superintendent. Upon his hiring, the superintendent said to Diego, "Be sure to make the school your own. Don't feel like you have to be Duncan." While Diego appreciated the confidence the superintendent's words suggested, he wondered what exactly was meant. When pressed to explain, the only additional direction that was offered was, "Start with the vision. I'm sure you'd like to make some changes."

Discussing the Case

- What appears to be working well at Rhoades?
- What might benefit from a change?
- If you were Diego, how might you approach this situation?
- Is a vision change needed?
- When entering a school as a new principal, what priorities should you value during your first year?

- How might you consider existing practices and policies as you identify your priorities?
- To whom might you turn for assistance and guidance?
- Would you want to take on a leadership role in a school you already knew well?
- Would you prefer to start from a fresh perspective?
- How are things different when you know a place well?
- What do you need to learn when you do not know a school well but have been appointed its new principal?

ACTIVITIES

ACTIVITY 2.1

Examining Mission and Vision: Looking Externally

Complete a Web search of school vision and mission documents and statements. Choose three to five examples that you find compelling and meaningful. Consider what each includes. What do they have in common? What do you like about each? How do they foster an inspiring future for the schools (or districts) they are written? What do you find lacking in these missions and visions? If you had been part of the writing team, what might you have included that they did not? In what ways do you think they might inform your vision and mission thinking?

ACTIVITY 2.2

Examining Mission and Vision: Looking Internally

Analyze the components of your school's or district's current mission and vision with an eye toward developing what it says or does not say, and what the mission or vision was intended to do. Interview members of your school community to determine how the mission and vision was developed, and in what ways it has been reviewed, revisited, revised, and implemented. Consider the following questions in your mission and vision analysis.

- How was the vision and/or mission written?
- How does your school "live" your mission and vision?
- Are there rituals related to your vision?
- What is included explicitly in the current mission and vision?
- What is included or understood implicitly?

continued . . .

- What is missing, vague, or needs to be explicitly articulated in the current mission and vision of your building and district?
- Whose voice was included in the crafting of this mission and vision? (Alternatively, whose voice or perspective wasn't included?)
- How might mission and vision work in your school be enhanced?

ACTIVITY 2.3

Revising and Reviewing Existing Mission and Vision

Imagine that you are the building leader or part of the leadership team and required to move forward with a review and revision of the current mission and vision. Presume you have all the resources and control, what would be the best vision and mission for your school?

- What would you need to do in order to get this work done?
- What values would you hope that your mission and vision featured?
- What conceptual understandings would you bring into your process?
- What are the leadership frames you will draw from?
- What data might be needed to inform your process?
- What barriers might you face?
- How will you build organizational capacity?
- Who would you include in the planning and why?
- How would you ensure equitable representation of diverse voices and perspectives in your school community?
- How might you assess and evaluate your process?

Write a mission and vision that you believe would be motivating and inspirational for a school. Describe in detail why you have included specific words and phrases, what they mean to you, and how you believe these will be operationalized in the practices of your school.

RESOURCES

The Internet is replete with resources to support mission and vision work. While much of this writing is focused on businesses, school leaders can learn a lot by studying how others have done this work and where they have succeeded and where they have failed. Here we offer several non-education volumes that consider the importance of vision in leadership work. We also want to stress that in offering these as resources we do not want to suggest that schools would be better off if they were run like businesses. Instead, we are suggesting that by stepping away from a more traditional school leadership literature, school leaders can gain leadership insights in new, fresh ways.

The Zappos Story

Zappos is a company that has long been recognized as leading from a clear central vision. While the company story and vision can be found at www.zappos.com/c/about-zappos, the story of the ways in which leadership worked to bring the company from nothing to the dominant on-line retailer it is today is instructive. We suggest two volumes (Michelli, 2011; Hsieh, 2010) that describe the way that Zappos leadership worked to create a strong organizational culture by fostering a clear and focused direction as embodied in their now famous core values:

- Deliver WOW service
- Embrace and drive change
- Create fun and a little weirdness
- Be adventurous, creative, and open-minded
- Pursue growth and learning
- Build open and honest relationships with communication
- Build a positive team and family spirit
- Do more with less
- Be passionate and determined
- Be humble

In each book the authors (Hsieh was the founder) tell the organizational growth story of Zappos and discuss the ways in which vision-centered leadership fostered success.

Hsieh, T. (2010). *Delivering happiness: A path to profits, passion, and purpose*. New York: Business Books.

Michelli, J. (2011). *The Zappos experience: 5 principles to inspire, engage, and WOW*. New York: McGraw Hill.

The Starbucks Story

Starbucks has a simple mission: *To inspire and nurture the human spirit—one person, one cup, and one neighborhood at a time.* Love the coffee (and company) or not, Starbucks has changed both the fast food and beverage landscape worldwide. In the process of doing so, adherence to their mission, vision, and core values made a difference in Starbucks's success. We acknowledge that the company has not been without fault, their presence has put many a local coffee house out of business and we acknowledge that some of their corporate efforts have fallen flat. Nonetheless, a lot has been written about Starbucks and much of it tells a compelling story of the centrality of mission and vision in leadership. Among the best are:

Gill, M.G. (2007). *How Starbucks saved my life: A son of privilege learns to live like everybody else*. New York: Penguin Group.

Michelli, J. (2013). *Leading the Starbucks way: 5 principles for connecting with your customers, your products, and your people*. New York: McGraw Hill.

continued . . .

Schultz, H. (2012). *Onward: How Starbucks fought for its life without losing its soul.* Emmaus, PA: Rodale Press.

Tech Thinking

There is no disputing that technology has changed the way we live. Yet, in most stories about famous companies, the story is centered around the charismatic leader who made them who they are today. As we all know, leadership, especially great leadership, is a team effort. In each of these books, the story is more about the ways people worked together to achieve great things and less about how one person got the company there. In each, mission and vision plays a starring role.

Galloway, S. (2017). *The four: The hidden DNA of Amazon, Apple, Facebook, and Google.* New York: Penguin Group.

Hoefflinger, M. (2017). *Becoming Facebook: The 10 challenges that defined the company disrupting the world.* New York: AMACOM, American Management Association.

Levy, S. (2011). *In the plex: How Google thinks, works, and shapes our lives.* New York: Simon & Schuster.

Stone, B. (2013). *The everything store: Jeff Bezos and the age of Amazon.* New York: Little, Brown & Company.

REFERENCES

Bratianu, C., Jianu, I., & Vasilache, S. (2007). Integrators for organizational intellectual capital. *International Journal of Learning and Intellectual Capital, 8*(1), 5–17.

Bryman, A. (2004). Qualitative research on leadership: A critical but appreciative review. *The Leadership Quarterly, 15*(6), 729–769.

Checkland, P. (1981). *Systems thinking, systems practice.* Chichester, UK: John Wiley & Sons.

Checkland, P., & Poulter, J. (2006). *Learning for action: A short definitive account of soft systems methodology and its use of practitioners, teachers, and students.* Hoboken, NJ: John Wiley & Sons.

Checkland, P., & Scholes, J. (1999). *Soft systems methodology in action.* Hoboken, NJ: John Wiley & Sons.

Collins, J.C., & Porras, J. I. (1996). Building your company's vision. *Harvard Business Review, 74*(5), 65.

Deal, T.E., & Peterson, K.D. (2016). *Shaping school culture* (3rd ed.) San Francisco, CA: Jossey-Bass.

DiPaola, M.F., & Hoy, W.K. (2008). *Principals improving instruction: Supervision, evaluation, and professional development.* Boston, MA: Pearson/Allyn & Bacon.

Fullan, M. (2014). *The principal: Three keys to maximizing impact.* Retrieved from: http://michael fullan.ca/wp-content/uploads/2016/06/14_The-Principal-Handout_Spring-Summer.com pressed.pdf

Gill, R. (2011). *Theory and practice of leadership.* London: Sage.

Gioia, D.A., Nag, R., & Corley, K.G. (2012). Visionary ambiguity and strategic change: The virtue of vagueness in launching major organizational change. *Journal of Management Inquiry, 21*(4), 364–375.

Glatthorn, A.A., Jailall, J.M., & Jailall, J.K. (2017). *The principal as curriculum leader: Shaping what is taught and tested* (4th ed.). Thousand Oaks, CA: Corwin.

Hall, G.E., & Hord, S. M. (2016). *Implementing change: Patterns, principles, and potholes.* Upper Saddle River, NJ: Pearson Education.

Hallinger, P., & Murphy, J. (1985). Assessing the instructional management behavior of principals. *Elementary School Journal, 86*(2), 217–247.

Haque, M. D., Titi Amayah, A., & Liu, L. (2016). The role of vision in organizational readiness for change and growth. *Leadership & Organization Development Journal, 37*(7), 983–999.

Heck R.H., & Hallinger, P. (2010). Leadership: School improvement. In Peterson, P.L., Baker, E.L., & McGaw, B. (Eds.) *International encyclopedia of education* (pp. 135–142). Oxford: Elsevier.

Heifetz, R. (1994). *Leadership without easy answers.* Cambridge, MA: Harvard.

Heiftez, R., Grashaw, A., & Linsky, M. (2009). *The practice of adaptive leadership: Tools and tactics for changing your organization and the world.* Cambridge, MA: Harvard.

Hord, S. (1997). *Professional learning communities: What are they and why are they important?* Austin, TX: Southwest Educational Development Laboratory (SEDL).

Hord, S. (2008). Evolution of the professional learning community. *Journal of Staff Development, 29*(3), 10–13.

Hoy, W.K., & Miskel, C.G. (2008). *Educational administration: Theory, research, and practice* (8th ed.). New York: McGraw-Hill.

Jackson, M. C. (2003). The origins and nature of critical systems thinking. In Midgley, G. (Ed.) *Systems thinking* (Vol. 4, pp. 227–253). London: Sage.

Johnson, J. (2007). *A mission of the heart: Leaders in high-needs.* New York: The Wallace Foundation.

Kruse, S.D. (2009). *Working smart: Problem-solving strategies for school leaders.* Lanham, MD: Rowman & Litttlefield.

Kruse, S.D., & Johnson, B.L. (2017). Tempering the normative demands of PLCs with the organizational realities of life in schools: Exploring the cognitive dilemmas faced by educational leaders. *Educational Management, Administration, & Leadership, 45*(4), 588–604.

Kruse, S.D., & Louis, K.S. (2009). *Building strong school cultures: A guide to leading change.* Thousand Oaks, CA: Corwin Press.

Kruse, S.D., Louis, K.S., & Bryk, A.S. (1995). An emerging framework for analyzing school-based professional community. In Louis, K.S. & Kruse, S.D. (Eds.) *Professionalism and community.* Thousand Oaks, CA: Corwin Press, pp. 23–44.

McLaughlin, M., & Talbert, J. (2001). *Professional communities and the work of high school teaching.* Chicago: University of Chicago Press.

Mendels, P. (2012). The effective principal: Five pivotal practices that shape instructional leadership. *Learning Forward, 33*(1), 54–58.

Mintzberg, H. (2009). *Managing.* San Francisco, CA: Berrett-Koehler.

Mintzberg, H. (2013). *Simply managing: What managers do and can do better.* Berrett-Koehler.

Murphy, J. (1990). Principal instructional leadership. In Lotto, L.S. and Thurston, P.W. (Eds.) *Advances in educational administration* (pp. 163–200), Greenwich, CT: JAI Press.

Murphy, J., Elliot, S. N., Goldring, E., & Porter, A. C. (2006). *Learning-centered leadership: A conceptual framework*. New York: The Wallace Foundation.

Murphy, J., & Torre, D. (2015). Vision: Essential scaffolding. *Educational Management Administration and Leadership*, *43*(2), 177–197.

Printy, S., & Marks, H. (2006). Shared leadership for teachers and student learning. *Theory into Practice*, *45(2)*, 125–132.

Sun, J., & Leithwood, K. (2012). Transformational school leadership effects on student achievement. *Leadership and policy in schools*, *11*(4), 418–451.

Timperley, H.S. (2005). Distributed leadership: Developing theory from practice. *Journal of Curriculum Studies*, *37*(4), 395–420.

Tschannen-Moran, M. (2014). *Trust matters* (2nd ed.). San Francisco, CA: Jossey-Bass.

Vaill, P.B. (1984). The purposing of high-performance systems. In Sergiovanni, T.J. and Corbally, J.E. (Eds.) *Leadership and organizational culture*. Urbana, IL: University of Illinois Press.

CHAPTER **3**

Curriculum, Instruction, and Assessment

Instruction lies at the very core of classroom practice. Fundamental to teachers' work, instruction has long been a central feature of schools and schooling. Certainly, instruction is not one thing. At times, large group lessons are appropriate. At other times, small group seminars or individual tutorials are a better match for student learning needs. Instruction might include interactive lectures, guided inquiry, discussions, and project- or problem-based approaches. No matter the form that instruction takes, it has long been accepted that instruction is the primary work that schools perform.

Yet, the idea that instructional leadership should be a primary task of school leaders is a relatively new idea (Hallinger & Murphy, 1985). Prior to the rise of the effective schools movement (Edmonds, 1979), instruction was largely considered teachers' work. Clearly, principals were responsible for managing the school and ensuring that teaching could occur, but they were only tangentially responsible for instructional practice. Moreover, prior to the release of the report *A Nation at Risk* (National Commission on Excellence in Education, 1983), student learning was viewed less as the responsibility of the teacher and school and more about individual student ability and motivation. Historically, principals had not been held accountable for student achievement.

Nevertheless, as pressure grew to address the concerns about the nation's schools raised in *A Nation at Risk*, so did the notion that principals should take on instruction as a leadership focus. Yet, as recently as 1980, there was scant research to suggest that school leaders could have significant impact on student learning (Andrews & Soder, 1987; Brewer, 1993). In this way, the idea that principals should have responsibility for student learning gained popularity in tandem with a growing research literature that suggested that school leaders *do* make a difference in the learning outcomes of students (Heck, 1992; Murphy, 1988). More recently and as Leithwood and Louis (2012) have confirmed, it is understood that *leadership is second only to classroom instruction as an influencing factor on student learning*. Therefore, the idea that principals are instructional leaders has become accepted and well established. The challenge for school leaders is how they might do this work and do it well.

KEY LEARNINGS

In this chapter, you will learn to:

* review and promote a rigorous approach to curriculum and instruction within the school;

* support an intellectually rigorous and coherent system of assessment to address areas of student strength and growth; and

* promote data-driven decision making that ensures student academic success and well-being.

FEATURED CASE

It's All About the Data

Beachside Superintendent Harold Jones had to look twice when he saw the state accountability report card grade for Palm Tree Elementary School. For the last five years, the school had been ranked as an F school and one of the lowest in the state of Florida. To be fair, they did improve last year, just missing a D grade by only a few points. After careful review, Jones confirmed that the school grade was, in fact, a C for the most recent academic year. Jones believed that much of the credit is due to his new administrative team, Principal Kelly O'Malley and Assistant Principal Stephanie Brown, both in their second year at Palm Tree Elementary.

Jones was proud of the duo because he was aware that Palm Tree has never been an easy school to lead. Situated in an established neighborhood with a high crime rate, Palm Tree's student mobility ranks among the highest in Florida. Approximately 1 percent of the student body is Caucasian, 5 percent is Hispanic, and the remaining 94 percent is African American. As a Title I school, 100 percent of the 785 students enrolled qualify for free or reduced price lunch services. Additionally, the district's per pupil spending is far below the state average. Furthermore, the school has had a high teacher turn-over rate. Jones and others believe the constant churn of teachers has contributed to the school's prior poor performance. Clearly, something had recently changed at Palm Tree and that change was for the better. Jones was excited to share the news with the school community.

Palm Tree's Story

After being hired and although O'Malley and Brown had not worked together in the past, they quickly bonded, taking time over the summer to review five years of testing data, school climate surveys, and continuous improvement plans for Palm Tree Elementary. Their approaches to the work varied slightly, as did their personalities, yet, O'Malley and Brown agreed to disagree privately and to present a united front to the teachers, students, and community at all times. Together, and based on their assessment of these data, they developed a leadership plan for the upcoming academic year. Knowing there was extensive work ahead of them if they were to address the poor performance of students at Palm Tree, they divided managerial tasks between themselves, considering each other's strengths as they assigned primary and secondary areas of responsibility. However, on one point they both believed they held responsibility. Instruction had to be their first priority. O'Malley and Brown agreed to visit every classroom, every day. This would be a non-negotiable for their team.

First Steps

As the school year began, O'Malley and Brown stayed true to their commitment. Many of the teachers were impressed by the way the two handled their classroom visits. Of particular note was the duo's efforts to learn student names and how they always took a moment to praise the children. However, the last few principals at Palm Tree had not come out of their offices much and although O'Malley and Brown didn't appear threatening, the teachers voiced some concern about their interest in classroom practice. O'Malley and Brown knew that they needed to establish trust among the teachers prior to implementing any changes. They took careful notes and met often to discuss the ways they believed classroom instruction might be improved. Finally, after several months and much discussion they decided to focus their first efforts on altering how teachers talked with each other about student learning.

As in many schools, Palm Tree teachers had dedicated planning time to discuss instruction, their curriculum, student discipline, and other classroom issues. According to Beachside policy, they were to use a portion of the time to analyze student learning data. The intent was that after review, teachers would respond to identified student need by differentiating their instruction, providing extended support, or reteaching content that students had not grasped. In practice, the conversations about data, known as data chats, were less about instructional response and more about the challenges to learning that Palm Tree students faced. Furthermore, many teachers at the school were unclear as to what to do with the data and how they might use it for classroom decision making. O'Malley and Brown knew that data alone was not enough to change classroom practice. They knew that the real power in data use came from the instructional decisions that were made based on the conclusions teachers drew from the data. Their concern was how to foster a deeper conversation about instructional choices and practices.

O'Malley and Brown decided that they could capitalize on this existing practice by modeling what they had been doing as a leadership team. They believed they could help teachers understand how to read the data and how it could drive instructional decision making. However, first of all they knew they would need to share what it meant to analyze the data without shaming or blaming teachers for what they didn't know. Additionally, they feared some resistance because at Palm Tree, prior principals had not engaged in this kind of close scrutiny of classroom practice.

Data Chats and Data-Driven Decision Making

O'Malley and Brown started to meet with teachers by grade level every week. Initially, they led and organized the sessions. Beginning by discussing student concerns, O'Malley and Brown slowly shifted the conversation toward aligning lesson and unit plans to student learning standards. Florida had recently revised its state standards, and O'Malley and Brown encouraged Palm Tree teachers to "do a close read" to see how the standards had changed. In particular, they focused teachers' attentions on linking what they taught to the kinds of assignments and assessments they provided for students. O'Malley and Brown encouraged the teachers to keep careful records of student performance and used these records to prompt data chats focused on how their students were performing in relation to the new standards.

At the same time, they began using faculty meetings to share school-level data. Using disaggregated school data, they asked the full faculty to examine where Palm Tree students were succeeding and where they were not. Understandably, several teachers were defensive and felt blamed for student failures. Yet, O'Malley and Brown stood firm. They encouraged teachers to "stop the blame game" and to think instead about what needed to change for students to learn and achieve. Additionally, they stressed that they were not alone in the challenge of instructing and achieving with a highly transient student population.

Significantly, O'Malley and Brown pressed a discussion among the teachers that tied the conclusions drawn from the data to classroom instructional practices. They encouraged teachers to think about how they were using district curriculum materials, their instructional time, and the ways in which they were following up with parents and care-givers regarding student progress. Furthermore, they pushed teachers to establish a common instructional language so that they could talk more effectively with each other about their teaching and advocated for deepening data chat discussion. As O'Malley shared, "We really wanted our teachers to challenge each other and not accept the easy explanation. We lobbied hard for the data chats to be places where teachers thought about how what they did affected what students learned."

A New Culture of Learning

By January, O'Malley and Brown believed that they had done much to change the culture of student learning at Palm Tree. Teachers were becoming more public about their practice and were using their planning time to share classroom instructional ideas and assessments. Furthermore, it was evident that the teachers were becoming more strategic in addressing the needs of students who were not proficient in specific standards. Special small group strategies and remediation exercises and activities were developed. The teachers worked to be as innovative as possible, using the skills and resources they had access to within Palm Tree Elementary. They began to press O'Malley and Brown for additional resources and professional development to enhance their efforts. O'Malley and Brown did what they could to support the faculty. Importantly, they confronted several reluctant teachers. Three teachers who were not on board with the data chats or change in general were encouraged to apply for transfers for the upcoming school year. One decided to retire early and the other two were happy to transfer elsewhere.

One big change at Palm Tree addressed the way that teachers interacted with their students. Based on the work of a small team of teachers, who had worked with their students to set individual goals for improvement, others began to guide students to establish goals and timelines for their own improvement effort. By March, a majority of students were setting learning goals for themselves. O'Malley and Brown promoted student goal setting by providing prizes and awards given out every Friday during lunch. At first, the prizes were popular juice drinks or snacks. Eventually, there was a shift to coupons for reward activities, including lunch with the principal, a half hour in the computer lab, extra time in the art classroom for crafts after school, and free reading books to take home. Students loved the rewards and the attention they received for meeting their goals. An added bonus was a small but significant reduction in the absence rate. It seemed that students were happier than they had been in years at Palm Tree.

In May, and as part of their annual evaluation process, O'Malley and Brown encouraged the teachers to write reflections. One veteran teacher shared,

> I learned more this year than I did in all of my years in the classroom. I am proud of the changes that I made. I felt like Kelly and Stephanie really supported me becoming a better teacher. They saw in me what I hadn't seen in myself. I am a believer in DDDM and my colleagues here at Palm Tree Elementary!

A second-year teacher wrote,

> I feel so proud of what we have accomplished this year. We made a difference. To be honest, I thought I knew how to analyze data and to teach my students well. Boy, did I learn a lot this year. I hope that we earned a decent school grade this year because we sure do deserve it.

Traditionally, at the end of each school year, parents and guardians were given a climate survey. In the past, Palm Tree Elementary rarely received positive comments or constructive criticism. This last year was different. Most parents were supportive of the improvements at Palm Tree Elementary. One parent shared,

> The school is working hard to make our community better. I think Mrs. O'Malley really wants to see positive change for our kids. She is using all of her energy to make a difference in our neighborhood. My son can't wait to go to school and loves the after-school program because he gets to do art and science projects. Mrs. O'Malley and Ms. Brown are really making a difference.

Unfortunately, not all parents were pleased with the data-focused approach of the school. Another parent quipped, "All they care about is test scores, not my kid. She ain't just a number, she's a kid. She needs more time to play outside and less time taking tests and studying." O'Malley and Brown felt they could do more in the coming year to reach out so that all parents understood what they were trying to achieve. Nevertheless, they were pleased with the responses.

Celebrating Success

Following confirmation of the school's improvement, Jones, O'Malley, and Brown planned a special ceremony for the students, inviting parents and community members to attend. At a staff lunch, personalized handwritten thank you notes were presented to each teacher. Each letter focused on specific changes or improvements made by the teacher, and included praise for the work they had accomplished and the ways it had impacted student learning. Additionally, Superintendent Jones presented each teacher with a $500 voucher to be used for classroom and instructional resources. Not surprisingly, the event was an emotional one. As one teacher stated, "It is just so good to be recognized for doing a good job." O'Malley and Brown were proud of the work they had completed and the results they had achieved. They realized that data-driven decision making was not the only intervention to implement. Yet, they agreed that it was an effective approach for their first year at Palm Tree Elementary. Their only concern was what they would do next.

INSTRUCTIONAL LEADERSHIP FOCI AND ACTION

Schools become exemplary when school leaders focus on what matters for student learning and success. The practice of doing so is instructional leadership. Broadly, instructional leadership requires that principals advocate for a school vision that fosters a learning-focused culture, support the improvement of instructional practice, allocate resources to provide for instructional programing, and manage the systems and processes to support student learning (Mendels, 2012; Rigby, 2013). Instructional leadership necessitates that attention be paid to issues related to curriculum, instruction, and assessment with the intent of assuring student learning. Yet, the achievement of positive student learning outcomes requires more than good intentions. It requires an *intellectually rigorous* approach be taken and decision-making efforts be directed toward ensuring the academic success and well-being of each student.

A Word About Rigor

When something is rigorous it is generally thought of as challenging or difficult. Yet, if something is too hard or there is too much of it, rather than persisting and succeeding most students simply tend to give up. Therefore, rigor is not about simply making things hard (or harder). Rigor is about providing appropriate challenge paired with appropriate support so that students learn what they are to learn in deep ways (Hechinger Institute, 2009). Leading with a mind toward rigor includes attention to what is taught (i.e., curriculum), how it is taught (i.e., instruction), and how it is evaluated (i.e., assessment). As such, rigor pairs high expectations for student learning, with appropriate instructional supports in the context of assessments that demonstrate that students have mastered what it was to be learned. Instructional leaders focus on making their schools better places for students by increasing rigor across all instructional settings in a school (DeMatthews, 2014; Murphy, 2016).

Rigorous Approaches to Curriculum

There are many ways in which to define curriculum. Curriculum might be thought of as a plan of academic goals, the program or programs offered to students, as a field of study and subject area content, or the foundation upon which pedagogical theories and principles are based (Eisner, 2002; Ornstein & Hunkins, 2013; Wiles & Bondi, 2011). No matter which definition any given leader embraces, rigor matters. School leaders who focus the attention of faculty and staff on the following research supported dimensions cannot help to increase rigor. Instructional leaders structure the school's curriculum so that it:

- builds upon and extends beyond a standard course of study (Leithwood & Louis, 2012; Ornstein & Hunkins, 2013);
- consistently addresses both content knowledge bases and skill sets (Erickson, Lanning, & French, 2017; Glatthorn, Jailall, & Jailall, 2017);
- focuses on problem solving (Brubaker, 2004; Scheerens, 2016);
- provides for an integrated, sequential course of study (Bradley, Curtis, Kessinger, & Meyers, 2018; Galtthorn & Jailall, 2008); and
- develops connections to the world beyond the classroom (Herrington, Parker, & Boase-Jelinek, 2014; Newmann, Carmichael Tanaka & King, 2015).

Yet, it is often difficult to determine what constitutes a rigorous curriculum. Knowing what is rigorous and what is not is difficult because learning is a cultural phenomenon. Learning varies across time, place, and people. No educational intervention works the same way in all instances and contexts. It is impossible to say if a teacher uses X curriculum, then Y will happen for every student. Yet, taken together the five dimensions listed above create the conditions under which students can be more deeply engaged in the content they are studying, better able to make connections between lessons and units, more likely to understand why they are studying what they are studying and, ultimately, how those ideas might be of use to them (Bell, 2010; Newmann, Carmichael Tanaka, & King, 2015). When school leaders support teachers toward these curricular objectives, rigor is increased.

Rigorous Approaches to Instruction

Rigorous instruction is unavoidably tied to rigorous curriculum. Inasmuch as curriculum comprises what is taught, instruction addresses how it is taught. Therefore, leading rigorous instruction calls for school leaders to focus attention on the ways teachers interact with students around their learning. Successful instructional leaders focus their attentions on the ways teachers employ curricular materials, using them to support student growth and achievement. If instruction is to be rigorous, it should be structured so that it:

- incorporates higher order thinking for every student so that students are challenged to interpret, analyze, and/or manipulate information and ideas (Mendels, 2012; Newmann, Carmichael Tanaka, & King, 2015);
- promotes deep substantive knowledge of content and disciplinary concepts (Bell, 2010; McTighe & Wiggins, 2013);
- encourages inquiry and problem solving (Kuhlthau, Maniotes, & Caspari, 2015; Scheerens, 2016);
- differentiates instructional formats with intent of providing a more diverse and interactive learning environment (Tomlinson, 2014; Tomlinson & Murphy, 2015); and
- fosters cultural competence and critical reflection (Banks, 2016; Khalifa, Gooden, & Davis, 2016).

As with rigorous curriculum, there are no silver bullets for rigorous instruction. Yet, if leaders are to support instruction that challenges and engages students, they must support teachers in employing research-based instructional strategies with the intent of improving instructional practices. Doing so requires that school leaders support teacher development by providing professional development, ongoing feedback, and coaching to ensure that rigorous instruction is occurring in all classrooms.

Rigorous Approaches to Assessment

A rigorous approach to assessment should be the natural outcome of rigorous curriculum and instruction. In fact, rigorous classroom assessment has the potential to promote student learning and measure student learning outcomes (O'Connor, 2018; Stiggins, 2014). Unlike external standardized or state-level tests, well-designed classroom assessment provides timely, detailed, personalized, and explicit feedback to students regarding their learning as well as important information for teachers to make instructional decisions. Instructional leaders who focus their attentions toward classroom assessment, guide teachers in the use of assessment in three key arenas—pre-instruction diagnosis, feedback concurrent to instruction, and post-instruction evaluation. Rigorous assessment occurs at all three stages of assessment and should be structured so that it:

- provides formative and summative feedback to students and their caregivers about their learning (Dixon & Worrell, 2016; Stiggins, 2014);
- informs instructional decision making (Datnow & Hubbard, 2015; Farrell, 2014);
- helps students set learning goals and/or self-assess learning goals (Chappuis, Commodore, & Stiggins, 2017; Stiggins, 2014);
- provides clear models and/or descriptions of what is expected for a student to demonstrate their learning in clear, understandable, and concrete terms (Gotch & French, 2014; Smit & Birri, 2014); and
- links assessment to meaningful standards and learning outcomes (O'Connor, 2018; Vatterott, 2015).

School leaders who champion rigorous assessment practices focus their attention toward the use of assessment data with the intent of supporting student learning. This entails focusing leadership effort toward continuous improvement and promoting thinking about classroom strategies for enhancing learning. It requires that school leaders are able to support teachers' understanding of high-quality assessment practice and the use of the data that assessments provide.

DATA-DRIVEN DECISION MAKING

As was demonstrated at Palm Tree Elementary, data use in schools generally focuses on observing how students perform on state-level tests in concert with day-to-day instructional tasks, while collecting and analyzing those results to inform instructional decisions (O'Neal, 2012; Roegman, Perkins-Williams, Maeda, & Greenan, 2017). Usually, formative and summative student data are used to identify areas of strength and need in individual students or student groups. Then, data are used to guide decisions regarding instructional remediation or supports for students. Yet, the process is rarely as linear as it appears. We begin with a short example.

Data Use at Harbourview

At Harbourview Middle School subject-specific teacher teams meet quarterly to review student performance data from short cycle, common assessments. The assigned task is quite simple—review the data to identify three trends. First, teachers are to identify the student learning objectives (SLOs) that have been mastered by the majority of students. Second, teachers are to identify specific students who have not yet mastered these same SLOs and to set aside the list for future individual remediation. Third, teachers are to identify any SLOs for which more than 50 percent of students scored poorly and set aside these SLOs for future group reteaching. The group's final task is to choose remediation activities and plan for future instruction based on their choices.

As intuitively sound as this process appears, it also highlights the strengths and limitations of data use in schools. In this case, and many others like it, the attempt is to use data to make sense of the complexity of teaching a large number of students with differing abilities and performance. Yet, it falls short because it fails to capture the circumstances and perspectives in which these data are generated and reside. By contrasting the ways that data can be used well and the areas where it falls short, the tensions inherent in data use can be better understood.

Complex Questions and Data Use

Data analysis such as that of Harbourview handles broad complex questions well. It allows teachers to isolate specific students in need of specific interventions and to develop teaching and learning plans for remediation. It helps to make sense of a large amount of student data and identify individual instances where intervention is required. It measures the quantity of who "gets it" and who does not. Where it falls short is in measuring the social complexity that exists within every school. It can tell us who is not learning, but it cannot tell us why they are not learning. These data cannot detect which students demonstrate uncooperative behavior, lack motivation to learn, their emotional state, or the climate of the classroom. In short, the quality of the learning experience can be left unexamined. Furthermore, when data are aggregated, individual differences can be masked, further complicating its meaning.

Data used in this fashion may do a good job of identifying the global context in which it is generated, but it misses the local context present within each classroom. Data struggles with context. It must be contextualized in order to mine its greater meaning. Data can identify where a specific topic is addressed less well across all classrooms; yet, it fails to tackle a circumstance where a single teacher may lack the knowledge or skill set to make learning clear for students. When global understandings are privileged over locally informed contextual understandings, the temptation to form sweeping conclusions and generate reactions ignores more nuanced narratives and choices (Datnow & Hubbard, 2015; Johnson & Kruse, 2009).

Furthermore, data helps us to locate small problems, but has the potential to miss bigger, more intractable problems. For example, at Harbourview while it is relatively easy to identify students in need of intervention, it is much harder to identify what intervention might serve the student best or what form of performance task a student might require to best demonstrate their knowledge. As one teacher shared, "this process makes it so I can tell you who doesn't get adding fractions, but I don't always know what I'm supposed to do to help them get it."

Additionally, data can surface instances where bias might be functioning. Individuals vary in their ability to interpret and make judgments based on the data at hand. At Harbourview, teachers are proud to note that by using this system for considering data, traditional tracking and grouping has been virtually eliminated. They credit their ongoing examination of student performance as "transforming" how they think about a given student's capability. Clearly, the potential for data to reduce, if not eliminate, biased explanations for student performance is significant. Yet, reducing student learning outcomes to easily tested low-level objectives has, in some schools, compromised meaningful learning (Gotch & French, 2014; Leithwood & Louis, 2012).

Finally, data has the potential to prompt teachers to identify issues and problems where none may exist. Take Harbourview's practice of reteaching SLOs on which students have evidenced poor performance. Doing so, without an analysis of the importance of the learning, the linkage of this construct to others like it in the curriculum, and identification of future opportunities in which reteaching this construct might naturally arise, teachers may find themselves playing a "constant game of catch-up" where they believe they are "reteaching too many things," without consideration for meaning and impact. In other words, attention to the detail that data can provide may well distract from what might be more meaningful issues and actions. This distinction is not entirely lost on Harbourview teachers. As one teacher provocatively noted, "there is a direct correlation between how far removed you are from a classroom and how much you talk about data." While we have yet to test this statement empirically, we recognize that this teacher was expressing frustration with the ways in which the work and thinking of teachers has become diverted from the core work of teaching (Stiggins, 2014; Vatterott, 2015).

Substantive and Symbolic Data Use

In light of this observation, and in the context of data use in the collective learning process, we suggest that school leaders need to be intentional in how they approach data use and data-based decision making. This means that school leaders must distinguish between *symbolic* data use and *substantive* data use. It also means managing both in strategic ways.

Substantive data use describes the process whereby educational personnel use data to inform instructional, curricular, and assessment choices in the school or district. The changes that ensue are the result of thinking about and using these data. The primary use of these data is formative, since data are used to monitor and evaluate core task performance on an ongoing basis (Kruse & Johnson, 2017). These data are used by those working at the core and is aimed at improving the performance quality of this task. In sum, it is the internal (i.e., within school or district), non-public, critical, and formative use of data embedded in an immediate school context.

Symbolic data use by schools or districts describes the process of generating, posting and using data for public consumption. These data are generated for public use and inspection or selective "data for show." Although subject to shifts over time, many of the data indicators used are consistent with the dominant institutional logics of the day and are often politically determined. These include such measures as pupil-teacher ratios, student enrollment and key demographic data, dropout rates, aggregated test scores, and common core assessments to name a few. In recent years, accountability reforms have placed schools in a position to report data they might otherwise not wish to report.

Symbolic data tend to be used for external summative school judgments (e.g., state report cards, school and district ranking). As such, they serve an important symbolic function. Whereas substantive data use is contextually embedded and interpreted, symbolic data use is abstracted and often interpreted apart from its context and discussions of instruction and curricular choices (Kruse & Johnson, 2017). While substantive data use is ongoing, internally oriented and formative, symbolic data use is periodic (e.g., annually), externally directed, and summative. These data often place the superintendent and principal in a position to interpret, defend, and field questions from various publics. Given that a school's quality is predicated on public perceptions generated by such data, it behooves the principal to manage and respond to these data in strategic ways.

We have presented these ideas as a caution to school leaders. Yet, we also believe strongly that when done well, data-driven decision making holds great promise for fostering student academic success and well-being. When considering data use in schools, the following points are worth remembering:

- *Successful instructional leaders use data to guide substantive discussion regarding teaching and learning.* The process of identifying, collecting, and analyzing data allows educational leaders to focus teachers' attention on the core work of the school. Doing so can provide a strong foundation for goal setting and focused instructional and assessment strategies.

- *Data are more than test scores.* As we have suggested above, if data use is to transcend the symbolic and become a meaningful part of a school's institutional practices, it must include attention to diagnostic and formative data alongside that of evaluative information. School leaders should work to systematize and institutionalize the collection and analysis of data through the school year and across various programs. This should include data related to student and community demographics, school climate as it is experienced by teachers, students and their families, as well as data related to instructional practices and policies.
- *Data collection and analysis is best accomplished in coherent ways.* To maintain coherence, leaders must align data collection and analysis efforts with anchors such as subject- and course-standards, school goals, lesson and unit student learning outcomes, instructional practices, and assessment demands. Finally, the development of a continuous improvement cycle is essential to high-quality data collection and analysis strategy. School leaders should start with a focus on a desired outcome, define a point of inquiry, identify data valid to desired outcomes, collect and organize the data, make meaning of the results, take action, and evaluate the results of those actions.

Conclusions

Sound curricular, instructional, and assessment leadership is an all-hands-on-deck proposition. While school leaders can chart the course of a school's instructional work, doing so does not guarantee that students will learn or learn well. Instead, instructional leadership requires that all members of the school community focus their attentions toward student progress and growth. School leaders must choose where to begin and then to persist. It is important to remember that leaders who have successfully transformed the instructional climate and culture of their schools did so by starting with one focus. It might have been data, or differentiation, or problem-solving. However, they simply kept moving from there. One success built on another and another. Not everything effective school leaders tried was a roaring success, but they kept trying. Successful instructional leadership requires that we keep trying as well.

CASES FOR ANALYSIS

CASE 3.1

Pinney Glade Elementary: Struggling and Succeeding

Pinney Glade Elementary School is a small school located in a community described as high risk. The school is home to 500 kindergarten through fourth grade students, most of whom qualify for free or reduced lunch. Test scores have steadily improved over the past five years, which is credited to the efforts of the principal and the assistant principal. Hired as a team, Mary Jane Allsmen and LaVon Merrywheather were brought in with the explicit charge of raising student achievement at Pinney Glade. Allsmen and Merrywheather had worked together at another elementary in the district and the results they had achieved with that faculty and staff had impressed district leaders.

The two had been wary of taking the new assignment. After finally settling into a phase where all they needed to do was maintain their good work at Maple Grove Elementary, they wondered how much energy they had to offer Pinney Glade at this late stage of their careers. Additionally, they worried that the staff at Pinney Glade would resent the district's intervention at the school. Yet, they welcomed the challenge and believed that the "magic" they had worked at Maple Grove could be replicated at Pinney Glade.

Allsmen and Merrywheather agreed to make the move contingent upon district support for staff development and professional learning. Specifically, they asked that they be able to hold a full staff two-day retreat prior to the start of school and build four days of time into the school calendar to provide for additional professional development. Allsmen proposed that, to start, these days would be paid for by the district and was clear about her plans to seek external grant funding to support additional work. She had been a prolific rainmaker at Maple Grove and the district was willing to gamble on her ability to produce similar results at Pinney Glade. Allsmen and Merrywheather also requested that they be able to meet with the faculty, staff, and the families of Pinney Glade students prior to making the move. They wanted to be sure that the school community would welcome them and that everyone was on board with what promised to be "serious business."

First, Allsmen and Merrywheather met with the faculty. After sharing data regarding recent test results, they did not mince words, suggesting, "you all can do better for these kids." They outlined an ambitious calendar of activities starting with the mandatory retreat in August. Reminding the teachers that this would be paid time, Allsmen noted that, "if you work hard, I'll support you." She also noted that consistent with the district's union contract, she had the right to require attendance at the retreat and would be exercising her management rights "to expect professionalism" at every turn. Allsmen and Merrywheather were also blunt about their interest in "taking the evaluation process seriously." As Merrywheather added, "We'll be in your classrooms, we'll work with you on the data, and we'll expect results with the kids. All you have to do is work with us."

For most of the teachers, Allsmen's and Merrywheather's approach was welcomed. Several knew teachers at Maple Grove and had heard positive things about the two. As one Maple Grove teacher put it, "They work you hard, no question, but they also support you." Another added, "I never had them not back me with a parent." Several stated that they believed in the Maple Grove "magic" calling it, "nothing more than solid good work" but also sharing that Allsmen and Merrywheather, "didn't take excuses from anyone." Following the meeting, a few teachers requested transfers to other schools in the district and several more suggested that "they'd try it for a year." Almost all were impressed by the focus that Allsmen and Merrywheather demonstrated and were happy for the added paid time.

At the parent meeting, Allsmen and Merrywheather took an equally aggressive approach. Although attendance was light, they outlined their expectations for student behavior, homework, and "engagement with their own learning." They stressed that every family at the school would be required to sign a family contract agreeing that they "understood the expectations of the school and would support the educators at Pinney Glade in making the school the best it could be." Allsmen ended the meeting telling the families that she "was on their side" and wanted "their kids to become great young men and women" but that to do so she "needed their support."

The summer prior to beginning at Pinney Glade was a busy one for Allsmen and Merrywheather. They reviewed the school data and, using already vetted district programs and policies, created a detailed strategic plan for improving student achievement and progress. As Merrywheather described, "We purposefully did this work the way we did. We didn't want to waste time and since we didn't do anything that hadn't already been approved by the district, we knew we couldn't be grieved." In fact, Allsmen and Merrywheather believed that a strength of their work was their ability to "simply use what was already in place, just require that it be done well."

The August retreat began with a complete review of the plan. Following the presentation, teachers were asked to identify personal goals and then set forth measurable outcomes for their students for each quarter of the school year. They were required to develop plans for differentiation and formative assessment of student learning. Allsmen and Merrywheather provided examples of how they might set goals and what kinds of data would need to be collected. They were careful to show how what they were requiring was already within the negotiated agreement and already part of the state mandated teacher evaluation process. As Allsmen shared,

> For me, school leadership is about doing what works. It's not about fancy or jumping on the newest thing; it's about solid instruction and looking at the results. My magic is simple—I set the standard and then make sure everyone meets it.

The two days were exhausting for the faculty. A lot had been expected and, as one teacher said, "it's easy to make plans, it's harder to make them happen." Yet, she added, "I know what I have to do and that's refreshing." Pinney Glade opened its doors in early September with an all-school assembly. Allsmen and Merrywheather began by introducing themselves and immediately reviewed the school's new rules. They told the students that "your job is to learn and our job is to make sure that happens." They cautioned that misbehavior would not be tolerated and that being sent to the principal's office was "not a fun thing." After dismissing the students to their classes, Allsmen and Merrywheather began to "make their rounds," stopping by each classroom, checking on how students were settling in, and working to learn student names. They both did lunch and recess duty as well as afternoon duty. Their intention was to model that they, too, planned on working as hard as everyone else. They stayed long into the evening, calling on the families of Pinney Glade students to check on how the first day had been received.

As the school year progressed, Allsmen and Merrywheather continued to press toward the goals set in the strategic plan. Teachers soon learned that a favorite question was, "What did you do to help kids learn today?" They also learned that a clear and detailed response was required and that having the data to back up that response was preferred. More often than not, Allsmen and Merrywheather could be seen following a teacher back to their classroom to review lesson plans or student learning data. Students soon learned that the principals would be a constant presence in the school hallways and that their opening question in any encounter would be "What did you learn today?" Parents grew used to regular phone calls and weekly letters home.

Although focused on structure, Allsmen and Merrywheather also worked to develop a sense of comradery among the teachers at Pinney Glade. They publicly acknowledged when teachers had achieved their goals and sought out mentors to support instructional and assessment efforts. Merrywheather made himself available to teach classes so that teachers might be able to observe each other and was always willing to co-teach if requested. Several times during the fall, he taught for an extended time so that teachers could visit other schools or collaboratively plan together. These efforts were appreciated and his work was widely recognized as "putting his words into action."

Allsmen spent less time in classrooms than Merrywheather, preferring to schedule one-on-one conferences with teachers to review lesson plans and instructional materials. She also worked hard to be present for parent discipline calls and conferences. As she stated, "I want my teachers teaching. All the rest, it's my job to clear the decks so that can happen." As winter break approached, the school felt different. It was clear that there was still a lot of work that needed to happen for Pinney Glade to become all that it could, but it was equally clear they were on the path to school success.

Discussing the Case

- How would you describe Allsmen's and Merrywheather's approach to curriculum, instruction, and assessment leadership?
- In what ways do Allsmen's and Merrywheather's practices reflect curriculum, instruction, and assessment leadership theories?
- Allsmen and Merrywheather took a top-down approach to managing the school. What do you think of those choices? Would such an approach work on your school or district? Why or why not?
- In your opinion, would including other stakeholders in decisions related to curriculum, instruction, and assessment benefit this school? Why or why not?
- What might Allsmen and Merrywheather do next to foster success?
- How might they maintain positive momentum? If this were your school, where would you direct attention?

CASE 3.2

Challenging Times at Challenger Alternative School

Challenger Alternative School is home to about 75 students ages 11 through 18. The small school was created to address the needs of students who, for any number of reasons, had been unsuccessful at the larger middle and high schools in the district. At Challenger, classrooms are rarely traditional, nor are the individual learning plans for each student. Interestingly, and because of Challenger's approach to individualized instruction, the school has become attractive as an open-enrollment option for nearby districts and has recently begun to accept additional students who are seeking an alternative approach to learning.

Not surprisingly, the teachers who choose to work at Challenger come from diverse backgrounds as well. Many welcome the freedom that working at Challenger offers to customize instruction and curriculum for and with small groups of students. Others appreciate the way in which Challenger offers a space for students to build their own instructional programs and to work according to their own pace. It is not unusual for Challenger students to "test out" of work or to spend extended time reviewing older material prior to beginning a new course of study. The school also offers the opportunity for students to utilize online resources for course credit and to use those resources for credit recovery efforts. Every student has a learning plan and must show progress toward learning outcomes on a quarterly basis.

Older students are free to come and go during the 7:00 to 4:00 school day, and many hold jobs, have children themselves, or play sports at their home schools. As a result, it is hard to know who might be in class at any given time or in what work they might be engaged. Younger students tend to be more predictable but, even so, their attendance is highly variable. For most students, pairing flexibility and individual attention works and the students are respectful of the school's policies. Yet, more recently, students have been taking advantage of the school's laissez-faire approach. Thus, faculty have begun to press for more structure and accountability at Challenger.

Leading the charge is veteran teacher Terry Licen-Davis who has prided himself on being a founding member of the school faculty and is openly committed to supporting, "the kind of kid who doesn't fit elsewhere." In his tenure at the school, he has focused much of his effort on developing students' literacy skills and is known for sticking with students until they master the material. Licen-Davis believed the issues the school faced could be remedied by working with students on issues of perseverance, determination, grit, and tenacity. He suggested that requiring that all students to choose character goals to complement their instructional goals would simultaneously bolster respect and achievement.

Licen-Davis had his supporters. Other teachers noted that they had observed an increase in behavior problems and "If behavior wasn't under control, learning couldn't happen." By teaching directly to character, it was reasoned that "all sorts of issues could be addressed" and students would "become more successful." However, Shayleen Reed, Challenger's assistant principal of three years, disagreed. She asserted that adding non-academic requirements for students would "slow academic progress" and "distract from the core purpose of schooling at Challenger." She contended that, "engaging curriculum and high-quality instruction were the best forms of classroom management." Instead of supporting Licen-Davis, she openly confronted teachers, claiming that "younger minds were needed" to "better connect with these kids." For

Reed, the issue was not about structure and accountability, but instead was about relevance and responsiveness. However, reluctantly, Reed agreed to support Licen-Davis's addition of character education to the Challenger program "as long as there was no loss of academic progress."

With the support of several other faculties, Licen-Davis moved forward with the adoption. He planned an all-school assembly and introduced the program. He developed a structure for students to set character goals and instituted a weekly awards program for students who met their character targets. At first, it appeared that Licen-Davis had steered the school in a positive direction. Students liked the program, attendance seemed steadier, and the school appeared less chaotic. Even more positively, teachers believed that students were learning more and doing better in their classes.

So, everyone was surprised when, at the end of the semester, school data suggested that in fact, fewer credits had been earned and overall less academic progress had been made by many of Challenger's students. After the data had been checked and rechecked, Reed appeared at Licen-Davis's door, stating, "I gave you permission to do this but only if it did not impact student learning. It has. Now what do you have to say for yourself?" Licen-Davis admitted he really didn't have an answer. Instead, he begged for more time, suggesting that getting the program off the ground may have taken more time than he realized. He promised that by next reporting period things would improve. Reed told him she would consider his request but "wasn't making any promises."

Discussing the Case

- What are the issues Challenger Alternative School faces?
- What aspects of curriculum, instruction, and assessment leadership are present in this case?
- Reed is an assistant principal. Should she have taken such a bold stance?
- If you were the principal, how might you address this issue with your leadership team and teachers?
- How can school leaders balance instructional and academic issues with competing priorities?
- How can a school leader navigate differences in beliefs and views among faculty and staff?
- What and whose work should be prioritized?

CASE 3.3

Common Assessments: Dynamic or Demonic?

In the past decade, teachers at Powers High School had developed a series of common assessment tasks (CATS) for students in the core subjects of mathematics, English, history and the sciences. Designed by a core group of teachers in each content area, the common assessments are linked to the Common Core State Standards and require students to demonstrate competency toward shared course learning goals. Led by the principal, Xin Tan, the thinking behind the common assessment project was that all students, no matter who they had as a teacher, would be assured that their coursework would be consistent with and aligned to collectively agreed upon outcomes. Although the number of assessments varied across content areas, it was a general rule that each unit of study would contain one or two cumulating common assessment tasks.

Furthermore, and important to the district curriculum director, the assessment tasks were linked to the annual continuous improvement process. Under Tan's leadership, teachers at PHS created both the assessments and a review and reporting process. Employing a backward design process, the teacher teams worked to create assessments that would respond to the complexity and specificity of the common core standards. After each common assessment was developed, teachers designed units of study focused on teaching the curriculum necessary to assure mastery of important content. Materials included in the units of study were generally consistent across the classrooms. However, teachers had some latitude in how they approached their instruction. Creativity was encouraged at PHS, just as long as teachers didn't drift too far from the agreed upon pacing and progression of the curriculum.

Known as the CATs, an additional source of pride among the teachers was the nature of the work each CAT utilized. Mirroring the state exam format, the CATs were traditionally formatted exams that included a flight of multiple choice items followed by short answer and extended response essays. Additionally, during the first years of the process, Tan insisted that the assessments be regularly modified in response to student performance. Items that students scored consistently well on were dropped as were items that, after review, were determined to be unaligned with the standards. Veteran PHS teachers were proud of the effort and believed that they were employing the best classroom assessments they could to assure student learning.

State and national testing data supported the teacher's assessment of their work. PHS students did well, regularly scoring in the upper quartile of the state and a significant number of national merit scholars graduated from PHS. However, more recently, state support for schools had taken a hit. Along with legislation that radically limited the rights of unions, budgets were slashed and the districts were hit hard. PHS was forced to reduce the amount of time that teachers had to meet and plan together, and Tan was no longer able to support the expense of shared planning time. Class sizes grew. Predicting that "things would get far worse before they got better," several veteran teachers chose to retire rather than teach under these new, more contentious and stressful, conditions.

Importantly, the district was forced to cut the number of preparation days that teachers were allotted prior to the opening of the new school year. As a result, Tan was unable to require that teachers continue to review and revise the CATs as regularly as they once did. Furthermore, grading the CATs had always taken more time than traditional exams and the teachers were lobbying to remove the short answer and extended response items in favor of retaining the easily graded multiple choice items. In fact, for the first time since the adoption of the CATs, teachers were beginning to question why they were "teaching to yet another test."

Tan was concerned. He believed that the common assessments were integral to the success of PHS students. Additionally, he also believed that the backward design planning process was important to high-quality instruction and assessment practice. Yet, he was uncertain how to sustain the process under more austere conditions. He doubted that he would gain much traction if he asked teachers to support the process on their own time. Discord among the teachers was high. Tan sympathized with their concerns and he agreed that the profession was unfairly under attack.

However, Tan also believed that he was responsible to the students of PHS. He feared that the slow dissolve of the CAT process would ultimately compromise student achievement, opportunity, and progress. He hated to think that the glory days of PHS had passed.

Discussing the Case

- What aspects of curriculum, instruction, and assessment leadership are present in this case?
- Are there compromises that Tan could propose to the teachers?
- Who else in the school might be available to support this work moving forward?
- Sustaining curriculum, instruction, and assessment reforms after initial adoption is challenging for many schools. How can high-quality practice be sustained after initial implementation efforts?
- In what ways can school leaders buffer teachers from external pressures and censure?

ACTIVITIES

ACTIVITY 3.1

Analyzing the Work of Curriculum, Instruction, and Assessment in Your School

Curriculum, instruction, and assessment leadership requires that attention be paid to selecting appropriate materials for the work, coordinating effort, and evaluating results. How does your school measure up? Use the tool below to evaluate where work is needed and who might do that work.

continued . . .

	Considerable development needed	Some development needed	Minor development needed	Individual work required	Team work required
Selection of curriculum materials and activities					
Selection of instructional and pedagogical materials and activities					
Selection of assessment materials and activities					
Coordination of curricular goals, objectives, and materials within grade level (or content area) courses					
Coordination of curricular goals, objectives, and materials across grade levels (or content area) courses					
Evaluation of the efficacy of curriculum materials and activities					
Evaluation of the efficacy of instructional and pedagogical materials and activities					
Evaluation of the efficacy of assessment materials and activities					
Modification to and revision of curriculum materials and activities					
Modification to and revision of instructional and pedagogical materials and activities					
Modification to and revision of assessment materials and activities					

ACTIVITY 3.2

Developing Your Curriculum, Instruction, and Assessment Checklist

As we have discussed, leading curriculum, instruction, and assessment efforts requires that school leaders keep current on activities and accomplishments as they occur in classrooms. We are aware that many school districts have formal, and at times negotiated, walkthrough protocols and procedures. However, as DeMatthews (2014) suggests, a good deal of curriculum leadership occurs while leaders informally interact with teachers and staff. We suggest that having a mental checklist of high-quality practices to look for and later discuss can go a long way to supporting your leadership efforts. Strong principals look for evidence of the following practices, as well as use these as conversation starters when discussing curriculum, instruction, and assessment practices with teachers and staff:

- research-based and essential teaching strategies
- purposeful student grouping
- technology that unambiguously supports student learning
- clear goals for student learning
- ample opportunities for formative assessment
- evidence of teaching at basic and higher order levels of knowledge
- teacher-led questioning designed to elicit creative and independent thinking
- supportive and instructive responses to student questions

Clearly, there are other items a school leader might wish to add to personalize the checklist. What would you think is important? How might you use these prompts to develop a coherent and consistent focus on student learning at your school? How might you support good practice when you see it? How might you confront practices that need attention and support?

ACTIVITY 3.3

Student Voices

Inasmuch as students are the ultimate beneficiaries of our curriculum, instruction, and assessment leadership work, determining what students think helps them to learn is important. There are any number of good ways to be sure as a school leader you are in touch with students' opinions about and evaluations of teaching in your school. Certainly, asking students "What did

continued . . .

you learn today?" when they are in the bus line, the hallways, or at events can provide a quick read of what they are experiencing. However, on occasion it is worth formally sitting down with students in interview or focus group settings. If you are uncomfortable with doing this yourself, it might be worth asking a trusted colleague to assist. In any case, be sure to invite a wide range of students into the conversation. Insights can be gained from students who easily succeed and those who struggle, from those who are popular and engaged in school activities and those who are not, as well as students who are new to the school and those who have generational ties. You might begin by asking the following items:

- Describe your best day at school.
- How do you learn best?
- When do you struggle at learning something new?
- What's your favorite subject? Why?
- If you had to describe this school in one word what would it be? Why?
- What do teachers do that helps you learn?
- When are you most proud of yourself as a student?
- If there was one thing about this school you could change, what would it be?

After listening carefully to the students, what themes do you notice? How might you use this information to inform your curriculum, instruction, and assessment leadership work? What hard truths might you need to confront? How might you share this information with parents, faculty, and staff? What benefits might accrue by making student interviews and focus groups a regular practice in your school?

RESOURCES

There are multiple outlets for resources related to curriculum, instruction, and assessment leadership. We include here information about long-standing reliable organizations and a few newer resources worth consideration.

ASCD: www.ascd.org

The Association for Supervision and Curriculum Development was founded in 1943. Dedicated to supporting educators through the development of professional knowledge and skills, ASCD is a member-driven organization. ASCD publishes *Educational Leadership* and *Educational Update* as well as a variety of books and on-line resources. The organization hosts a yearly conference on teaching excellence and another on educational leadership.

continued . . .

Common Core State Standards (CCSS): www.corestandards.org
A one-stop site for information about the CCSS, this website offers information about the standards, material for parents, links to states that have adopted the standards, and resources to support the use of CCSS in classrooms and schools. Videos for individual and faculty/staff use are available free of charge to support your CCSS efforts. The website is also available in Spanish.

Edutopia: www.edutopia.org
The website of the George Lucas Educational Foundation, Edutopia is home to a broad community of educators. Focused on supporting efforts to implement project-based learning, social and emotional learning, comprehensive assessment, teacher development, and technology integration, Edutopia serves as a clearinghouse to support high-quality instructional and curricular innovation. All the materials, including access to numerous blogs and videos, are available for free. Placing yourself on Edutopia's email list ensures that you will receive immediate alerts when new materials and resources are created.

SEDL: www.sedl.org
Originally begun as the Southwest Educational Development Laboratory, SEDL became a national organization with broad reach in the past 30 years. In 2015, SEDL merged with the American Institutes for Research (www.air.org). However, all of SEDL's excellent professional development resources are still archived at the original site.

McREL: http://mcrel.org
McREL is a non-profit education research organization that has, for over 50 years, worked to support educators in improving their practice. McREL operates as consultants to schools and districts partnering to locate solutions to local instructional and curricular challenges. The webpage also offers free resources, including webinars, the *Changing Schools* biannual magazine, and access to free survey materials to access your school's progress toward what matters most.

REFERENCES

Andrews, R.L., & Soder, R. (1987). Principal leadership and student achievement. *Educational Leadership*, 44(6), 9–11.

Banks, J. (2016). *Cultural diversity and education* (6th ed.) New York: Routledge.

Bell, S. (2010). Project-based learning for the 21st century: Skills for the future. *The Clearing House*, 83, 39–43.

Bradley, L.H., Curtis, S.A., Kessinger, T.A., & Meyers, D.M. (2018). *Curriculum leadership: Beyond boilerplate standards* (2nd ed.). Lanham, MD: Rowman & Littlefield.

Brewer, D.J. (1993). Principals and student outcomes: Evidence from US high schools. *Economics of Education Review*, 12(4), 281–292.

Brubaker, D.L. (2004). *Revitalizing curriculum leadership* (2nd ed.). Thousand Oaks, CA: Corwin Press.

Chappuis, S., Commodore, C., & Stiggins, R. (2017). *Balanced assessment systems: Leadership, quality, and the role of classroom assessment.* Thousand Oaks, CA: Corwin.

Datnow, A., & Hubbard, L. (2015). Teachers' use of assessment data to inform instruction: Lessons from the past and prospects for the future. *Teachers College Record, 117*(4), 1–26.

DeMatthews, D.E. (2014). How to improve curriculum leadership: Integrating leadership theory and management strategies. *The Clearing House, 87*(5), 192–196.

Dixon, D.D., & Worrell, F.C. (2016). Formative and summative assessment in the classroom. *Theory into Practice, 55*(2), 153–159.

Edmonds, R. (1979). Effective schools for the urban poor. *Educational Leadership, 37*, 15–24.

Eisner, E. W. (2002). *The educational imagination.* Columbus, OH: Merrill.

Erickson, H.L., Lanning, L.A., & French, R. (2017). *Concept-based curriculum and instruction for the thinking classroom.* Thousand Oaks, CA: Corwin.

Farrell, C.C. (2014). Designing school systems to encourage data use and instructional improvement. *Educational Administration Quarterly, 51*(3), 438–471.

Glatthorn, A.A., Jailall, J.M., & Jailall, J. K. (2017). *The principal as curriculum leader: Shaping what is taught and tested* (4th ed.). Thousand Oaks, CA: Corwin.

Gotch, C.M., & French, B.F. (2014). A systematic review of assessment literacy measures. *Educational Measurement, 33*(2), 14–18.

Hallinger, P., & Murphy, J. (1985). Assessing the instructional leadership behavior of principals. *Elementary School Journal, 86*(2), 217–248.

Hechinger Institute (2009). *Understanding and reporting on academic rigor.* New York: Teachers' College Press.

Heck, R.H. (1992). Principals' instructional leadership and school performance: Implications for policy development. *Educational Evaluation and Policy Analysis, 14*(1), 21–34.

Herrington, J., Parker, J., & Boase-Jelinek, D. (2014). Connected authentic learning: Reflection and intentional learning. *Australian Journal of Education, 58*(1), 23–35.

Johnson, B.L., & Kruse, S.D. (2009). *Decision making for educational leaders: Under-examined dimensions and issues.* Albany, NY: SUNY.

Khalifa, M.A., Gooden, M.A., & Davis, J.E. (2016). Culturally responsive school leadership: A synthesis of the literature. *Review of Educational Research, 86*(4), 1272–1311.

Kruse, S.D., & Johnson, B.L. (2017). Tempering the normative demands of PLCs with the organizational realities of life in schools: Exploring the cognitive dilemmas faced by educational leaders. *Educational Management, Administration, & Leadership, 45*(4), 588–604.

Kuhlthau, C.C., Maniotes, L.K., & Caspari, A.K. (2015). *Guided inquiry: Learning in the 21st century* (2nd ed.) Santa Barbara, CA: ABC-CLIO.

Leithwood, K., & Louis, K.S. (2012). *Linking leadership to student learning.* San Francisco, CA: Jossey-Bass.

McTighe, J., & Wiggins, G. (2013). *Essential questions: Opening doors to understanding.* Alexandria, VA: ASCD.

Mendels, P. (2012). The effective principal: 5 pivotal practices that shape instructional leadership. *Journal of staff development, 33*(1), 54–58.

Murphy, J. (1988). Methodological, measurement, and conceptual problems in the study of instructional leadership. *Educational Evaluation and Policy Analysis, 10*(2), 117–139.

Murphy, J. (2016). *Leading school improvement: A framework for action.* West Palm Beach, FL: Learning Sciences International.

National Commission on Excellence in Education. Department of Education (1983). *A nation at risk: The imperative for educational reform: A report to the nation and the Secretary of Education.* Washington, DC: United States Department of Education.

Newmann, F., Carmichael Tanaka, D.L., & King, M.B. (2015). *Authentic intellectual work: Improving teaching for rigorous learning.* Thousand Oaks, CA: Corwin.

O'Connor, K. (2018). *How to grade for learning: Linking grades to standards* (4th ed.) Thousand Oaks, CA: Corwin.

O'Neal, C. (2012). *Data-driven decision making: A handbook for school leaders.* Eugene, OR: International Society for Technology in Education.

Ornstein, A.C., & Hunkins, F.P. (2013). *Curriculum: Foundations, principles, and issues* (6th ed.). Upper Saddle River, NJ: Pearson.

Rigby, J. (2013). Three logics of instructional leadership. *Educational Administration Quarterly, 50*(4), 610–644.

Roegman, R., Perkins-Williams, R., Maeda, Y., & Greenan, K. A. (2017). Developing data leadership: Contextual influences on administrators' data use. *Journal of Research on Leadership Education,* 1–27, doi: 10.1177/1942775117719452

Scheerens, J. (2016). *Educational effectiveness and ineffectiveness: A critical review of the knowledge base.* New York: Springer.

Smit, R., & Birri, T. (2014). Assuring the quality of standards-oriented classroom assessment with rubrics for complex competencies. *Studies in Educational Evaluation, 43,* 5–13.

Stiggins, R. (2014). *Revolutionize assessment: Empower students, inspire learning.* Thousand Oaks, CA: Corwin.

Tomlinson, C.A. (2014). *The differentiated classroom: Responding to the needs of all learners.* Alexandria, VA: ASCD.

Tomlinson, C.A., & Murphy, M. (2015). *Leading for differentiation: Growing teachers who grow kids.* Alexandria, VA: ASCD.

Vatterott, C. (2015). Rethinking grading: Meaningful assessment for standards-based learning. Alexandria, VA: ASCD.

Wiles, J., & Bondi, J. (2011). *Curriculum development: A guide to practice* (8th ed.). Boston, MA: Pearson.

CHAPTER 4

School, Family, and Community Partnerships, Involvement, and Engagement

PSEL STANDARD 8—MEANINGFUL ENGAGEMENT OF FAMILIES AND COMMUNITY
Effective educational leaders engage families and the community in meaningful, reciprocal, and mutually beneficial ways to promote each student's academic success and well-being.

We have all heard the proverb, "It takes a village to raise a child." The notion that schools, parents, and the community should work together to enhance student learning is not surprising. Nor is it new. It has long been understood that raising successful, happy children takes the support and resources of multiple agencies, organizations, and groups. Moreover, research supports that strong partnerships can create positive outcomes for students (Epstein, 2011; Hamlin, & Flessa, 2016; Molina, 2013; Sanders, 2003). Yet, there is a gap between knowing that engagement with families and the community is a good idea, and knowing how to go about creating and sustaining partnerships that produce their intended results.

The knowing/doing gap is wide and deep. Students today come from highly diverse families and backgrounds. Differences in the socioeconomic, racial, ethnic, linguistic, and cultural backgrounds of students, families, and communities complicate this work.

Long gone are the days where communities appeared to be mono-cultural and mono-linguistic, racially homogeneous, or socioeconomically consistent. Note that we used the word "appeared." Difference, at least in terms of race, ethnic, and socioeconomics has always influenced student achievement; it is only in recent decades that educators and society have viewed this with concern (Spring, 2015).

Furthermore, difference itself is a complicated thing. When we don't know something, it is easy to fall prey to stereotypes, biases, and prejudices. It is easy to fall back on what "worked" for us, the ways we think people and families "should" be, and to romanticize the past. It is easy to dismiss others' realities, to marginalize their experiences, and disregard important influences on children's lives that are outside a school's control. Yet, study after study suggests that high-quality school, family, and community partnerships can mitigate these challenges and promote student academic success and well-being (Epstein, 2011, Jeynes, 2012; Weiss, Lopez, Rosenburg, 2010; Wang, Deng, & Yang, 2016).

Research across the United States and in other nations suggests that high-quality partnerships are distinguished in three ways. First, members engaged in high-quality partnerships create *opportunities for engagement in meaningful work* (Molina, 2013; Stacer & Perrucci, 2012). Second, partner members *capitalize on family and community strengths*, creating opportunities for reciprocal and mutual work (Baquedano-Lopez, Alexander, & Hernandex, 2013; Castro, Exposito-Casas, Lopez-Martin, Lizasoain, Navarro-Asencio, & Gaviria, 2015). Finally, partner members organize efforts to *make the work collaborative and productive* by advocating for shared goals and outcomes, in turn, enhancing a sense of belonging in the community for all (Hamlin & Flessa, 2016; Osterman, 2000). In this chapter, we will examine how partnerships like these can be built and sustained as well as how the character of partnership differs across diverse settings. We begin by examining a partnership at Rumford Heights Schools.

KEY LEARNINGS

In this chapter, you will learn to:

- create and sustain positive, collaborative, and productive relationships with families and the community for the benefit of students;

- engage in regular and open two-way communication with families and the community about the school, students, needs, problems, and accomplishments; and

- understand, value, and employ the community's cultural, social, intellectual, and political resources to promote student learning and school improvement.

FEATURED CASE

Family Resource Centers in Rumford Heights

Rumford Heights is a semi-rural community located just 15 miles north of a large metropolitan city. Historically, verdant fields of corn and soy beans have sustained the families of Rumford Heights. However, the recession hit the community hard and the town is still fighting to recover. In the past decade, the Rumford Heights experienced a shift in wealth as family farmers have struggled and local, small businesses have closed. Additionally, as housing prices in surrounding areas have risen, Rumford Heights has, more recently, become the site of affordable housing and homes for service workers who commute into the city for employment. Enrolment of families new to the district has increased by over 15 percent in the past two years.

Never a rich community, Rumford Heights is now solidly lower to lower middle class. The average home in town costs just under $100,000 and rental properties are readily available. Foreclosed farms can be purchased for pennies on the dollar, while many lie fallow. A small number of farms have been purchased by new investors interested in developing a local farming community with attention to sustainability and organic practices. Many in the community are excited about the potential for community renewal, yet at this juncture, success is more aspirational than real.

As the community changed, teachers and school leaders in Rumford Heights Schools (RHS) have noticed that families in the community and students in the school have expressed increasing need. Applications for free and reduced price lunches were up by 15 percent and students appeared "generally less well prepared for school." Additionally, teachers reported that fewer students have the required school supplies or at home support for homework and other activities, and more students say that they no longer have consistent Internet access at home.

Principal James Christopher of Grover Middle School (GMS) found these stories troubling. He was aware that the community was changing. Christopher also knew that more families were inquiring about access to community supports when they enrolled their children at GMS. He was also aware that he and the staff did not have the necessary internal resources to meet the growing needs of the 500 students who attend GMS. Yet, he empathized. Christopher was the first in his family to go to college.

Christopher was quick to explain,

Growing up in a town like I grew up in, all of us were poor. There were some who had a little more money because their dad had a little better job at the mine or smelter, but most of us lived in that same kind of place. I think my disadvantage, or my family's disadvantage, was my folks just getting married at 16 and not having time to really get their feet under them and get a house or get something before they had children. They were always behind a little bit in those kinds of things. Other than that, we didn't even know it. We just lived like everybody else did. My mom and dad were very bright. They knew what they had given up. Back then, you didn't finish school when you got pregnant. You were out—period. They knew they gave up an education and they knew that they would pretty much put themselves in a spot for the rest of their life that they didn't want to see any of their kids live. Education was always really important to them. We never talked about getting out of high school. We always talked about getting out of college.

Christopher adds,

I went to a school with good guys. We won the state basketball championship four or five times in six or seven years. We had a lot of pride in the high school as far as the athletic program was concerned—not real high standards academically. It wasn't important because most people who left high school were going to go work at the smelter, mine, or zinc plant. I was lucky because I ran with my best friends, who were mostly athletes. They came from professional families. So, I had that to see as an option. It helped. Their dads also helped. The town made a difference in my life. I worked at the smelter because one of my best friend's dad was superintendent at the smelter and he made sure I had weekend work. He made sure I had summer and vacation work because he knew where we were. Ted took care of us. Because of all of them, I am who I am today.

Christopher stressed, "I spent my life in education working so that kids could have options. I know what's it like to need them. So, when I started to see these changes I knew it was my turn to step up and do what I could."

Reaching Out

Christopher called together his governance council. The GMS governance council included a representative from each of the school's seven teaching teams, the president of the parent organization, the district curriculum director for STEM initiatives, and as this year's community representative, the new owner of one of the start-up organic farms. Christopher was careful to outline the issues the school was facing, emphasizing his interest in creating a school-based resource for families. He began the meeting recounting the story of how his community had supported him as a youth. He lamented that Rumford Heights and most communities that he knew of were no longer the kinds of places that would spontaneously support families and students in need.

The members of the council agreed. Most of the first meeting was spent brainstorming all the ways they might be able to provide help. At the end of the two-hour session they decided that GMS should focus on developing both on-site and referral services. They decided that opening a Family Resource Center (FRC) made good sense and that they might start small using space within the school to house the infant organization. The council believed that on-site support and resources should include, at a minimum, school supplies, winter coats and other clothing, weekend backpacks, computer, printer, and Internet access, and after-school tutoring. They also believed that the FRC should offer referral services to connect families to community agencies that could provide additional food and clothing, childcare and parenting resources, early childhood education, counseling services, employment and continuing education resources, medical, vision, and dental care and information regarding public assistance.

At the conclusion of the first meeting, Christopher felt excited. He believed they were heading in the right direction. In a post-meeting conversation with the organic farmer and the parent representative, they both promised to begin looking into potential community donations and grant funds to get the initiative off the ground. In the meantime, Christopher began to look for a small space in the building that he could house the new center.

Growing Pains

The FRC started small and quietly. Donations from faculty, staff, and community members created an initial cache of clothing and school supplies. Working with the local food bank, the team modeled a weekend back-pack program on that of a successful national program (see www.hungerfreecommunities.org for details). The STEM coordinator repurposed several computers and printers. A cozy Internet access and reading area was established in a small space.

Henry Oscar, the community representative and start-up organic farmer, began volunteering his time to staff the FRC. He was often there early in the mornings, with a pot of coffee at the ready and boxes of his "ugly produce" for the taking. Additionally, Henry was active in soliciting donations from area businesses. He was careful to keep track of where contributions were distributed and which families the FRC was serving.

His data was impressive. According to Henry, within the first two months of school, the FRC had served over 50 families, providing clothing and school supplies to 58 GMS students and, in many cases, their younger brothers and sisters as well. Donations had topped the $1,000 mark. Additionally, since mid-September, the center was averaging three dozen backpacks each weekend. Over 500 pounds of food had been provided to GMS students and their families.

Proud that the effort was succeeding, Henry also was privately troubled. As he shared at the November governance council meeting,

> We're doing good work here. But we can't sustain this kind of need and it's clear that this isn't only a middle school problem. I mean, I know, we never say no to anyone, but a lot of what we're doing is about the family and the neighborhood. I know we're already serving more than GMS kids. I fear when more people learn about the FRC. We're also heading into the winter. That will change need. We need to start thinking about how we scale up and how we adapt.

Christopher agreed. He was also aware that the fledging group was overly reliant on a few volunteers. He feared that should Henry decide to invest his energies elsewhere, staffing the FRC would prove tough. Christopher also knew that the superintendent, Marsha Gates, was impressed with the FRC. Gates was watching the program carefully and had made overtures that perhaps, the district might be interested in expanding the effort to the elementary and high schools.

On one hand, this was good news. On the other, Christopher knew that a small number of faculty and the community were not fans of the FRC. He had heard that among some teachers there were concerns that the school was not "holding families responsible" for expected parenting behaviors, the FRC "was giving handouts," and resources that were going to running the FRC were "detracting" from other school programs. Yet, even the disbelievers admitted the program was working. Kids were better prepared for class—they had materials that had been lacking before. The afternoon and evening hours afforded students access to supports and resources that were not available before. More parents had come to conferences. As the tutoring program grew, more homework was being completed. Yet, Christopher was aware that they had just begun to scratch the surface of need in Rumford Heights.

He knew that the quiet start the FRC had enjoyed was quickly coming to an end and that long-term plans needed to be established if the effort was to sustain itself. The last thing Christopher wanted to happen was to have to close the center. He knew that he would lose the trust of his families if, after promising this service, he needed to take it away. As a busy school principal, he had to admit that the effort was taking more of his time than he thought it would. Christopher was uncertain about what to do next. As he saw it, he had several choices: he could try to find a community partner to more fully support the FRC; he could apply for grant money to sustain the program as a Rumford Heights Schools program; or he could continue to operate the FRC as he was doing and hope for the best.

A Resolution

Christopher took the weekend to think about his options. He returned to GMS on Monday with renewed hope and an appointment with the superintendent. He would, at least for now, move forward on several fronts. To begin, he asked that the FRC be formally adopted by the board as a district program housed at GMS. He reasoned that as an official district effort, the FRC would have increased standing and importance within the community. It would "provide credibility" as well as "make clear the district's commitment to the work." Next, he asked Gates to partner with him to expand the center and he requested that she help seek additional sponsors and partners. Christopher was willing to be the voice of the FRC, but he requested that the superintendent "be the connector" as he reached out beyond his initial contacts. Finally, Christopher requested that she provide a small amount of funding so that he could hire Henry as a grant writer to locate solid support for the FRC and as a working partner to ensure continuity in the coming months as the FRC became more formalized. Gates agreed to all of Christopher's requests. A plan was set in motion. By early January, Christopher had gained traction on much of his new agenda.

Five Years On

At this writing, the FRC is now entering its fifth year of operation. GMS is now led by Christopher and two assistant principals. The new administrative configuration allows Christopher between 10 and 20 hours a week to serve as Assistant Superintendent for Outreach and Community Engagement. The FRC has expanded to a full-time, year-round effort and is now housed in donated space on the main street of Rumford Heights. Additional partners include several area doctors and dentists who provide pro-bono health services and screenings. Summer programming includes credit recovery courses for high school students, GED programs for parents, and mentoring and tutoring opportunities for GMS and RHS students. Henry's organic farm is taking hold, he supplies area restaurants with produce and each spring elementary students plant potatoes at his farm. They harvest the crop each fall and donate the produce to the local food bank.

SCHOOL COMMUNITY RELATIONS, INVOLVEMENT, ENGAGEMENT, AND PARTNERSHIPS DEFINED

Before we begin unpacking the ways that high-quality, successful partnerships are developed, a word on terms. Over the decades, the ways in which school, family, and community work has been discussed has evolved. To be clear, the goal of the relationship has always been to achieve positive outcomes for students. Yet, the orientation of the work, and in turn, the vocabulary that has been used to discuss this work has evolved. In early educational administration texts (Sears, 1950; Grieder, Pierce, & Jordon, 1961), the emphasis was on communication that informed parents, and to a lesser extent the community, of the work occurring in the school. Known as *school community relations*, this iteration of the notion focused the development of plans that sent word from the school about those things the principal and, at times, teachers, felt were important for parents to know. This communication was almost always one way and focused on telling, rather than including, others about the school's work.

Next, the term *school community involvement* gained popularity (Sergiovanni & Carver, 1973). In this version, a nod was given to the variety of ways that parents, mostly stay-at-home mothers, might participate in school events, assist their children in school work, and generally support the school's agenda. Involvement in schools took on many forms. For example, when parents volunteered in classrooms as "helpers," baked cookies for the school carnival, or fundraised for new band uniforms, they are clearly involved in the school. Undoubtedly, in each of these examples there is a good deal more inclusion for parents and families in the day-to-day work of the school than in earlier iterations of the notion. Yet, these early conceptions of involvement were still, fundamentally, a one-way street and the role of "outsiders" remained largely passive and limited.

More recently, the term *school community engagement* has gained popularity (Christenson, 2001; Weiss, Lopez, Rosenburg, 2010). When someone is engaged in something, they are expected to be an active participant or even a partner in that effort. Engagement, as a stance toward school community work, implies that this is a joint effort. Embedded within the construct of engagement is the notion that unlike bake sales or classroom "help," the engaged parent shares responsibility for the success of the school. As a school reform strategy, it suggests that parents, families, and the community are not outsiders in the educative effort. Rather, they are integral to the success of the goals and objectives the school sets for itself. Engagement challenges the ways in which everyone in the school community interacts, holds and exercises power, and innovates to make the school a better place to work and learn.

Like school community engagement, the term *school community partnership* has recently gained currency (Epstein, 2011; Molina, 2013). Whereas the research on engagement has largely focused on parents and families, the research literature on partnerships is more inclusive, incorporating community resources, businesses, agencies, and nonprofit concerns. In this construction, the emphasis is on the ways that schools and the communities in which they are embedded can work together to provide a network of supports for students and their families so as to improve the well-being of the whole.

Furthermore, the literature suggests that successful partnerships are intentionally focused on three collaborative principles designed to foster family and community empowerment. It is suggested that intentional partnerships require school leaders to embrace parents and community members as genuine partners (Bryan, 2005; Ishimaru, 2012). Second, school leaders need to purposefully diminish their roles as the experts and respect families' and community members' knowledge and insights (Bryan & Henry, 2008). Third, family and community members should be involved in decisions about partnership goals, activities, and outcomes, and encourage families and communities to define issues that affect their children (Nelson, Prilleltensky, & MacGillivary, 2001; Higgins, Ishimaru, Holcombe, & Fowler, 2012).

Underlying these principles are the mutually reinforcing and interconnected frameworks of empowerment and social justice. Whereas empowerment focuses on increasing participation and voice for families in the partnership process and in their children's education, social justice focuses on increasing access to resources, information, skills, and knowledge for families (Nelson et al., 2001). In social justice-focused partnerships, school leaders and other partners collaborate to ensure that families participate in school and community decisions and policies, especially those that often affect their children negatively, such as disciplinary referral policies (Furman, 2012; Higgins, et al., 2012).

Moreover, partners intentionally tackle pressing social justice issues, such as closing achievement gaps, reducing disproportionate disciplinary referrals among affected student groups, and providing in-school and out-of-school supports for students. As we saw in Rumford Heights, when schools reach out to support families in ways that make it easier for children to participate in classroom and school work, and for their families to trust that the school is focused on supporting them and their children, progress toward important goals can be made.

In short, consideration of the role of parents, families, and the community in the school has developed over the past century. Attention has shifted away from one-way informative communication to interaction and participation that invites and honors many voices. Similarly, when approached from this understanding, high-quality school, family, and community partnership relationships are, by definition, meant to be more inclusive, and to include topics and agenda of broad interest. Of particular importance is the shift from an agenda defined and controlled by the school to one that is co-constructed and shared by parents, families, communities, and the school.

Because the Professional Standards for Educational Leaders (NPBEA, 2015) uses the term *engagement* when describing family and community agenda and work we, too, shall employ the term engagement when discussing these topics. We do so knowing that there is considerable difference within the broader literature of its use and acknowledging that your school may use different words to define similar work. We shift our discussion to the setting of the school, and how where your school is located matters in considering school, family, and community efforts.

SETTINGS: URBAN, SUBURBAN, AND RURAL

Context matters. Elementary schools differ from high schools. Urban schools are different than suburban schools, and rural schools have their own uniqueness. Understanding how setting and context affects school community engagement is important for successful school leadership.

Urban Schools

A good deal of current research is focused on parental engagement in urban schools (Bower & Griffin, 2011; Jeynes, 2012; Williams & Sanchez, 2012). Due to the general agreement that, in urban schools across the US, academic proficiency and growth, attendance, and graduation rates lag behind national goals, while discipline infractions, suspensions and expulsions are greater than national averages, a good deal of school reform research has been focused on the urban school environment (Henderson & Mapp, 2002; Mapp, et al., 2008). Attention to parental engagement is no different. In the hopes of increasing student achievement and decreasing negative outcomes for urban children, many educators believe that engaging parents holds great promise for urban school reform.

Yet, urban schools have unique challenges. Generally, but not always, they tend to be large bureaucratic systems fraught with long-standing financial and political problems. Students who attend urban schools have often experienced enduring poverty. Lower income families experience significantly higher levels of material hardship than middle income families. Food, housing, and work insecurity are common, as are lower levels of overall familial educational attainment. Low income families may also struggle with access to medical care, transportation, and other forms of support. Absent the financial resources of middle income parents, lower income parents may experience *time poverty*, where their energy is expended maintaining basic aspects of day-to-day life with little remaining energy to dedicate to their children's education. In short, the challenges that urban schools face are systemic and generational. In this way, the challenges of and for parent engagement in urban schools differ because they run more deeply and encompass greater and more acute need. For school leaders, this means that engagement plans and activities must acknowledge the challenges faced by urban families and act in ways that are responsive and sensitive if they are to see results.

Suburban Schools

We use the term *suburban* to mean those schools that serve a largely middle-class population (Bauch, 2001; Epstein, 2011; Minnotte, 2012). We do not want to suggest that engaging families in middle-class neighborhoods is easy or that middle-class children do not come to school with a host of problems, concerns, and issues of their own. However, we do want to stress that in studies of middle-class, suburban school parental engagement, on the whole, it is clear that suburban schools enjoy positive outcomes as a result of robust parental engagement (Christensen, 2001). Middle-class parents generally have greater resources to support the school and their children. To generalize, middle-class families tend to have increased monetary resources that allow them to provide greater day-to-day security as well as access to additional enrichment opportunities (e.g., vacations, entertainment, enrollment in extracurricular sports, etc.). Additionally, middle-class parents tend to have attained more education than lower income parents, and this knowledge and skill set translates into an increased ability to successfully support their children both in and out of school. On the surface, the challenge of engaging suburban parents within school agenda and programs may seem more straightforward. However, suburban schools can still struggle with engaging parents in the kinds of high-quality efforts known to increase student well-being and academic growth (Hamlin & Flessa, 2016; Molina, 2013).

Rural Schools

According to the National Center for Educational Statistics (2017), 57 percent of school districts in the US are rural, 32 percent of schools are in rural areas, and 24 percent of all students attend a school in a rural area. A smaller percentage of students in rural schools live below the poverty line (19 percent) than those in urban cities (25 percent) yet, rural poverty is a real and increasing concern. As a category, rural schools are under-researched and under-accounted for in discussions concerning education in the US (Bauch, 2001; McHenry-Sorber, 2014).

Additionally, rural America is not the same place as it was in the past. Nostalgic images of tight-knit, harmonious communities stand in sharp contrast to today's images of rurality. Declined agricultural production, increased migration of younger people from rural communities, and greater class distinctions within these areas have all contributed to changes in how rural communities thrive and function. Just as all cities and suburbs are not the same, not all rural communities can be categorized as one way or another. Yet, more often than not, schools in rural communities are marked by dense regional networks, strong intergenerational values and norms, and an abundance of place-based social capital within the community (McHenry-Sorber, 2014). All of these factors can serve to enhance school community engagement in the rural environment. On the other hand, issues of distance and polarization within a community can distract from a school's agenda.

As we move to a discussion of high-quality engagement practices, we encourage the reader to keep these differences in mind. All leadership is contextual. However, attention to context is heightened when issues of school community engagement are in play. Leadership practice must be responsive to the community in which you are working and knowing your community matters. Best practice can only be best practice if it meets the needs of your context, school, and community.

HIGH-QUALITY ENGAGEMENT

We have stressed that high-quality parent and community engagement matters for academic success and the well-being of students. Research suggests that in schools where parental engagement is strong, student achievement is improved. In a meta-analysis of 37 studies of parental engagement Castro, et al., (2015) found that involvement in homework, supportive and shared expectations for student learning and behavior, reading at home with elementary aged children, and parental attendance and participation in school activities all contributed to increased educational successes for children. Not surprisingly, these results held across all grade levels. In more focused work, Bryk et al. (2009) described that in Chicago Public Schools parental engagement, when paired with strong school leadership, sound instructional practice, high-quality professional learning opportunities, and a school climate supportive of student learning, was essential to student success. Henderson and Mapp's research (2002) validates that family and community engagement in schools improves overall student academic achievement, attendance and graduation rates, and enrollment in post-secondary education. Taken as a whole, it appears clear that parental and community engagement is an important focus for school improvement efforts.

Yet, across the US, family and community engagement efforts are often random and unconnected to other school improvement efforts (Weiss, et al., 2010). As we suggested earlier in this chapter, historically, educators have treated families and community members as bystanders to, rather than partners in, the educational processes of the school. When the strengths that parents and communities bring to the school are overlooked, and in many places marginalized, it is impossible for children to reap the benefits. Family and community engagement must be a coherent, aligned, and sustained part of every school leader's vision and agenda.

Coherent engagement efforts include those that are intentionally designed into the systemic practices of the school. Coherence suggests that there is a consistency between and across grade levels within the school and schools within a district in how parents, families, and communities are included in educational goal setting and ongoing improvement efforts. When family and community engagement are *aligned*, the work that teachers do in classrooms is united with the effort of parents and families at home and in the community. Alignment suggests that homework policies are responsive to family ability, that ample opportunity is provided to all families to participate in the education of their children, and that school structures and processes are aware of and responsive to the community. Finally, these efforts must be *sustained*. Families and community members need to be able to count on and plan for their participation in and with the school. By doing so, school leaders have the opportunity to powerfully impact student learning and well-being.

We acknowledge that these tasks are formidable. Additionally, we acknowledge that there are no silver bullet programs or one-size-fits-all approaches to this work. However, research suggests that there are several ways in which strong family and community engagement can be achieved. First, effective partnerships create opportunities for *engagement in meaningful work* (Molina, 2013; Stacer & Perrucci, 2012). By deliberately broadening who is included in the work of the school, collective responsibility for success can be enhanced. This means that parents and community leaders should be brought to the table for the purpose of making a difference in the school. As we saw in Rumford Heights, as members of the community took ownership of the FRC, they increased their involvement in and commitment to its success.

We have witnessed this over and over in our studies of schools. Recently, one of us was in conversation with the HR director of a local technology firm. His story was simple. In prior years, schools across the region had come to him with requests to partner in after-school tutoring programs, fund new equipment, and to provide internship opportunities for students. He stated, "I always turned them down. It's not that I didn't want to help. I just felt like there wasn't much in it for me or my company." In the past year, an area superintendent came to him with a different request. He asked that instead of a "hand-out" what he wanted was input into how the schools could partner to assure the success of students after graduation.

The HR director felt that, "This was a request I could honor. I felt like I was being asked to contribute something with more of a half-life beyond a one-shot deal. I signed up for a slot on the district's strategic planning team." After a year of his participation, company employees are now involved with after-school tutoring at the middle school and offer internship opportunities for high school students. They have made a sizable donation for computer equipment as well. The difference? The HR director laughs, "So this time it was my idea—that helped. But more so, I understood why I was needed and the real impact we could make." In other words, his partnership efforts were made tangible and meaningful.

Second, effective partnerships *capitalize on family and community strengths*, creating opportunities for reciprocal and mutual work (Baquedano-Lopez, et al., 2013; Castro, et al., 2015). Strengths-focused partnerships focus on identifying, using, and enhancing strengths in children, families, and communities for the overall good of students (Crowson & Boyd, 2001; Ishimaru, 2014). In these partnerships, schools, families, and community partners focus together on protective factors that build resiliency in children, foster caring adult relationships, increase meaningful student participation in their schools and communities, and hold high expectations for students' success (Bryan & Henry, 2008).

All communities hold the potential to support the school. When school leaders focus on what they have in common with the community they serve, student learning outcomes are enhanced. All too often educators rush to quick fixes. Then they are disappointed when their efforts fail to produce the intended results. Learning the strengths of a community takes time. Patience is required and trust needs time to develop. In a nearby community it was observed that parents of English language learner (ELL) students wanted to support the school. They wanted their children to succeed. The majority of these parents struggled with speaking English themselves. Many also worked long hours at work—mostly in landscaping and house-cleaning services. It was tiring work and more importantly, they wanted more for their children.

A savvy district leader saw the potential of engaging these parents. His response was, with the support of a translator and the school community liaison, to create a parent leadership network. The ten-week leadership workshop began with a conversation focused on what the parents found difficult and frustrating about working with the school. Based on this feedback, a curriculum was built that taught parents how they could better work with the school, the resources that were available to them and their children, and the ways in which they could understand how to support their students at home. Role-playing and other activities were used to allow parents and volunteer school employees to practice their skills. Space was created at each event for knowledge and skill building, as well as for conversation and friendship. At the end of the ten weeks a celebration was held to award certificates. At that event, the initial parent group shared that they knew of dozens of other parents in this district and surrounding districts who wanted to attend workshops like these in the future.

Plainly, these parents brought an investment in their children's future to the table. They wanted to work with the school to see their children succeed. What differed in this instance was that they were invited to a table that welcomed them. Once there, they were able to participate in the very work the school wanted them to be part of. These results should not be surprising. Research has long suggested that people participate in new activities when *someone they know and trust* asks them to go (Warren, Hong, Rubin, & Uy, 2009). What seems to get people in the door and to make the first steps is the feeling that someone cares about them and their children. In this case it was easy—both these parents and the school cared about their kids.

The take-away here is clear. Relationships matter when participation matters. If schools are to build strong networks of support and to engage parents and others in the school's work, an investment in building relationships is required. It is imperative that school leaders learn where the strengths lie among those with whom they wish to partner.

Finally, partnership work is made more collaborative and productive when members advocate for commonly held goals and agreed upon outcomes. In turn, a sense of *belonging in the community* is developed among and enhanced for all members (Block, 2009; Hamlin & Flessa, 2016; Osterman, 2000). Community can be considered in one of two ways. The first suggests that community is formed by geographic boundaries. In this example, we are a community because we share a zip code. Our ties are therefore relatively weak.

The second definition of community is more salient to our discussion. In this case, community is relational. We are bound together by intellectual, social, and emotional ties. Community exists because we feel connected and we care about others to whom we are connected. This is not to say that within a community there is no discord or disagreement. On the contrary, it is within strong communities that discord can be voiced, disagreement can be resolved, and tensions acknowledged and addressed. When community is more than a label, when it is real and felt, commitment to the work needed to sustain belonging is enhanced (Block, 2009).

Studies show that when strong supportive relationships with students and their families are built, student motivation is enhanced, a sense of competence and confidence in one's ability to succeed is developed, and prosocial school behaviors are more evident (Osterman, 2000). When students and their families feel a sense of belonging to the school community, several positive outcomes may be realized. First, parents and students are more willing to hold themselves and others accountable for the well-being of the larger collective (Block, 2009). Schools are filled with these kinds of behaviors. When students choose to self-regulate their choices, even in the face of great temptation (e.g., when a substitute is present), they are demonstrating their investment in the larger collective. We acknowledge that there are multiple other reasons for good behavior when a teacher is absent. Threat of punishment or promise of reward are great motivators. Here, however, we are referring to instances where students do the right thing, absent clear punishment or reward.

Second, conversations shift away from focusing on the problems a school is currently experiencing to discussion where possibility and potential are central to deliberation (Kruse & Louis, 2009). What is evident when this seismic shift occurs is the tenor of the conversation. Excuses, blame, and rationalities fall away and members take real and serious ownership for the state of the school and their role in making it a better place in which to work and learn. When the school district referenced previously chose to listen to the parents of ELL students and to work with them, addressing their concerns, the conversation shifted. Other examples abound. When teachers work to implement new curriculum or pedagogies struggling through the hard months of learning new skills they are embracing possibility. When teams come together to problem solve in earnest ways, doing the hard work of choosing the best option rather than the easiest, they are focused on potential. In all these examples, community is developed and a sense of belonging to the greater whole is enhanced.

Third, a sense of dignity in ones' work is fostered (Bryk, et al., 2009). As community belonging emerges, the purpose for engaging in the work broadens. Success among students, engagement with families, and communal support for the schools becomes, in many ways, its own reward. It is well understood that many teachers and school leaders feel that their efforts go unappreciated. Certainly, education, and by extension those who work in the field of education, have been publicly held to account for many of the nation's ills. We are not suggesting that negative press will magically disappear or that high-quality school community engagement is easy. We are, however, asserting that the reward is well worth the effort.

CASES FOR ANALYSIS

CASE 4.1

Homework Hassles

> As I see it, it's an equity issue. We have families who cannot help their kids. We have families who don't have the resources for kids. We have families that don't have extended, nightly time to help their kid—even when they want to. For those reasons, I am asking that homework not be assigned on a nightly basis. If a kid doesn't finish class work and *if* they can do the work on their own, it can go home as homework. Other than that, no homework.

Superintendent Daria Hobbs was pleased with her pronouncement at the annual August back-to-school teacher meeting. Hobbs had just returned from a national conference on student learning and she was ready to implement what she had learned. There she learned that the research (Flunger, Trautwein, Nagengast, Ludtke, Niggli, & Schnyder, 2017; Galloway, Conner, & Pope, 2013) concerning the benefits of homework was mixed, and negative effects had been found for students from disadvantaged backgrounds (Barnett & Stevenson, 2016). Hobbs also knew that, in her schools, there were significant differences in how teachers assigned and graded homework. Some teachers were already following the policy that she had recommended. Others assigned homework as a regular, daily practice. Some graded all homework. Others graded a student's attempt to complete the assignment. Still others used a system that graded each homework assignment but only assigned 10 percent of a student's overall grade to homework. For Hobbs, the inconsistency was troubling.

Furthermore, she knew from the district's recent data analysis of student learning outcomes that meaningful disparities existed when student achievement was compared among subgroup populations. Hobbs knew that more was at play in these data than the district's stance on homework. Yet, she knew, as a parent in the district, that a good deal of what was sent home for homework had little instructional value. She had also had more than her share of tear-filled evenings, last-minute "surprise" projects, and late nights to know that homework was a stressor for families. As she said, "I'm the superintendent, my kids have to do their homework. The last thing I want is for a teacher to think I'm not supporting learning. But, honestly, most nights I really hate it."

Hobbs expected push back related to her announcement. She expected calls and emails from teachers challenging her decision. She expected principals, whom she had informed prior to her announcement, to take "a lot of heat on this one." She assumed she would hear from some parents. She also knew that some teachers would continue to provide homework anyway. As she said, "I know what will happen is some teachers will just ignore me and others will just double the classwork, and then shrug and say it was classwork the kid didn't finish. It wasn't really homework. I expect that. I can deal with that."

What she didn't expect was a call from an area business partner, Derric Tayler, CEO of Unified Shipping and Trucking. A long-time supporter of the schools, Tayler's company regularly sponsored athletic teams, high school student internships, and other school events. Tayler could always be counted on to support levies and bonds. He had sponsored Hobbs for a seat at the Rotary Club when she first joined the district. They had kids about the same age and enjoyed a personal, as well as professional relationship.

It wasn't unusual for Tayler to reach out to Hobbs to offer support for district initiatives. However, it was rare that he intervened on matters of policy or decision making. So, when he began to probe, Hobbes listened closely. His concern with the new policy was, he thought, simple. He began,

> It's about teaching responsibility. I mean, I know, in the real world it's your job to get your work done. Self-discipline matters, being able to suck it up and do the work, even when you don't want to is something we all need to learn. Kids today—hell, people today—they're lazy. If we don't teach them that their effort is important, what's gonna happen on the job? I have these parents, they're the ones that call in sick, don't come to work, don't know how to be professional. It's hurting me, my company. If the district can't support what business needs maybe business shouldn't . . .

Hobbs cut Tayler off and thanked him for the call. She reiterated that her decision had been made with the best interests of student learning in mind. Hobbs knew she believed in what she started. Yet, in her excitement to do what she thought was best, maybe she had gone too far, too fast. Maybe there was a better way to handle her decision.

Discussing the Case

- Hobbs unilaterally made the decision to change district homework policy. Should Hobbs have included district and community members in this decision?
- If so, how might she have handled that process?
- What might she do now to remedy the situation?
- What aspects of high-quality community engagement were present, or absent, in this case?
- What is the role of community in setting policy in schools?
- Should powerful community members be able to set policy and practice?
- How might school leaders walk the narrow line when disagreement among and between school stakeholders occurs?

CASE 4.2

Listening and Learning

East Mount Township High is a neighborhood at the crossroads of several major freeway interchanges. The buildings that surround East Mount are tall, gray, and old. Timeworn homes and apartment buildings line the mostly treeless streets. Township High has struggled. Four-year graduation rates hover around 60 percent; yet after six years they rise to almost 75 percent. Of particular concern to school and community leaders are the number of young men who seem overly street-wise and unreachable. Teen pregnancy in the East Mount Township neighborhood is higher than surrounding areas of the city and teen fathers are rarely involved with their children.

In early 2015, three members of the local community center approached the principal of Township. Interested in developing a group to support urban youth, they asked if they might work with the school to develop an evening program at the center that would encourage "better life choices." They intended to identify about two dozen low-performing at-risk youth, invite them to weekly meetings, and "offer alternatives they might otherwise not realize they had." Goals for the meetings were twofold: goal one was to encourage students to stay in school, to graduate, and to have stated life goals. The second was to teach these young men what they "ought" to learn about relationships. The team believed that they would be able to use a curriculum that included mentoring and "a fair amount of tough love and straight-talk." As an incentive to attend the group, the students would receive a meal at every gathering, referrals for local employment, and occasional tickets to concerts and movies as rewards for participation.

Included in the team of three, were two 40-something men who had grown up in the city but not in the Township neighborhood. Two, Ty Reed and Dwayne Georges, had worked in the neighborhood center for over a decade and believed that it was time to "pull kids in" rather than "waiting for them to find us." The third, Geoff Freeman, was, in his own words, "an over-educated white guy" who "wanted to make a difference." He had been volunteering at the center for the past few years. Together the group carefully planned recruitment and meeting activities, working to balance "their lessons" with time for the young men to also speak. The principal of Township vetted the curriculum, offered a few changes, and provided the names of students he believed would benefit from the program.

Shortly into the effort, Ty and Dwayne realized that, even though attendance was generally good, the meetings lacked "the energy we were hoping for." As Ty said, "They kept showing up, but like they really weren't there." Geoff continued, "We knew it would be hard but something was off." Dwayne, said it this way, "Kind of honestly, we were just more talking heads, we wanted to connect but there was no trust." They decided that "unless we started listening more than we talked," they would never understand who these young men were. A plan was made to abandon the planned curriculum in favor of "hanging out" with the youth.

They opened the next meeting by asking for ideas about what the group might do together. Predictably, DVD and poker nights were suggested, as was holding a rap battle and a poetry slam. Once a week, for over six months, the group met absent a planned agenda. Some nights there was an organized activity, others there was just talk. Slowly, the young men started opening up. In particular, the poetry slam events surfaced hard stories and heartbreaking truths. A few teachers learned about the effort and committed to providing course credit when a student offered up a performance.

Throughout it all, Ty, Dwayne, and Geoff listened. They resisted the urge to, as Ty said, "correct, teach, or preach." Over time, the conversation changed. The young men started coming to the center with questions about how they might handle a conversation or situation, they began to bring schoolwork and job applications to be completed, and they began to bring other young men with them to the weekly group meetings. After a year, none of the original participants had left school, all were holding jobs, and none had become teen fathers. By listening, the conversation they had hoped to hold happened of its own accord.

Discussing the Case

- Is this an example of a school community partnership? If not, how might the school have been more involved? Should the school have been more involved?
- What aspects of high-quality community engagement were present, or absent, in this case?
- What stands out for you as an important lesson that might be learned from the partnership?
- Where might a program like this go from here? What new goals might be adopted?
- Check out https://poetryslam.com. In what ways do programs like this offer opportunities for school community engagement and partnership? What are other external agencies and initiatives like poetry slam that might enhance student learning?

CASE 4.3

Katherine Johnson K8 Learning Center's School/Community Partnership Plan

Katherine Johnson K8 Learning Center (KJLC) opened in 2014–2015 to great excitement and fanfare. Housed in a newly built space, the K8 Learning Center was designed to provide a comprehensive education for the school's 800 kindergarten through eighth graders. Prior to opening KJLC, students in grades kindergarten through fourth had attended an elementary school and students in grades fifth through eighth attended a middle school in a separate location in the district.

KJLC was designed as a K8 school to better meet the needs of students in the district. Among the intended benefits was the reduction in the number of transitions a student would need to make throughout their schooling, increased continuity and community for students and faculty, and an expansion of honors courses, arts, music, band, and foreign language education. By constructing a new school, the district was able to customize architectural spaces that separated students into K–3, 4–6, and 7–8 units, but still allowed for shared and expansive common areas. KJLC was completed in July of 2014 and the district had opened the building for numerous community tours. Everyone seemed excited to begin using the new school in the fall.

Opening the K8 building required that the faculties of the former elementary and middle schools should come together and begin to work as a unit. Faculty were paid additional salary for summer meetings and were tasked with a variety of projects to ready the school for opening. Among those was the development of a School Community Partnership Plan (SCPP). The teaching team that developed the plan included a teacher representative from each grade level, the music teacher, and an assistant principal. The team worked diligently over the summer months and, just prior to September of 2014, presented the plan to the full faculty for review and discussion.

The plan began with a preamble that stated:

> Research is clear that quality family and community engagement is critically important for student progress, success, and well-being. We view family and community engagement as a foundational value for KJLC. We believe that engagement means involving families in every aspect of their child's education, including planning for learning and success, assessment and evaluation of progress and growth, and the development of life, social, and citizenship skills and behaviors. We believe that to do so we must welcome every family to our school, employ two-way communication, support student success, and collaborate with the community.

The plan then proposed three levels of objectives for the school, family and community, as follows.

School Level

- Welcoming every family

  - Establish a parent resource room.
  - Host inclusive celebrations.
  - Distribute a family-friendly school handbook.
  - Share information on how parents, caregivers, grandparents, and others can support the school.

- Employ two-way communication

  - Provide parents with grade-level expectations, report cards, conferences, email, and other correspondence to inform them of student progress and need.
  - Utilize multiple communication systems and formats—Web page, Twitter, email, newsletters, and Robocalls, to keep parents informed.
  - Encourage regular and meaningful communication.
  - Encourage both formal and informal interactions between families and teachers.
  - Provide clear information regarding school expectations, offerings, opportunities, and educational options for students.
  - Regularly distribute student work for comment and review.

- Support student success

  - Encourage the use of homework hotline.
  - Provide information about testing.
  - Sponsor parent workshops to increase understanding about how students can be helped at home.
  - Provide an annual school calendar.
  - Provide opportunities for parent volunteers to work in and outside of the classroom.

- Collaborate with the community

  - Make local agencies and businesses aware of school events.
  - Recruit volunteers for in-school and parent leadership events.
  - Make use of community resources for learning.

Community Level

- Welcoming every family

  - Participate in unified efforts to educate parents and families in the community.

- Employ two-way communication

  - Assess needs and share information about opportunities to work with the school.

- Support student success

    - Develop partnerships to enhance student learning and well-being.

- Collaborate with the community

    - Work across community agencies for the betterment of students, families, and the community.

Family Level

- Welcoming every family

    - Build relationships with the school faculty and staff.

- Employ two-way communication

    - Provide parents with information that will enhance student learning and well-being.
    - Inform teachers when your child has difficulty learning or in other areas of school or home life.
    - Read materials sent home from school and ask questions when items are unclear.

- Support student success

    - Set and monitor student learning goals.
    - Attend school meetings, conferences, and events.
    - Read every day with your child.
    - Create regular routines at home.
    - Provide guidance, not answers, for homework.

- Collaborate with the community

    - Thank local businesses who support the school.
    - Encourage community service.

At the conclusion of the presentation, there was a short discussion about each of the bulleted objectives. The general sense was that the team had done a good job and that although extensive, and lacking some detail concerning how the objectives might be executed, the plan was a good place to begin and that the team "should continue working" to refine the plan and present that work at the October faculty meeting.

Discussing the Case

- Critique the plan as proposed. Where is it strong? Where is it weak?
- In what ways does the plan incorporate high-quality engagement practices?
- Choose one area of the plan to enhance. How might you develop activities to support the chosen objective? How might you evaluate success?

- The principal assigned the development of the plan to an internal team. How might that have been handled differently? Should it have been handled differently?
- How does this plan compare to the plan at your school? How are they alike? How are they different?

ACTIVITIES

The following activities will further expand your understanding concerning how to create and sustain meaningful relationships and engagement with families and communities.

ACTIVITY 4.1

School Communications Inventory

Take an inventory of your school's communications to families. Reflect on the ways you might strengthen family–school communications and engagement. In the table below, note the areas you believe are strengths in your school. Note where further development might be required. Is your communication balanced? Are there opportunities for multiple-pathways of communication? Do you see any patterns in your communication? Do you over- or underuse any one form of communication? What leadership work might be needed to strengthen your communications? How might you go about doing that work? Who might need to be included that is not currently part of your communications team?

School Communications Inventory			
Communication regarding:	Who initiates the communication?	Who receives the communication?	How is the information communicated?
General school polices			
Homework policies			
Discipline and behavior policies			
Dress code policies			
School events and celebrations			
Classroom events			
Grade-level or team events			
Athletic events			

continued . . .

School Communications Inventory			
Communication regarding:	Who initiates the communication?	Who receives the communication?	How is the information communicated?
Music and art programs and events			
Individual student progress, growth, and achievement			
Individual student well-being			
Whole-school student progress, growth, and achievement			
Whole-school student well-being			
Individual student goals, hopes, wishes, and dreams			
Student illness or absence			
Informal learning activities for at home			
Formal learning activities for at home			
Informal community resources			
Formal community resources			

ACTIVITY 4.2

School Community Asset and Priority Assessment

This activity offers you the opportunity to assess the strengths and weaknesses of your school community relationships. It can also help you to prioritize goals and purposes for your school community work. You may want to consider input from others as you complete this assessment.

continued . . .

School Community Goal Setting					
Our school community relationships benefit our students by . . .	Asset Assessment		Priority Level		
	Strength	Weakness	High	Moderate	Low
Increasing our knowledge and understanding of and about each other					
Including parents and other community members in decision making and problem solving					
Creating a sense of belonging for students and families					
Fostering student achievement and well-being for all children and youth					
Building collaborative relationships with community members and families					
Generating multiple pathways for communication					
Constructing productive relationships between the school and the community					
Supporting learning in and out of school					
Forming alliances to support students and their families throughout the community and across the calendar year					
Helping students and their families gain access to needed resources					
Celebrating student accomplishments, milestones, and achievements					
Advocating for the priorities of students, families, and the community					

ACTIVITY 4.3

Community Inventory: Knowing your Community Matters

Identifying the assets and needs of a community can be a first step to strengthening school community relations, engagement, and involvement. Develop a community profile by researching and answering the following questions. What issues arise? Where might you partner to make a difference?

- What are the demographics of your community (e.g., average age, race, income, available housing)?
- When was your community first founded? How has your community changed over time? What are the trends for the future?
- What community organizations are active in your community (e.g., social clubs, religious organizations, civic or community development associations)?
- What kinds of public institutions are present in your community (e.g., libraries, museums, hospitals) and what kind of community programs do they sponsor?
- What is the current status of the local economy?
- Are there locally owned businesses with roots in the community?
- How do people get around in your community? Is public transportation or non-car transportation available and realistic?
- What are the dominant land uses in your community? How does land use impact the quality of life for students, families, and community members?
- How do people get food in your community? Where does the food come from?
- What is the ecological state of your community? Are families and community members confronting significant challenges to maintaining their health and well-being (e.g., air or water pollution crisis)?
- What are health services like in your community? Are there enough services for families (e.g., doctors, dentists, mental health and addiction counselors or programs)? What are the wait times to see a health professional?

RESOURCES

Getting started is often the hardest part of developing a new family, school, and community partnerships. The following are foundations known for grant funding and other ways to begin your work.

continued . . .

The Annie E. Casey Foundation: www.aecf.org
The foundation works across the US, Puerto Rico, and the US Virgin Islands with the intent to support children and families at risk of poor educational, economic, social, and health outcomes. Their website provides many free resources for schools and community agencies. Grant programs focus on long-term strategies and partnerships with the potential to strengthen families and communities.

The National Education Association (NEA): www.nea.org
The association offers quick links to articles and leadership resources related to parent and family involvement in schools. It is not necessary to be a member to gain access to their reports and resources. Additionally, NEA offers grants to support schools, educators, students, and communities. The kind of opportunities vary. However, the site is worth checking regularly since they tend to generously fund successful projects.

Philanthropy News Digest (PND): http://philanthropynewsdigest.org
The PND provides links to any number of grant possibilities. PND serves as a free service for nonprofit and grant-making organizations across a variety of areas. Look to their RFP pull-down menu and choose either education or children and youth. One of the best features of this site is the wide variety of grant opportunities they post, ranging from small dollar amounts to larger more generous awards.

The W.K. Kellogg Foundation: https://wkkf.org
The foundation accepts grant applications that support new and innovative ideas to ensure that children and their families have the opportunity to reach their full potential. Unlike other foundations that offer grants at specific times and for specific initiatives, the Kellogg Foundation has an on-going open application process with quick turn-around and helpful assistance. Grant applications are available in both English and Spanish.

The Robert Wood Johnson Foundation: www.rwjf.org
The foundation focuses its efforts on creating healthy communities. Although not directly education oriented, they have resources related to childhood obesity, early childhood development, and family and social support. They offer funding opportunities for communities looking to build a culture of health across any number of public and non-profit agencies.

The National Network of Partnership Schools (NNPS): http://nnps. jhucsos.com
The NNPS at The Johns Hopkins University provides a one-stop hub for research and professional development regarding school partnerships. Many of their materials are free. However, joining the alliance provides even greater access to many wonderful resources. In particular, the publication *Promising Partnership Practices* features dozens of one-page descriptions of ideas

continued . . .

school leaders might employ to boost family and community involvement in their school. An added bonus is that the guide is regularly published and up-to-date. If your school is an NNPS member, you can add your ideas to the yearly publication and gain significant attention for your efforts.

The National Endowment for the Arts (www.arts.gov)
The organisation provides links to Web pages for asset mapping. Search for *Exploring Our Town* to learn if an asset map of your city has already been developed. If not, use the asset mapping resource guide to learn more about the resources and opportunities in your region. Doing so is a great way to work with parents, families, and community leaders to partner on projects to enhance the lives of your students.

REFERENCES

Baquedano-Lopez, P., Alexander, R.A., & Hernandez, S.J. (2013). Equity issues in parental and community involvement in schools: What teacher educators need to know. *Review of Research in Education, 37*(1), 149–182.

Barnett, B., & Stephenson, H. (2016). Leading high poverty urban schools. In Clarke, S. & O'Donoghue, T. (Eds.) *School Leadership in Diverse Contexts*. New York: Routledge.

Bauch, P.A. (2001). School-community partnerships in rural schools: Leadership, renewal, and a sense of place. *Peabody Journal of Education, 76*(2), 204–221.

Block, P. (2009). *Community: The structure of belonging*. San Francisco, CA: Berrett-Koehler Publishers.

Bower, H.A., & Griffin, D. (2011). Can the Epstein model of parental involvement work in a high-minority, high-poverty elementary school: A case study. *Professional School Counseling, 15*(2), 77–87.

Bryan, J. (2005). Fostering educational resilience and achievement in urban schools through school community partnerships. *Professional School Counseling, 8*(3), 219–227.

Bryan, J., & Henry, L. (2008). Strength-based partnerships: A school-family-community partnership approach to empowering families. *Professional School Counseling, 12*(2), 149–156.

Bryk, A.S., Sebring, P.B., Allensworth, E., Luppescu, S., & Easton, J.Q. (2009). *Organizing Schools for Improvement*. Chicago: University of Chicago Press.

Castro, M., Exposito-Casas, E., Lopez-Martin, E., Lizasoain, L., Navarro-Asencio, E., & Gaviria, J.L. (2015). Parental involvement on student academic achievement: A meta-analysis. *Educational Research Review, 14*, 33–46.

Christenson, S.L. (2001). Promoting engagement with school and learning: A resource for Check & Connect mentors to enhance student success. Early Risers "Skills for Success" Project, University of Minnesota, Minneapolis, MN.

Crowson, R.L., & Boyd, W.L. (2001). The new role of community development in educational reform. *Peabody Journal of Education, 76*(2), 9–29.

Epstein, J.L. (2011). *School, family, and community partnerships: Preparing educators and improving schools* (2nd ed.). Boulder, CO: Westview Press.

Flunger, B., Trautwein, U., Nagengast, B., Ludtke, O., Niggli, A., & Schnyder, I. (2017). A person-centered approach to homework behavior: Students' characteristics predict their homework learning type. *Contemporary Educational Psychology, 48,* 1–15.

Furman, G.C. (2012). Social justice leadership as praxis: Developing capacities through preparation programs. *Educational Administration Quarterly, 48*(2), 191–229.

Galloway, M. Conner, J., & Pope, D. (2013). Nonacademic effects of homework in privileged, high-performing high schools. *The Journal of Experimental Education, 81*(4), 490–510.

Goodlad, J. (1984). *A place called school.* New York: McGraw-Hill.

Grieder, C., Pierce, T., & Jordon, E.F. (1961). *Public school administration.* New York: Ronald.

Hamlin, D., & Flessa, J. (2016). Parental involvement initiatives: An analysis. *Educational Policy.* Available at: http://journals.sagepub.com/doi/abs/10.1177/0895904816673739

Henderson, A.T., & Mapp, K.L. (2002). *A new wave of evidence: The impact of school, family, and community connections on student achievement.* Austin, TX: Southwest Educational Development Laboratory (SEDL).

Higgins, M., Ishimaru, A., Holcombe, R., & Fowler, A. (2012). Examining organizational learning in schools: The role of psychological safety, experimentation, and leadership that reinforces learning. *Journal of Educational Change, 13*(1), 67–94.

Ishimaru, A. (2012). From heroes to organizers: Principals and education organizing in urban school reform. *Educational Administration Quarterly, 49*(1), 3–51.

Ishimaru, A. (2014). When new relationships meet old narratives: The journey towards improving parent–school relations in a district-community organizing collaboration. *Teachers College Record, 116,* 1–49.

Jeynes, W. (2012). A meta-analysis of the efficacy of different types of parental involvement programs for urban schools. *Urban Education, 47*(4), 706–742.

Kruse, S.D., & Louis, K.S. (2009). *Building strong school cultures: A guide to leading change.* Thousand Oaks, CA: Corwin Press.

Mapp, K.L, Johnson, V.R., Strickland, C.S., & Meza, C. (2008). High school family centers: Transformative spaces linking schools and families in support of student learning. *Marriage & Family Review, 43,* 338–368.

McHenry-Sorber, E. (2014). The power of competing narratives: A new interpretation of rural school-community relations. *Peabody Journal of Education, 89,* 580–592.

Minnotte, K.L. (2012). Family structure, gender and work–family interface: Work-to-family conflict among single and partnered parents. *Journal of Family and Economic Issues, 33*(1), 97–105.

Molina, S.C. (2013). Family, school, community engagement, and partnerships: An area of continued inquiry and growth. *Teaching Education, 24*(2), 235–238.

National Center for Educational Statistics (2017). *Percentage of distribution of public elementary and secondary students, schools, districts and locale.* Retrieved from: https://nces.ed.gov/programs/coe/indicator_tla.asp

National Policy Board for Educational Administration. *Professional Standards for Educational Leaders* (2015). Retrieved from: www.npbea.org/wp/wp-content/uploads/2014/11/ProfessionalStandardsforEducationalLeaders2015forNPBEAFINAL-2.pdf

Nelson, G., Prilleltenshy, I., & MacGillvary, H. (2001). Building value-based partnerships: Toward solidary with oppressed groups. *American Journal of Community Psychology, 29,* 649–677.

Osterman, K.F. (2000). Students' need for belonging in the school community. *Review of Educational Research, 70*(3), 323–367.

Sanders, M. (2003). Community involvement in schools: From concept to practice. *Education and Urban Society*, *35*, 161–180.

Sears, J. (1950). *The nature of the administrative process*. New York: McGraw-Hill.

Sergiovanni, T., & Carver, F. (1973). *The new school executive: A theory of administration*. New York: Harper & Row.

Spring, J. (2015). *American education*. New York: Routledge.

Stacer, M.J., & Perucci, R. (2013). Parental involvement with children at school, home, and community. *Journal of Family Economics*, *34*, 340–354.

Wang, Y., Deng, C., & Yang, X. (2016). Family economic status and parental involvement: Influences of parental expectation and perceived barriers. *School Psychology Journal*, *37*(5), 536–553.

Warren, M.R., Hong, S., Rubin, C.L., & Uy, P.S. (2009). Beyond the bake sale: A community-based relational approach to parent engagement in schools. *Teachers College Record*, *111*(9), 2209–2254.

Weiss, H.B., Lopez, M.E., & Rosenberg, H. (2010). *Beyond random acts: Family, school, and community engagement as an integral part of education reform*. Cambridge, MA: Harvard Family Research Project.

Williams, T.T., & Sanchez, B. (2012). Parental involvement (and uninvolvement) at an inner-city high school. *Urban Education*, *47*(3), 625–652.

CHAPTER 5

School Climate, Culture, and Professional Community

> **PSEL STANDARD 7—PROFESSIONAL COMMUNITY FOR TEACHERS AND STAFF**
> Effective educational leaders foster a professional community of teachers and other professional staff to promote each student's success and well-being.

As we walk into places—a school we are visiting or one where we work, a doctor's or dentist's office, or our mechanic's garage—we immediately get a sense about where we are. Some places exude warmth. We might experience this as we take in the bold artwork on the walls, the comfortable waiting room, or the smile of a cheerful welcome. Others feel less friendly. Sometimes it is hard to put your finger on why a place feels cold. It might be the amount of time it took for someone to acknowledge you, a lack of a shelf to rest your belongings, or simply your discomfort with the reason for your visit. In any case, how we feel about a place makes a difference in the ways we interact with the people there, our experience while we are there, and, in the case of schools, how students learn.

Additionally, from this perspective, schools are unique. While we can choose another mechanic, doctor, or dentist, our relationships with schools are less malleable. For students, the school they attend is assigned geographically or by program criteria. Reassignment often requires extensive justification and appeal. For teachers, assignment may be less rigid than for students but is often inflexible and less open to individual choice.

Yet, how we feel about where we learn and work matters. Our patterns of experience with an organization, our sense of like or dislike, reflect the *climate* of that place. Climate is generally thought of as our experienced feelings about a place. A range of terms is used to describe climate, including atmosphere, tone, setting, or milieu (Cohen, McCabe, Michelli, & Pickeral, 2009). Generally speaking, school climate refers to the ways in which the character of the school is expressed. It reflects the values, norms, interpersonal relationships, levels of trust, and the organizational structures on which daily life within the school is experienced.

Furthermore, beyond our felt experience, schools, and other organizations, also have a *culture*, often expressed as the ways in which organizational identity is expressed and shared. It is the "who we are" and the "how you know it" aspects of school organization. Culture is deeply embedded in the minds of faculty and staff, current students and alumni, and others who interact with the school. It forms the foundation for how members of the school community act and what they believe.

Yet, neither climate nor culture is unchangeable. Admittedly, neither are easy to alter but neither is fixed. Furthermore, both have been tightly linked to school and student performance (James & Connolly, 2009; Kruse & Louis, 2009; Stoll & Louis, 2007). In this way, understanding the differences as well as understanding how leadership influences school climate and culture matters for success. We begin with an example of a leader who, in the face of district unrest, made developing a strong school culture a leadership priority.

KEY LEARNINGS

In this chapter, you will learn to:

- develop workplace conditions for teachers and other professional staff that promote effective professional development, practice, and student learning;
- provide opportunities for collaborative examination of practice, collegial feedback, and collective learning; and
- encourage faculty-initiated improvement of programs and practices.

FEATURED CASE

George Washington Elementary: Building a Strong Culture

After the retirement of Teddy Lopez and years of working in another school in the district, Celine Frist was transferred to George Washington Elementary. Lopez had led Washington Elementary for over a dozen years. Lopez had been well loved and

Washington Elementary was considered a good place to work. In many ways, Washington was like a small family—the faculty and staff had been relatively stable and knew each other well. Conflicts rarely happened and when they did were easily and professionally resolved.

Yet, at the district level relationships were less idyllic. Recent contract negotiations were volatile. Teachers had not gotten a significant raise in the last contract and, as a result, were paid less than teachers in neighboring districts. The teacher's union entered negotiations with the intent of catching up.

However, the district was facing financial woes of its own. A property-poor district, historically, the board had relied on state funding to balance the books. Yet, state funding to the district had not been increased in over a decade. District administration had little to work with as they entered the boardroom and began negotiations with the intent of making their best offer at the start of the negotiation process. In doing so, the superintendent believed she could bargain with transparency, "open the books," and make clear that the offer on the table was both honest and real. She also believed that she could not "sell the schools out" by bargaining a contract that was unsustainable in coming years.

The union, supported by state leadership, rejected the initial offer. Instead, they chose to take their case to the press, arguing that administrators were overpaid and that the district had been mismanaged. In response, the superintendent simply restated that she believed this was the only offer the district was able to make. Progress stalled. Months passed. A mediator was brought in. Over and over, the district presented its single best offer.

September to December

As Frist began her first year at George Washington without a teacher's contract, the previously close faculty was feeling strained. Start of school activities and district professional learning planning had been cancelled or reduced. Teachers were pressured to "do your job and nothing more." Within the staff at Washington, there were teachers who were strong union supporters. Others were less engaged with the union agenda but felt they needed to "band together."

Frist felt unable to establish personal or professional relationships with faculty outside of the ongoing tensions. Eager to establish herself as supportive, Frist made efforts to connect with her new staff. Monday mornings she brought muffins, doughnuts, and fresh fruit to the staff room. She greeted buses, working to learn student names as she welcomed children to the school. She visited professional learning community (PLC) meetings and classrooms, limiting the time she stayed, so as not to be perceived as acting in an unauthorized evaluative role. She left notes in teacher's boxes praising the student work she observed in hallways and passing on compliments shared by parents. At Halloween, she organized the student costume march, careful to ask teachers how it had been handled in the past, but not asking for additional help outside of the contracted day. She shared, "It was like doing the job blindfolded in a minefield. I kept feeling my way ahead not wanting set someone off."

Additionally, Frist felt constrained by the lack of professional learning time she was accustomed to using to review data, talk about instruction and curriculum with teachers, and plan improvement efforts. As she stated,

Had I been in the school before all this, maybe I would have been able to get more done. I don't know. What I do know was I didn't want to do something I'd never be able to recover from. I figured I might lose some of this year, I didn't like that, but it was better than having to dig out later.

As Thanksgiving approached, union leaders began to press for a strike vote. Many teachers believed the district had been negotiating in good faith and wanted to settle. A small group began to lobby for the union to allow a vote on the contract, as presented. Sensing that she might prevail, the superintendent contacted local news media and in an on-camera interview suggested that the union was failing to represent the teachers. Not surprisingly, this move was viewed by union leadership as overtly aggressive. In early December, the union called for an immediate strike vote. It failed by a small margin. Within days, a contract vote was held and a new contract ratified. Exhausted, the faculty and staff left for Winter Break. Frist hoped she might find a fresh way to start the new year and leave the tensions of negotiations behind.

January

Frist worked over the break to design a welcome back her teachers would appreciate. She knew "I couldn't pretend we hadn't all just been through this fall. I knew that this wasn't the school it used to be either. I needed a bridge to get us to the next place." She decided to reach back into the school's past as a way to move forward. As she shared, "I thought if I could remind them, and learn myself, who they had been, we could start fresh." She invited Lopez to welcome the teachers as they entered the school the first day back from break. She contacted former, retired George Washington teachers and asked that they email a favorite Washington memory and a photo. She created a rotating slide-show of the photos and comments she received and added photos of past classes and recent pictures of the school.

On January 2, Frist sent an email to faculty and staff asking that they "consider arriving a bit early" on January 5, the first day back, so that she might have a brief meeting in the library and "share a few thoughts." She promised that in addition to her usual faculty room offerings, she would provide breakfast and coffee from the local gourmet roaster.

At each place setting were two index cards. The first asked, "What have you loved about working at Washington?". The second asked, "What do you hope we can become?"

SCHOOL CLIMATE AND CULTURE

As the recent organizational climate and culture literature (Hogan & Coote, 2014; Louis & Lee, 2016; Schneider, Ehrhart, & Macey, 2012; Thapa & Cohen, 2016) suggests both have long been considered key variables in understanding change and improvement. Yet, climate and culture differ and attention to each is important for effective school leadership.

Climate

Climate is generally thought to be evidenced in the atmosphere or tone of the school. In this way, climate is unavoidably experiential in nature. Climate is reflected in the ways in which norms, values, interpersonal relationships, levels of trust with one another, and organizational structures of the school are experienced. When students or teachers describe the school as a caring place, they are suggesting something about the climate of the school. The sense that they are cared about, or care about each other, may be the tangible result of a school's value for the individual worth and dignity of each member. It may also be related to the ways in which teachers reach out to students as advisers and mentors, how counseling services are provided, or how discipline is handled. One's experience of the climate of any given school is additive— that is, rarely does any single attribute define a school's climate. Rather, it is the sum total of a variety of distinct qualities or attributes of the school that creates a distinctive, supportive climate.

We are rather fond of the metaphor thinking about climate offers for understanding schools. Climate, as meteorological phenomena, is by definition the statistics of weather. The climate of a region is determined by measuring variations in temperature, precipitation, wind and other naturally occurring atmospheric events over long periods of time. On the other hand, weather is our short-term experience of climate. Weather changes daily. The politics of climate change aside, climate is a steadier feature of a region.

Yet, much like regional micro-climates exist, school climate is not experienced equally by all members. Climate is tightly linked to the individual perception. Therefore, a student who rarely is disciplined experiences the school's climate very differently than the student who has a regular seat in the principal's office. As such, climate is not a monolithic construct. Especially in large schools, consensus concerning how climate is perceived may be more fragmented than united. Additionally, as we saw at George Washington Elementary, school climate can become unsettled, as a result of larger system pressures.

Yet, as we stress throughout this volume, leadership matters. Leaders play important roles in shaping school climate. Additionally, research suggests that a school leader's attention to school climate matters because it plays an important role in student achievement. Attention to developing a school climate that features an emphasis on academic press (Hoy, Tarter, & Bliss, 1990), academic support for students (Hallinger & Heck, 2010), and trust (Bryk & Schneider, 2002; Hoy & Tschannen-Moran, 2003; Tschannen-Moran, 2014) strongly correlates to positive student learning outcomes.

Academic Press

Understandings of academic press emphasize attention to the ways in which academic achievement is prioritized within the school. The degree to which a school attends to the development of academic standards, hold high expectations for students toward meeting agreed upon standards, and examines student learning outcomes as a result of instruction and curriculum have all been positively linked to student achievement. Academic press is evidenced in schools that give clear priority to academically focused initiatives. When teachers work to develop challenging curriculum, differentiate instruction, or provide extensive and meaningful formative assessment, the importance of student learning is communicated. In turn, the values that underscore school climate are clarified and illuminated. The result is a workplace where teachers are clear about what matters and student learning is enhanced.

Academic Support

Prioritizing academic achievement suggests that principals and teachers attend to creating learning opportunities that benefit all students. However, academic press without academic support is counterproductive. Key to understanding the role of academic support is distinguishing between supports that are designed to enhance student well-being as distinct from those designed to support student learning. Clearly, student well-being matters. When students experience the school as a safe and happy place, they are better able to learn. Caring, especially when expressed as an important relational value of the school, matters because it suggests that educators express an ongoing interest in each student's welfare.

However, investments in student well-being are not sufficient to ensure positive student learning outcomes. In addition to student well-being, a focus on academic support suggests that intellectual progress and growth must be a primary feature of leadership attention. Practically speaking, this means that alongside initiatives that provide students tangible evidence of care (e.g., breakfast and lunch programs or acknowledgment of birthdays and celebrations of other meaningful events), the school should emphasize initiatives that support engagement with school work. Strong support for student learning might be evidenced by before or after-school tutoring programs, community-based homework help, or a variety of student clubs and activities designed to motivate and enhance student learning and authentic achievement.

Trust

Trust has long been thought of as the glue that holds interpersonal relationships together. In schools, trust is considered to result when members of the school demonstrate competence, integrity, reliability, and concern for others. Competence suggests that members know what to do and follow through on doing what is needed at appropriate times. Integrity, sometimes referred to as honestly or fairness, is present when members act in ways that consistently honor and support the work of others within the school. Reliability or consistency suggests that as a feature of school climate, members act in ways that can be counted upon by others, including parents, students, and support personnel. Finally, concern for others is experienced as benevolence or compassion, where kindness is practiced and is a central feature of school climate. Trust, as a feature of school climate, suggests that the school is a place where people can come together in ways that enhance their ability to achieve shared goals. When trust is high, faculty-initiated efforts are able to thrive, and programs and practices designed to meet student need are fostered. In this way, teachers' professionalism is enhanced and becomes a central feature of school climate.

Culture

School climate encompasses those aspects of the school that are experienced by teachers, parents, students, and staff. School climate can be shaped, resulting in better academic outcomes for the students it serves by focusing on academic press, academic support, and trust for the school itself as well as for those who work within it. If efforts to shape a school's climate are to be successful, understanding the school's culture is necessary.

Unlike climate, which can be palpably experienced, culture is subtler. To illustrate this point we draw on Schein's (1992) definition of culture. Schein suggests that culture consists of "a pattern of shared beliefs, assumptions and value systems among a group of people" (p. 18). Important to Schein's definition is the emphasis on shared patterns of values and beliefs. It is not enough for an individual, or even a small group, to hold a belief or value for it to have cultural power—the value must be communally and publicly held.

In turn, school culture shapes the foundation of meaning making within the school. It provides members of the school community (e.g., teachers, parents, students, and external partners) a rationale for why "stuff gets done the way it does" within the school. If, for example, collaboration is robustly present among a school faculty, the underlying cultural value might be one that regards shared (as opposed to individual) effort as important to achieving a school's goals. Similarly, if a school's culture values professional learning, one is likely to see open classroom doors, ample time for teachers to discuss instructional and curricular choices, and plentiful opportunities for professional development.

Admittedly, as we noted in our discussion of climate, culture is not a monolithic construct. Even in small schools, subcultures are always present and cultural uniformity is rare. Yet, a school's culture can be thought of as strong when, even among the variation, there are clear understandings and interpretations of the primary goals to be addressed. In this way, even though culture might be thought of as defining "who we are" and "how we do things," we all do not need to be exactly the same and things do not always need to be achieved in identical ways.

Culture is something an organization *is*. Originating from studies in anthropology, the idea that culture is deeply rooted in an organization's DNA privileges a conception of culture that links understanding organizational culture to understanding organizational identity. It is this conception of culture that Celine Frist tried to draw on when she organized the back to school breakfast and asked the question, "What have you loved about working at Washington?"—the perspective that suggests that culture is something we share and individually interpret.

Unsurprisingly, Frist received a variety of responses. Teachers suggested that they liked the kids and families who attended the school and the people they worked with as well as feeling proud of what they accomplished at the school. While the specific details of each response varied, the general message was the same—Washington was a good place to learn and work because of the people who learned and worked there. Furthermore, as Frist discovered, Washington had a longstanding culture that focused on supporting each other at the school; they prided themselves on "being there for each other," no matter the circumstance. Theirs was a culture that valued relationships. Personal meaning for the work and an individual's role in that work was defined, at

Washington, by the ways they worked together. This was, in part, one of the reasons the fall had been so difficult for the school staff. In many ways, the tensions of negotiations had not only created stress for each individual at the school, it threatened the foundations of what bound the faculty together.

Researchers (Deal & Peterson, 2016; Erčulj, 2009; James & Connolly, 2009) of organizational culture suggest there are several key ways in which culture is expressed. These include symbols, stories, and ceremonies distinct to the school organization. We examine each as they provide insights into how workplace conditions can be enhanced to promote effective professional learning, practice, and student learning.

Symbols

Symbols are representations of tangible and real values. They can transcend language and cultural barriers, evoke memories, or convey significance. Symbols have the power to inspire feelings and to remind people of the things that matter most. Countries have flags, companies have logos, and sports teams have mascots. As symbols, they are simply pictures. For example, an apple is a piece of fruit. Yet when it drawn in a particular way, with that C-shaped bite taken out of the right side, we know we are seeing the Apple apple. Symbolically, that bite is purposeful.

Take a minute to think of stories where taking a bite from an apple holds great consequence. Snow White and the Bible probably come to mind. In each telling, taking a bite of an apple symbolizes the impact of surrendering to temptation. Additionally, once the apple has been tasted, one is never the same. The Apple logo symbolizes that their computers and other electronics are vehicles for new knowledge and enlightenment. Graphically, it is a powerful and purposeful use of an iconic symbol.

Importantly, cultural symbols include not only those explicitly designed to convey meaning. Cultural symbols can be experienced in implicit ways as well. A school with a central library sends the message that the school was designed with learning at its core. Similarly, a school with a prominent and large football field sends a clear and very different message about its priorities. When student work lines the hallways, we see a school that values what kids do. When the displayed work is a series of identical worksheets, the message is very different than when individual or unique student work is exhibited.

How visitors are greeted is symbolic. A warm smile and a statement of welcome send the message that whoever has arrived matters within the school community. It is important for school leaders to be aware of and openly confront symbols that undermine the cultural message the school wants to embrace. Often, schools have features that cannot be mitigated. It is important that schools are safe places. Locked doors and metal detectors are now commonplace in many schools. Sending the message that the school is a safe place matters. At the same time, neither a locked door nor a metal detector is welcoming. Awareness of and intentional leadership action is needed to mitigate this mixed message.

Stories

Stories communicate our school culture. They help us shape our narratives about what life is like in the school to ourselves, our students and their families, and the community.

They help to unite us. Stories allow us to publically assert who we are and what we stand for. Stories single out who we respect, what we think is important, and memorialize effort, large and small. Stories allow us to share what matters to us with others and serve as cultural bridges between what has passed and what is to come. When Celine Frist asked for teachers' memories, she was looking for the stories that bind teachers into a faculty. When she asked them to share their hopes for the future, she was laying the foundation for what was to come next.

Foundational to developing a strong school culture is our ability to create shared meaning. Stories help us to reinforce our core values and beliefs, share knowledge about the school and community, and build trust. As teachers, students, staff, and parents become clear about what it means to be part of a school, what it means to be part of the school changes. Importantly, when people work and learn in an environment where they understand what is valued and find meaning in that work, they will put forth greater effort. This is true for teachers and students. Furthermore, it goes beyond individual gain or investment. When people feel bound to the community that surrounds them, they are more likely to broadly support the organization and more likely to believe that they play an important part in making the school what it is. Stories help people find their cultural place.

Ceremonies

Ceremonies are formal observances and commemorations occasions. They provide a time for celebration, remembrance, recognition, and reflection. Perhaps the best known form of ceremony in schools is graduation, but others exist. Opening day ceremonies serve to welcome old and new members of the school community back after the summer holidays, concerts and recitals recognize the talent and skills of students, and memorial ceremonies remember the contributions and struggles of others. Successful ceremonies serve to deepen a school's culture by reinforcing the values of the school, rewarding members for achievements, and highlighting how and why being part of the community matters.

In summary, attention to both school climate and school culture are required of school leaders. Neither are something stable and nor should they be taken for granted. Instead, climate and culture are constantly being re-created and reshaped not only due to external influences, but also through people's knowledge, experiences, and beliefs. Belonging and feeling like one belongs is important for members of the school community. Forming strong school climate and culture provides leaders significant advantage because each represents a course for creating understanding, credibility and support for leadership work.

PROFESSIONAL COMMUNITY

Our discussion, thus far, has focused on the ways that schools, both as workplaces of teachers and places of learning for students, cultivate strong climates and cultures. We have introduced the core features of school climate—academic press, academic support, and trust—and school culture—symbols, stories, and ceremonies that support student learning. We turn now to thinking about the professional culture of school and explore the ways in which collaborative practice, collegial feedback, and collective learning enhance a school's communal practice.

McLaughlin and Talbert (1993) introduced the construct of professional community as an organizing theory for developing a supportive and engaging work environment in which educators might concentrate on improving pedagogy. The professional community was characterized by a focus on student learning and collaborative professional inquiry and reflection. However, McLaughlin and Talbert suggested that even within a structure designed to foster change, traditional practice was difficult to mitigate. Distinguishing between professional communities—where work was focused on *reinventing* practice and shared professional growth—and traditional community— where work was focused on *coordinating* effort to reinforce conventional practice— McLaughlin and Talbert noted that improvement was more likely to be found as educators' attentions focused on their own learning.

Research into professional community (Hord, 1987, 2009; Huggins, Scheurich, & Morgan, 2011; Kruse, Louis, & Bryk, 1995; Louis & Lee, 2016) stressed that the development of professional community provided school leaders the opportunity to increase efficacy among faculty and staff, promote personal dignity, and enhance collective responsibility for the values and goals of the school. Key to creating these beneficial outcomes was a collective focus on reflective dialogue (Schon, 1983), deprivatization of practice (Louis & Lee, 2016), and a focus on student learning (Stoll & Louis, 2007).

Reflective Dialogue

Reflective dialogue, as opposed to other forms of professional conversation, focuses attention on the collaborative examination of practice, offering collegial feedback and support for improved pedagogy. It centers on the notion that when teachers engage in deep discussion regarding their work with students, faculty-initiated improvement is more likely to occur. In addition to a climate and culture of trust within the school, reflective dialogue requires time to meet and talk, and gain access to expertise for dialogue to result in learning. School leaders can make time for reflective dialogue as a regular part of the school schedule by providing shared preparation periods, opportunity for discussion in faculty meetings, and promoting professional development that, as part of its design, provides teachers time to discuss what they are learning and how it might enhance their classroom practice. Similarly, for teachers to learn what they need in a "just-in-time" manner, access to expertise either from within the school or from external sources must be encouraged. In schools where reflective dialogue is strong, and conversation about practice is common, "not knowing" is encouraged and viewed as an opportunity where everyone can benefit from collective focused problem-solving.

Deprivatization of Practice

As teachers talk more openly about their work, it only makes sense that they would need and want to observe how their colleagues manage and work in their own classrooms. Deprivatization of practice fosters collective and collegial learning through watching others teach and, in turn, learning from the successes and failures of others. In schools where deprivatization is robustly present, classroom doors are open rather than closed and teachers regularly co-teach or team teach. Schools that have effectively deprivatized have done so in multiple ways. Co-teaching assignments make pedagogy public, as does scheduled peer observations and coaching commitments. Usually, such arrangements are made in like grades or subjects, but considerable collaboration and learning can occur in vertical teams and cross-content partnerships.

Focus on Student Learning

As dialogue and deprivatization are developed in a school, so is the sense that student learning is a shared responsibility of all organizational members. Certainly, teachers must take primary responsibility for the learning of students assigned to their classrooms. Yet, being a strong professional community suggests that the school as a whole bears responsibility for the learning outcomes of all students, including those who are not formally assigned to a teacher's current classroom. To enhance a school's focus on student learning leaders must begin to place questions about student learning at the top of their physical and metaphorical agenda. We know principals that do both. School leaders we admire begin each faculty meeting with the item, "What did you do to help kids learn and feel important today?" followed by 10–15 minutes to share answers and ask questions about practice. In other cases, school leaders we respect are more understated. Yet, they too focus teachers' attention on the reasons behind the instructional choices that get made and the kinds of work that students are asked to complete. Either way, there is no question that in those schools a strong professional culture has been built and is simply a way of life.

In conclusion, we would be remiss if we did not draw an important distinction between the research on professional community and the literature of professional learning communities. Professional community research has always placed communal learning at the core of teachers' professional work. Yet in the early 1990s, professional community researchers were not the only researchers pondering the ways in which schools and other organizations might become more effective if communal organizational learning was enhanced (Argyis, 1992; Louis & Kruse, 1995; McLaughlin & Talbert, 1993; Senge, 1990).

Organizational learning stresses that in complex places like schools, reliance on what individuals know is insufficient to ensure widespread organizational success. Organizational learning focuses on the ways in which new ideas are brought into a school organization, how they are considered and adopted or rejected, and the ways in which schools use the knowledge generated from them. Given the relative similarity of these constructs, it made sense to combine the two, and so the professional learning community, or PLC, was born.

Yet, as the construct became popularized (DuFour, 2008), PLCs became the code for many types of organizational structures (e.g., grade-level teams, subject area collaboration, multi-level conferences). As schools struggled to create PLCs, they often did so in ways that were out of sync with current school climates and cultures. Absent trust, how can teachers open their doors to others? Absent the knowledge and skill set to support academic press and support, how can teachers be expected to engage in meaningful, collegial feedback or reflective dialogue? Absent a communal story that features successful collaborative work, how can teachers and others know what their practice might look like? In this way, the PLC became, in many schools, a "thing we did" and failed to produce the intended results (Kruse & Johnson, 2017).

We remain hopeful that as new school leaders understand the importance of developing strong, productive school climates and school cultures, it becomes possible that true professional community can be built across our nation's schools. Yet, to do so school leaders must intentionally provide opportunities for collaborative practice, feedback, and learning. Additionally, they must encourage faculty-initiated improvement of programs and practices. Finally, school leaders need to employ the tools of climate and culture development in ways that focus on collective learning and success. Doing so has the potential to enhance the educational outcomes of all students.

CASES FOR ANALYSIS

CASE 5.1

We Are the Champions

Trout Creek High School (TCHS), home of the Red Eagles, is like a lot of large semi-urban high schools. Over 1,700 students attend the 9–12 school. TCHS has a student body that reflects the community that surrounds the campus. Approximately 11 percent of the students identify as Hispanic or Latino, 19 percent identify as black, 16 percent identify as biracial and the remaining students identify as white. Impressively, the school boasts a 98 percent graduation rate and a two- or four-year college attendance rate of over 90 percent. Among classroom teachers, 74 percent hold an M.A. or Ed.M. degree. In each classroom, teachers proudly display their high school and college diplomas.

Of the 70 classroom teachers at TCH, 62 identify as white and eight identify as black. Of the black faculty, five are men and although they all teach in different subject areas, each has a secondary affiliation as either a head or assistant football coach. Of the group, the longest tenure is held by coach Peru Jones, known locally as the "winningest" high school coach in the region. The Red Eagles have won numerous state championships in both football and basketball. However, no matter the season, Coach PJ is seen as the heart of TCHS athletics.

Jones, still an imposing man at 56, works hard to ensure that his team members excel on the field and in the classroom. He begins each football season in early August with three practices a day. The first two look like traditional team practice–sprints, blocking and tackling drills, weight work, and stretching. The third is held in a classroom. Alongside the coaching staff, school counselors work with each student athlete, identifying four college choices—two "safe schools" and two "stretch schools." Together, students research entry requirements, draft admissions essays, seek out scholarship opportunities, and explore campus visit days. Attention is paid to the developing course schedules so that players are enrolled in classes that will help them to achieve their academic goals. With the help of the booster club, student athletes are provided college T-shirts for each of their identified schools. It is these T-shirts that players wear to practice.

In coach Jones's words,

> If I do a good job, we win on Friday nights. If I do the job I ought to—the great job— these kids excel in life. I tell them, I really tell them, I blew out my knee playing college ball. Most kids don't make it to even play at that level, and those that do, like me, don't make it beyond that. It's what happens between your ears that will take you to the next place. What's there is important.

Once the school year starts, team members are required to complete weekly academic reports. If a student's grades slip, the student doesn't play on Friday night and the coaching staff arranges for tutoring. More often than not, the tutor is an upper classman from the team. If another player is not able to assist, Jones approaches other faculty asking that his player be paired with a student who can provide the needed help. In return, students are awarded a coveted number 99 Fighting Eagle jersey. At Friday afternoon game day, pep assemblies both team members and student-tutors walk out on the gym floor.

As principal Harris explains, "We create champions—on the field and off. None of us gets to where we want to be alone. Here at TCHS we just make it clear that everyone who supports someone else's goals deserves recognition." He goes on to note, "I know it sounds cheesy, but we're really a family here, and we work hard to make sure everyone feels like they matter."

Harris is also aware that "not all kids care about football." He is careful to add that although the school and community is rightfully proud of the ways in which student athletes are supported, all students need support and they "need it in ways that work for them." As he adds,

> It'd be bad if only my student athletes got this kind of attention. So, we work to find ways to make sure on the team or not you get what you need here. Our school vision has all the fancy words it should, but it comes down to this—learning matters, period. That's why we're here.

Discussing the Case

- What values are apparent at Trout Creek High School?
- What is made clear about the culture of the school?
- What features of the school's culture are less apparent?
- In what ways is professionalism reinforced?
- In what ways are academic press and academic support evident?
- How might communal learning be enhanced at Trout Creek?
- What questions would you have of coach PJ and others if you were to visit the school?
- What potential issues might arise for Trout Creek if coach PJ were to leave?

- Who might feel excluded by the culture that Trout Creek has created? In what ways might the culture become more inclusive?

CASE 5.2

Are We Warriors?

From its inception in 1930, Colkegan Falls High School had been the home of the Warriors. Over the past 20 years, the team logo has slowly changed in appearance. With each change, the resemblance to the original "Indian" has been softened and the latest version has been replaced entirely by a stylized and feathered letter W.

Yet, the team name remained. To many members of this tightknit California coast community, remaining the Warriors is a nod to tradition, to the roots of the region, and to the school's history. To others, it is a vestige of a past that should be finally and completely removed. Russell Meyer, Colkegan Falls High School Principal is among those who believe it is time to retire the name and all its associated logos and replace it with "something less charged." He adds, "Even though we've removed the caricature, we're still retaining a name that is racist. We're still using a feather, which can have special significance. It's an appropriation, it's offensive, and it's wrong."

Meyer credits his education concerning the name and mascot to the Student Diversity Council. They came to him with a request to change the name and logo with a carefully prepared presentation. In short, they argued that "in a school where diversity is claimed to be a value, and we're learning to be racially sensitive and inclusive and aware, we cannot continue to pretend our use of the name the Warriors is not shameful." They went on to note that even though the school no longer used the caricature, headlines in both the school and local papers like "Warriors scalp Bears" and "Warriors savage Knights" reinforced damaging stereotypes. Finally, the students noted that they knew that "as a term the word 'Warriors' was not itself defamatory, but the context of its use is the problem."

Meyer was impressed with the students' thinking, presentation, and argument. He believed that the time was right to make a change. Working with the student group, he asked that they make their presentation to the superintendent and her staff, CGHS faculty and then to the student body. He also pledged to support a contest for a new name and mascot. Meyer believed that by including all levels of the organization in early planning and conversations the change, although potentially controversial, would be supported.

Each presentation went well. The students were persuasive and professional. The contest was announced in March with categories, for a new name, a new mascot, and a new logo. A final winner would be determined by a student body vote and additional prizes would be awarded for creativity, artistic merit, and inventiveness. Additionally, Meyer secured the services of a local graphic designer to support the winner in developing a final concept. All in all, students were excited for the opportunity to make a change. As one student stated, "We could have a really cool modern name and mascot. It would be awesome if we weren't boring." Within the month, six completed entries were submitted for consideration. Choices included:

- The Fighting Artichokes
- The Golden Falcons
- The Screaming Toads
- The Mountain Gorillas
- The Evergreen
- The Hawk Rats

On the Friday before the spring break, the local paper ran a story about the impeding mascot change and the finalists. Meyer returned from a week away to a full voice mailbox and dozens of emails. As he described it, "I had no idea anyone would care. I had my office assistant print out all the email, I felt I had to listen to the calls myself but honestly, I thought it was all rather odd."

Meyer developed a system to group the responses. One bucket included those that were uniformly supportive. As he noted, "It was the smallest pile. I mean I get it, if you're fine with something you don't call or write the principal." A second included those emails that acknowledged a change was probably needed but that he should consider the "rich tradition" of the school before "making a mistake." In regard to this feedback, Meyer stated, "These folks mostly just thought a lot of the choices were kinda stupid. I saw it as a real disconnect between my high school kids and older generations." The third and largest group included comments that accused Meyer of being "politically correct" and "having lost my mind."

Meyer decided to share the feedback with the Student Diversity Council as well as with the students who had submitted entries. In his words, "I decided this was a teachable moment. You know, like we're doing something good here, and still not everyone thinks so. Not everyone will see things like you do. But in the end, I trusted my kids. I thought they'd done a good job and they'd make a good choice." Meyer returned all the email correspondence and as many of the calls as he could. In each he was to the point, thanking the person for the feedback and promising to take it "into consideration." For the moment, things seemed to calm down.

When in mid-May the ballots were tallied and the Fighting Artichokes won, Meyer was prepared for some community backlash. To him, the name made sense given the agricultural roots of the town. Additionally, the newly designed cartoon mascot was very cute. He could see its appeal to his student body. However, he knew that many in the community would not be pleased. Meyer also assumed that while some folks might not like it, they would either forget about it or simply move on to something else. As he put it, "After all, we do have a college with a Banana Slug as a mascot in this state."

What he was not prepared for was the call from the board president asking that he nullify the results of the election. As she stated, "We let you all play out this game and now it's time for the grownups to step in. We cannot be humiliated. We will not be demeaned in this way." Meyer was stunned. In conversation with the board president, he learned that privately the board had opposed the change and was gambling that a more traditional name would win. As she said, "We never agreed that the Warriors should go. We thought it was all rather silly and assumed you'd come to your senses and make them choose something respectful." She ended the conversation, with the statement, "We haven't finalized your new contract, you know."

Meyer was astounded by her threat. He had been proud of this effort. He believed that the students had acted appropriately adding, "They took what I thought was a moral stand. They had solid reasons for making a change. The fact that the board didn't even see that shocked me."

Meyer knew that he needed to back the students. But how?

Discussing the Case

- What are the issues that underscore this conflict?
- What aspects of culture are at play in this case?
- How can the voices of all members of a school community be heard?
- What might Meyer do next?
- How might he draw on symbolism, stories, and ceremonies to be effective?
- How can school mascots support the intellectual and academic goals of the school?

CASE 5.3

Spirit Dressing

Harmony Elementary school PTA includes an active group of parents. Many volunteer in classrooms, helping teachers assemble bulletin boards, transcribing early and strug-gling readers' stories, and supporting individual students with tutoring and mentoring. Others support the school by organizing fundraisers, the school carnival, and field day each May. Their efforts have resulted in the purchase of new playground equipment, an iPad cart at each grade level, and a 3D printer for the school library. They meet regularly to, as their charter suggests, "promote student learning, health, and well-being for the purpose of enriching our students' educational experiences."

The current president of the group, a stay-at-home dad, Curry Addamson, takes his role as president seriously. Not only does he sponsor an after-school coding club for fourth through sixth grade students, but he takes an active role in making the school a "fun" place to be. Building school spirit matters to Addamson and it is important to him that each month includes a special event at the school.

A staple of Addamson's tenure as president has been the increasing number of theme days—Crazy Hat Day, Harry Potter Wizard's Week, Pajama Day, and consecutive '60s, '70s, and '80s dress-up days. In most cases, students appear to like the opportunity to come to school out of the usual required uniform of khaki pants and navy polo shirts. Additionally, students enjoy small prizes that were awarded for the "most creative," "most original," or "most inventive" costume, as well as having their picture on the school's Web page after each win.

However, increasingly, parents have begun to grumble about the pressure to produce a novel, home-crafted, and school-appropriate costume on a regular basis. As one parent noted, "It's hard enough to get my three daughters out each morning with their homework, a lunch, and anything else they need. There are days this just pitches me over the edge." Another added, "I'm a single working parent. It seems like this is about getting cute pictures on Facebook or one-upping. I'm not crafty. I hate that my kid always looks like I just threw something together, 'cause most months that's what I do."

Finally, just after Dress Like an Explorer Day, a group of parents approached Thom Wittington, Harmony's principal, asking that "perhaps, we could dial this back a bit." The principal listened closely, taking care to make note of the group's most pressing concerns regarding cost, time, and the energy that costuming takes away from homework help or other family time each month. As the conversation drew to a close, Wittington took a moment to remind the group that the PTA had provided the school many resources and absent their support, the school would be unable to afford such "extras" going forward.

In an effort to gain another perspective, Wittington decided to ask a few teachers what they thought of these concerns. In many cases, teachers agreed. As one shared, "I mean, they look cute and all that but at times it does seem like it has more to do with the parents than the kids." Another shared, "I think, sometimes, it does divide the kids a bit. Like, I know it's about school spirit and all but whose school is this?" Still another mentioned, "I know some of my kids love these days. They're super outgoing and it's an opportunity for them to express that part of them. But I get it, last year we had 12 dress-up days—maybe that's too much."

Wittington knew it was time to call a meeting with not only Addamson but the full PTA board. Privately, he knew that he had allowed the PTA more latitude than he probably should have and that, at least in this case, things had gotten a bit out of hand. He worried, though, about offending this group of influential and dominant parents.

Wittington began the conversation praising Addamson and the rest of the board for the "energy" they put into the school. Wittington acknowledged that without the PTA the school would not "be what it is today." Yet, he emphasized that school activities needed to be inclusive and that "we should all be sensitive to the stresses other families have in raising their kids." He suggested that "maybe we could reduce the number of dress-up days in the next few months" and focus on other priorities, including the development of a lunchtime robotics club and other more academically focused efforts. Addamson and the board agreed to consider his suggestions. Wittington left the meeting with an uneasy feeling, one that was reinforced as he watched the group gather in the parking lot for a post-meeting conversation.

Discussing the Case

- Are events like Spirit Day important for school culture?
- What kinds of values do they reinforce?
- If you were Wittington, what would you do next?
- What decisions need to be made?
- Can culture building programs and events undermine academic and other goals of the school?
- How can school leaders be assured that all school programs are focused on supporting shared and valued goals?

ACTIVITIES

The following activities will further expand your understanding of school climate, culture, and community, and apply those ideas to your own school and practice.

ACTIVITY 5.1

Examining Your School Culture

One way in which culture is expressed in schools is by the ceremonies, events, and occasions that are part of the school calendar. Principal Frist used ceremony, from the way she handled the Halloween costume march, to the opening welcome back breakfast to honor what the school was and to prompt consideration of what it might become. At TCHS, there was a pep rally for athletes and their student tutors who helped them to maintain eligibility to participate in sports.

Consider the following questions as they relate to your culture. What might surface as a cultural leadership goal?

- What are your ceremonies, events, and occasions?
- Who participates in them? Who is left out?
- What values are expressed as a result of participation in these ceremonies, events, and occasions? What displays, artifacts, banners, or exhibitions are left behind as a result?
- Most schools have a mascot. How is your mascot part of your ceremonies or events? Do all events get equal time from the mascot? Or does the mascot only appear in a limited fashion?
- What kind of new ceremony would you create at your school? Why would you create it? What values do you hope it might instill or reinforce in your school's culture?

ACTIVITY 5.2

Visible Symbols of Your School Culture

School culture can be understood by the ways in which symbols and signs are present or absent in the school. Symbolic artifacts can vary, yet, they always tell a story about what and who the school values. What do your artifacts say about your school? Is it a message you believe in?

Are your mission and vision displayed? If so, what do your mission and vision suggest about your school culture? If not, what message is sent given their absence?

continued . . .

Does your school display student work? Which student work gets displayed? Do these displays honor subject-matter learning, artistic talent, collaborative or individual effort and success? If work is exhibited, where is it featured? How long is it displayed?

Do you have a hall of honor, a notable alumni wall, or showcase of historical school memories? What is included? Who is included? Are these artifacts a part of school life or are they ignored?

What does your website tell the community about your school? Is website

ACTIVITY 5.3

Strengthening Communal Work for School Success

Reflect on the ways to strengthen communal work that we have introduced in this chapter. In the table below note the areas you believe to be strengths of the professional community in your school. Also note where further development might be required. What leadership work might be needed to strengthen communal work and, in turn, school climate and culture? How might you go about doing that work? Who might you include in your efforts? Upon what resources might you draw?

	Current Strength	Development Needed	Support Personnel and Resources
Learning, rather than managerial tasks, is the focus of communal work.			
Leadership roles within the school are shared among members.			
Instruction, curriculum, and assessment are central features of communal conversation.			
Teachers share common goals for, expectations about, and norms for classroom practice.			
Healthy disagreement is encouraged, with the intention of pushing teachers to deeper understandings about their work.			

continued . . .

	Current Strength	Development Needed	Support Personnel and Resources
Teachers share instructional and other resources to enhance student learning.			
Teacher teams are provided opportunity to work with other teams within the building, cross-pollination of work is encouraged.			
Measures of student progress and achievement are shared, understood, and agreed upon by teachers.			
Classroom practice, in public, allows opportunity for teachers to co-teach and/or observe each other's practice.			
Excellence within the school is celebrated. When one teacher succeeds, the team takes pride in their success.			

RESOURCES

Many good resources for developing a positive school climate and culture are available online. We recommend using google to locate a school culture survey that best meets your individual needs. Even if you do not use the ones you locate as they are designed, it may be possible to use pieces of each to inform your understanding of your school culture. Our search turned up these resources we think are worth looking at:

www.mssaa.org/gen/mssaa_generated_bin/documents/basic_module/ School_culture_triage.pdf

www2.cortland.edu/dotAsset/1398c968–7af6–43bb-9ec9–076f78107a19.pdf

cms.azed.gov/home/GetDocumentFile?id=5669f9e7aadebe188002bee5

www.state.nj.us/education/students/safety/behavior/njscs/NJSCS_Staff_ Q2.pdf

continued . . .

Do not forget to include students and parents in your school culture exploration. Here are some resources you might use to find out how they experience your school:

www.surveymonkey.com/r/LQJQRMG

https://k2classroommanagement.wordpress.com/student-climate-survey/

www.state.nj.us/education/students/safety/behavior/njscs/NJSCS_ Parent_Q.pdf

REFERENCES

Argyris, C. (1992). *On organizational learning.* Boston, MA: Blackwell.

Bryk, A.S., & Schneider, B. (2002). *Trust in schools: A core resource for improvement.* New York: Russell Sage.

Cohen, J., McCabe, E., Michelli, N.M., & Pickeral, T. (2009). School climate: Research, policy, practice, and teacher education. *Teachers College Record, 111*(1), 180–213.

Deal, T. E., & Peterson, K. D. (2016). *Shaping school culture: The heart of leadership* (3rd ed.). San Francisco, CA: Jossey-Bass.

DuFour, R. (2008). *Revisiting professional learning communities at work.* Bloomington, IN: Solution Tree Press.

Erčulj, J. (2009). Organizational culture as organizational identity: Between the public and the private. *Organizacija, 42*(3), 69–76.

Hallinger, P., & Heck, R.H. (2010). Collaborative leadership and school improvement: Understanding the impact on school capacity and student learning. *School Leadership and Management, 30*(2), 95–110.

Hogan, S.J., & Coote, L.V. (2014). Organizational culture, innovation, and performance: A test of Schein's model. *Journal of Business Research, 67*, 1609–1621.

Hord, S. (1987). *Evaluating educational innovation.* London: Croom Helm.

Hord, S. (2009). Educators work together toward a shared purpose – improved student learning. *Journal of Staff Development, 30*(1), 40–43.

Hoy, W. K., & Tschannen-Moran, M. (2003). The conceptualization and measurement of faculty trust in schools: The omnibus T-scale. In Hoy, W.K. & Miskel, C.G. *Studies in leading and organizing schools* (pp. 181–208). Greenwich, CT: Information Age Publishing.

Hoy, W.K., Tarter, C.J., & Bliss, J.R. (1990). Organizational climate, school health, and effectiveness: A comparative analysis. *Educational Administration Quarterly, 26*(3), 260–279.

Huggins, K., Scheurich, J., & Morgan, J. (2011). Professional learning communities as a leadership strategy to drive math success in an urban high school serving diverse, low-income students: A case study. *Journal of Education for Students Placed at Risk, 16*(2), 67–88.

James, C., & Connolly, M. (2009). An analysis of the relationship between the organizational culture and the performance of staff work groups in schools and the development of an explanatory model. *International Journal of Leadership in Education, 12*(4), 389–407.

Kruse, S.D., & Johnson, B.L. (2017). Tempering the normative demands of PLCs with the organizational realities of life in schools: Exploring the cognitive dilemmas faced by educational leaders. *Educational Management, Administration, & Leadership*, 45(4), 588–604.

Kruse, S.D., & Louis, K.S. (2009). *Building strong school cultures: A guide to leading change.* Thousand Oaks, CA: Corwin Press.

Kruse, S.D., Louis, K.S., & Bryk, A. (1995). An emerging framework for analyzing school-based professional community. In Louis, K.S., and Kruse S.D., *Professionalism and community: Perspectives from urban schools.* Thousand Oaks, CA: Corwin Press.

Louis, K.S., & Kruse, S.D. (1995). *Professionalism and community: Perspectives from urban schools.* Thousand Oaks, CA: Corwin Press.

Louis, K.S., & Lee, M. (2016). Teachers' capacity for organizational learning: The effects of school culture and context. *School effectiveness and school improvement.* Available at: http://dx.doi.org/10.1080/09243453.2016.11899437

McLaughlin, M.W., & Talbert, J.E. (1993). Contexts that matter for teaching and learning: Strategic opportunities for meeting the nation's education goals. Stanford, CA: Center for Research on the Context of Secondary School Teaching (ED357023).

Schein, E. (1992). *Organizational culture and leadership* (2nd ed.). San Francisco, CA: Jossey-Bass.

Schneider, B., Ehrhart, M.G. & Macey, W.H. (2013). Organizational climate and culture. *Annual Review of Psychology*, 64(1), 361–388.

Schön, D.A. (1983). *The reflective practitioner.* San Francisco, CA: Jossey-Bass.

Senge, P. (1990). *The fifth discipline.* New York: Doubleday.

Stoll, L., & Louis, K.S. (2007). *Professional learning communities: Divergence, detail and difficulties.* London: Swets & Zeitlinger.

Thapa, A., & Cohen, J. (2016). A review of school climate research. *Review of Educational Research*, 83(3), 357–385.

Tschannen-Moran, M. (2014). *Trust matters* (2nd ed.). San Francisco, CA: Jossey-Bass.

CHAPTER 6

Equity and Opportunity

PSEL STANDARD 3—EQUITY AND CULTURAL RESPONSIVENESS
Effective educational leaders strive for equity of educational opportunity
and culturally responsive practices to promote each student's academic
success and well-being.

What does it mean to "strive for equity of educational opportunity and culturally responsive practices?" Kruse, Rodela, and Huggins (2018) have suggested that leadership studies without an explicit equity lens, while necessary, are insufficient to support leaders to work within the multidimensional settings of contemporary educational practice. They and others (Brown, 2004; Cambron-McCabe & McCarthy, 2005; Dantley & Tillman, 2010; Marshall & Oliva, 2010) note that when leaders fail to embrace understandings and practices that foster equitable and inclusive practices they often, perhaps unknowingly, reproduce the very inequities they hope to mitigate. The inequalities of schools fall along racial and socioeconomic lines and include a lack of access to experienced teachers and advanced curriculum (Adamson & Darling-Hammond, 2012), adequacy of school funding (Darling-Hammond, 2004), discipline actions (Gregory, Skiba, & Noguera, 2010), and the ways in which low-income families and students of color are perceived by teachers and school leaders (Valencia, 1997). Because of persistent and enduring inequity, educational opportunity for students of color and those who come from low-income families lags behind that of their peers (Larson & Murtadha, 2002).

In the U.S., these opportunity gaps result in differences of student achievement. For example, whereas Asian/Pacific Islander students graduated at a rate of 93 percent and white students at a rate of 84 percent, African American, Latino, and Native American students experienced graduate rates of 68 percent, 76 percent, and 68 percent respectively (Kena et al., 2014, p. 138). In response to these chilling statistics, researchers

(Brooks, et al., 2008; Capper, Theoharis, & Sebastian, 2006; Capper & Young, 2014) call for the promotion of educational opportunity and culturally responsive practices in our schools. In turn, promoting educational opportunity and culturally responsive practices requires that school and district leadership be intentionally and purposefully equity oriented.

Gaining traction on these issues requires an understanding of two complementary forms of leadership. *Equity-oriented leadership* (EOL) focuses on transforming educational policies and practices toward improved outcomes for all students. Equity-oriented leaders possess critical knowledge and skill sets concerning the systemic inequalities present in schools, particularly those related to race, income, gender, religion, disability, and lesbian, gay, bisexual, transgender, questioning (LGBTQ) issues (Brown, 2006; Furman, 2012; Theoharis, 2007). Furthermore, they are able to lead in ways that seek to alleviate those inequities.

Culturally responsive leadership (CRL) requires an awareness of diverse communities and students. More importantly, culturally responsive leadership is self-reflective (Khalifa, Gooden, & Davis, 2016; Milner, 2011; Ladson-Billings, 2011). EOL and CRL are distinct analytical concepts. Yet, they work in tandem, resulting in leaders who deeply reflect on their own sociocultural positionality. These leaders simultaneously advocate for systemic policy and programmatic changes to advance equity for all students, particularly those who have been historically marginalized in US schools (Bertrand & Rodela, 2018).

In this chapter, we will present the key themes of this research and place them in the context of school leadership practice. We do so with the knowledge that research (Kraft, Marinell, & Yee, 2016) suggests that good teachers leave schools when educational leadership is considered ineffective. This is especially true in urban schools and other challenging environments, the places most likely to be home to students of color and low-income families. Therefore, it is an imperative for schools in the US to develop high-quality leaders who understand equitable leadership practice so they can serve students well.

KEY LEARNINGS

In this chapter, you will learn to:

- address matters of equity and cultural responsiveness in all aspects of leadership;
- act with cultural competence and responsiveness in interactions, decision making, and practice;
- ensure that each student is treated fairly, respectfully, and with an understanding of each student's culture and context.

FEATURED CASE

Confronting Uncomfortable Realities

Keansmonk had seemed like a perfect location for Louis Sabetii when he accepted the position of high school principal five years ago. Several years prior to Sabetii's employment, Semiconductor Equipment Tek (SET) had opened a technology manufacturing plant in Keansmonk and brought many good paying entry-level jobs to the community. Since the jobs were primarily industrial in nature, many positions at SET required only a high school diploma. A generous benefit package, including a tuition reimbursement program, made working at SET attractive, as did the lure of being part of the bourgeoning "American-Made" tech industry.

SET brought a large number of blue- and white-collar jobs that decreased the unemployment rate in the region. A promise to promote from within paired with the tuition reimbursement program instilled a sense of loyalty to the company and community. There was a strong corporate culture established by SET, which benefited the Keansmonk Schools in several ways. Free and reduced lunch applications and student mobility declined, while parental attendance at school-sponsored events increased.

Sabetii was pleased that the high school was showing signs of increased academic achievement as well. With hopes of employment at SET, more students were enrolling in career and technical education (CTE) courses. Sabetti understood that there was a strong correlation between those enrollments and his increasing graduation rate. Even the high school football team was winning. The future looked bright.

So, it came as a surprise when Sabetii's phone rang late on a Saturday night. On the other end of the line was his associate principal (AP), Margot Elderberry, a veteran faculty member of KHS. Elderberry had been promoted to the role of AP after completing a school leadership program and had proven herself to be a valued and responsive member of the administrative team. Teachers, students, and parents trusted her judgment and respected her level-headed approach to problem solving and decision making. She was known for her ability to see issues from multiple lenses, while crafting compromise in situations that others found hopeless. Elderberry quickly got to the point of her call, sharing the news that earlier this evening the police were called to a party held by a recent graduate and former member of the football team. It appeared that several neighbors had complained about the noise, suspected under-age drinking, and reported damage to several cars parked along the narrow street.

To make matters worse, upon seeing the police arrive, about eight students had run out the backdoor and down the alley-way behind the home. Of the eight, five were caught, resulting in the arrests of three. The arrested were all members of the defensive line and all were black. Elderberry lacked additional details but shared that she found the incident concerning.

Monday morning the school was abuzz with stories of the party and the arrests. It was interesting to note that the police decided to arrest only three of the five students who were caught. More than one student noted that the two linemen who were not arrested included Sky Tenino and Mike Weints. Rumor had it that Sky got off because he was white and Mike, who was black, was not detained because his father was a prominent doctor in Keansmonk. Predictably, the arrests were being openly discussed on several social media platforms. The postings did not mince words, calling the arrests "racist and classist."

There was a lot of discussion about the district's zero-tolerance policy, requiring the suspension of any student who had been arrested. Elderberry was reluctant to suspend the three students as the arrests appeared "selective" to her. In her mind, it was clear that the players' actions endangered no one at the school and suspending the students would only deprive them of educational opportunities.

A quick conversation with Sabetii confirmed her thinking. Neither Sabetii nor Elderberry wanted to play a part in exacerbating racial tensions at KHS. With the support of the superintendent, Sabetii and Elderberry chose to allow the three to attend classes pending further advice from the district's legal counsel. They shared their decision with the players and stressed, no matter the decision on suspension, it was unlikely they would be playing football next Friday night.

Sabetii had cautioned faculty and staff to be vigilant to potential disruptions. Over the next few days Elderberry made her presence known around the school. She made it a point to be seen talking with the football coach and many members of the team. She kept her conversations light, talking about everything but the party and the arrests. She did not want to be perceived as gossiping about or interfering in the matter. However, she was able to glean that the players were truly embarrassed by what had happened and where horrified that the arrests had occurred. By Thursday afternoon, confident that the situation was under control, she returned to her office to catch up on neglected email and paperwork.

Just as she was about to settle into reviewing the paperwork for an upcoming individualized education program (IEP) meeting, Sabetii knocked on her door. He began with the words, "I have good news and bad news, which you do want first?" Elderberry opted for the good news. Sabetii was pleased that legal counsel was supportive of suspending the zero-tolerance policy and not the students. He noted that the law firm the district worked with realized that policies such as the one in Keansmonk exacerbated inequities and did little to increase school safety, the purported purpose of the zero-tolerance policy. In fact, the recommendation was that the board should vote to remove the section from district policy as soon as they possibly could.

Sabetii also reported that he had had a conversation with the chief of police and it was likely that charges against the students would be dropped in favor of some minimal community service. Further investigation suggested that, after running "a very short distance," the students had not resisted the police and the prosecutor's office suggested that the arrests had been "unwise" and "perhaps premature." The formal report also noted that none of the arrested students had been drinking. Interviews with the students suggested that one of the reasons they ran was that, in fact, they had not been partying and panicked. Elderberry smiled. She believed that while uncomfortable, the situation would soon resolve itself. She then asked, "So, what's the bad news?"

Sabetii closed the office door, "We have some teachers who are pitching a fit. They want the students suspended." Sabetii explained that a representative of the group had dropped by his office and asked that an "example" be made of these students. He went on to say that the teachers had referred to the boys as "thugs" and were suggesting that "not suspending these students sends the message that we condone under-age drinking and criminal activity." Sabetii added that he expected that the news of the dropped charges would not be well received. Elderberry noted that, "They don't have all the facts." She also worried aloud that, "We appear to be getting very lucky here, why would they want to push the matter?"

EQUITY-ORIENTED LEADERSHIP

Despite the fact that school improvement and educational reform has been a key theme of research and public policy for over 40 years, significant disparities in student achievement still endure. Over the past four decades, teachers and school leaders have invested considerable effort toward understanding and mitigating disparities in student academic performance. Yet, change efforts are often hindered because educators are unwilling to assume responsibility for students' low achievement. Research (Garcia & Guerra, 2004; McKenzie & Locke, 2009) suggests that even within schools working toward improvement, these efforts are impeded by teachers' and principals' tendencies to blame students, families, and communities for poor student outcomes. When attention is focused on student deficits rather than examining the links between school practices and student learning, it is difficult to look for solutions within the school system itself.

Clearly, schools are not alone in perpetuating deficit thinking about low-performing students. To be fair, deficit thinking permeates our national discourse (Valencia, 1997), which is echoed by educators. Additionally, we acknowledge that the vast majority of school leaders and teachers are compassionate and caring individuals. Yet, we also suggest that many are unaware of the ways in which their own cultural identities have significant influence on their decision making regarding classroom practice (Garcia & Guerra, 2004). Additionally, it is not enough to focus on remediating personal individual bias and prejudices, although clearly there is much work to done in that arena. Rather, professional attentions should be directed toward critically examining the systemic factors that perpetuate inequality and inequity in schools. Doing so requires that the long-standing myth that schools function as a meritocracy providing universal opportunities for students regardless of regional, ethnic, racial, or other differences be rejected.

Equity-oriented leadership (EOL) focuses on transforming systemic factors and educational policies and practices toward improved outcomes for each student. As Adamson and Darling-Hammond (2012) conclude, on every tangible measure of school quality, those who serve students of color have significantly fewer resources than schools serving a majority of white students. Minoritized students are disadvantaged in many ways that may compromise their educational opportunities. They often lack consistent access to effective and high-quality teachers, as well as classroom and technological resources in comparison to white students.

Inasmuch as a student's academic success is strongly correlated with parental income, wealth, and educational attainment, these inequities have become generational and pernicious. Certainly, there are additional and longstanding economic and social barriers to achievement outside of the influence of the school. Yet, equity-oriented leaders recognize that through inequitable practices, schools themselves contribute to and perpetuate existing inequalities. Furthermore, equity-oriented leaders work to transform their schools into places that support student learning by addressing, through intentional and purposeful actions, the systemic inequalities present in schools, particularly those related to race, income, gender, religion, disability, and LGBTQ issues (Brown, 2006; Furman, 2012; Theoharis, 2007).

CULTURALLY RESPONSIVE LEADERSHIP

Whereas EOL builds on a school leader's broad understandings of systemic inequality, culturally responsive leadership (CRL) requires that school leaders develop an awareness of and knowledge about the diversity present in their communities and students. Furthermore, and more importantly, CRL requires that school leaders engage in self-reflective practice concerning their own cultural identity, position, and privilege (Khalifa, Gooden, & Davis, 2016; Milner, 2011; Ladson-Billings, 2011). By engaging in self-reflection and understanding the values and beliefs they personally bring to their work, leaders are better able to orient their work toward the success and well-being of each student.

Central to the development of CRL are the tandem constructs of cultural knowledge and cultural leadership behavior. Cultural knowledge is informed by knowing students' languages and literacies, ethnic and spiritual orientations, and authentic behaviors and cultural wisdom. Furthermore, if we are not to essentialize students, families, and their communities (i.e., reduce the complexity of a culture to one or two key features), our knowledge base should be developed within and about the community in which one leads. By building on our understandings of the nuances of lived cultures within the boundaries of our school community, our leadership work can be oriented toward activities and foci pertinent and important to the broader school community.

Cultural leadership behaviors—those activities and performances that compromise culturally *responsive* leadership—require more than knowing about your community or advocating for inclusivity or fairness. The performance of cultural leadership is more involved and complex. CRL is active work. To be responsive is to *act* on that which we know and experience. Central to the practice of culturally responsive leadership is an understanding that creating a "good school" is not enough to gain traction on historic disparities and inequalities (Santamaria, 2014; Theoharis, 2007). School leaders seeking to become culturally responsive must first begin by developing self-awareness and reflectivity concerning the ways in which they have benefited from and been privileged by the systems in which they work.

Such reflectivity surfaces the assumptions and biases we bring to our work. Surfacing our own deep awareness and understanding of the values and beliefs we all hold about ethnicity and race, wealth and poverty, and difference, allows us to better respond to those around us. To this end, critical self-reflection (Capper, Theoharis, & Sebastian, 2006; Furman & Shields, 2005; McKenzie et al., 2008) asks that we all make sense of the ways in which our past education, family, and other significant influences have shaped our own deeply held values (see Activities 6.1 and 6.2 at the end of this chapter as a place to begin this work). As Brown (2004) notes, critical self-reflection creates the conditions in which school leaders may expand their world view. The result is the deliberate consideration of the ethical implications and effects on their leadership practice. Critical self-reflection requires that school leaders identify the ways in which our identities enhance or detract from our ability to see, understand, and consider alternative perspectives in and for leadership practice (Santamaria, 2014).

For example, in the case of Keansmonk High School, when Sabetii and Elderberry chose not to automatically suspend the three arrested linesmen in favor of waiting further detail concerning the situation, they chose to reflectively consider the ethical implications of their decision. By considering the negative implications of a suspension in concert with the minimal risk to student safety that allowing the three to remain in school posed, they demonstrated culturally responsive leadership behaviors favoring a choice that did not create further inequity. This example also serves to demonstrate how EOL and CRL work in tandem to create better outcomes for students. Absent the broad national discussion about disparate discipline and suspension data, Sabetii and Elderberry would have lacked the equity-oriented leadership knowledge that was fundamental for them to make a culturally responsive decision.

IMPLICATIONS FOR LEADERSHIP PRACTICE

There are many ways in which school leaders can favor equity-oriented and culturally responsive practices. These distinctions include actions that specifically and directly address leadership decision arenas through an equity lens. Traditionally, school leadership has been posited to include at least five core activities—visioning, mentoring and coaching, problem solving and decision making, instructional and curricular leadership, and mediating conflict and dispute (Johnson & Kruse, 2009). We examine each for the ways in which EOL and CRL offer a fresh perspective for leadership activity and work.

Visioning

Visioning builds a collective understanding of and direction toward school improvement and success. This is good practice. However, from EOL and CRL perspectives, visioning must also include discussions concerning how students who struggle can be provided learning experiences that assure they receive adequate academic and social supports so that they can achieve and succeed alongside their more privileged peers. Similarly, as we stressed in Chapter 4, visioning activities, inclusive of this orientation, would include the voices of parents and caregivers, community and other leaders, as well as those members of the school community in its development. Doing so high-lights the ways in which inclusive instructional, curricular, and behavioral practices might be employed to assure the success of all students and included in visioning goals and objectives (Cambron-McCabe & McCarthy, 2005; Jean-Marie, Normore, & Brooks, 2009).

Furthermore, visioning from an equity lens requires that school leaders create compelling narratives that embrace a vision of success that is relevant to the community and students the school serves (Ladson-Billings, 2011). Visions that are vague (e.g., create citizens for a constantly changing global community) do little to foster a sense of inclusion among families who may feel excluded or marginalized by existing school policies and practices. Visions that are overly prescriptive (e.g., all students will go on to college) may disregard equally positive life choices for students. This is not to say that students from marginalized populations should not aspire to college or that they would not be successful once there. Rather, it reflects the reality that for many first-generation and historically marginalized students, college attendance is financially prohibitive and often the social capital (e.g., needed guidance, information, and support) necessary for students to effectively navigate the college search and application process is also lacking. EOL and CRL thinking prompts leaders to consider the ways in which vision statements are read by the communities the school serves and to work toward creating inclusive vision statements. In turn, inclusive vision statements should be paired with comprehensive goals and activities that include the majority of the school community in their implementation.

Mentoring and Coaching

As leadership practices, mentoring and coaching are key to the development of expertise within a school. The terms are often used interchangeably. However, some general definition is important as we consider the development of EOL and CRL knowledge and skills. Mentoring is generally, but not always, considered less formal than coaching and more focused on guidance toward aspirations identified by the mentee (Mullen, 2009). Loosely defined, a mentor is a trusted adviser who offers support, guidance, and wise counsel in matters professional and personal. As Garvey, Stokes, & Meggison (2018) suggest, a mentor works with an interested mentee sharing wisdom, self-knowledge, and reflection on the work or situation at hand. Mentors often tell stories about their own practice and experiences, employing their personal narratives as an example or models. Additionally, while not always the case, often the best mentors come from within the same organization or profession as the mentee. As a result, they understand the cultural and organizational climate of the mentee, allowing advice, when offered, to be directly informed by their insider status, and therefore immediately applicable to the issues the mentee faces (Gray, Garvey, & Lane, 2016).

On the other hand, coaching is often a more formal relationship. Commonly, it is directive and technical in nature (Gray, Garvey, & Lane, 2016). Whereas mentors give advice and expert recommendation, coaches act more as facilitators enabling others to discover new skills and knowledge as a result of their own work and effort. Employing a universally accepted and understood knowledge and skill set, coaches can bring a fresh perspective to the circumstances the coached face. Additionally, coaching focuses more centrally on organizational goal attainment, and often on the advancement of organizationally defined and informed understandings and actions—for example, a new employee might be coached so that they are better able to align their work with the policies and practices of their new organization.

When considered from an equity lens, the distinctions between mentoring and coaching matter because one, mentoring, stresses understanding the local as well as attending to individual aspirations. Coaching accentuates more universal understandings and actions. The concern for school leadership development is clear. It is well documented that the principalship still attracts a majority of white men and women (Hill, Otten, & DeRoche, 2016), while the demographics of the national student population are becoming increasingly more diverse (McFarland et al., 2017).

These differences matter. Research (Egalite, Kisida, & Winters, 2015; Gerhenson, Holt, & Papageorge, 2016) suggests that there are strong and persistent academic benefits when students and teachers share the same race and ethnicity. While the mechanisms as to why this happens remain unclear, it is theorized that these benefits manifest themselves because teachers of like race and ethnicity may be better able to serve as mentors, role models, academic advocates, and cultural translators. Similar effects have been posited for school leaders (Foster, 2005; Gooden, 2005; Willie, Edwards, & Alves, 2002).

Additional research suggests that Latinx leaders, acting as mentors for students, may have enormous benefits on student outcomes, including setting high expectations for Latinx students by rejecting deficit perspectives (Hernandez, Murakami, & Quijada Cerecer, 2014), reducing Latinx dropout rates (Murakami, Valle, & Méndez-Morse, 2013), understanding the notion of extended family (Martinez, Marquez, Cantú, & Rocha, 2016), understanding how to harness the power of the Spanish language (Hernandez, Murakami, & Quijada Cerecer, 2014), increasing family involvement (Pedroza & Mendez-Morse, 2016; Hernandez, Murakami, & Quijada Cerecer, 2014), recognizing resilience among Latinx students and families (Murakami, Valle, & Méndez-Morse, 2013), and having shared cultural experiences with students (Hernandez, Murakami, & Quijada Cerecer, 2014). However, other less encouraging research (Martinez et al., 2016; Murakami et al., 2016; Peterson & Vergara, 2016) suggests that leaders who fall outside the traditional model are less likely to be "tapped" for leadership positions. In part, this is because the longstanding practice of "tapping" or targeting perspective teachers for leadership roles is, in part, forged through the informal mentorship process.

Teachers of color are often disadvantaged by this system because they are less likely to have formed primary mentor relationships in schools where they are in the minority (Foster, 2005). Simply put, informal mentorship tends to favor the familiar. Absent informal mentorships that would surface the leadership aspirations of minoritized teachers, their potential goes unrecognized. Similarly, more formal coaching supports those who are already identified as leaders or are already in leadership roles. Here again, those positions are more likely to be inhabited by white teachers (Hill, Otten, & DeRoche, 2016). Leading from ELO and CRL lenses suggests that these entrenched structures must be purposefully challenged and upended by the broader and more purposeful recruitment and mentorship.

Problem Solving and Decision Making

When approached from an EOL and CRL lens, problem solving and decision making can address two equally important concerns. The first centers on the ways in which problems are framed and decisions are generated. The second focuses on who is included in problem-solving and decision- making arenas, and the extent to which their input is valued. Traditionally, problems are framed by those within the broad educational community. Additionally, problems are usually identified by actors external to the school setting but with a vested interest in the school (e.g., policy makers) or actors within the school or district itself (e.g., principals, teachers) (Furman, 2012; Johnson & Kruse, 2009). EOL and CRL thinking shatters those distinctions and suggests that problem identification and subsequent decision-making efforts should be intentionally structured to include a wider and more inclusive set of actors.

By shifting the problem-framing perspective, two things happen. First, new windows are opened, providing insight into the way the school is experienced. Second, as alternative frames are generated, problems can be framed in innovative and inclusive ways. Economic theory suggests that problem-solving efforts go wrong in predictable and avoidable ways. Among these are attribution (Jones & Harris, 1967) and misdiagnosis errors (Kim & Grunig, 2011). When value is ascribed incorrectly, an attribution error has occurred. When it is assumed that parents do not attend school conferences because they do not care about their child's learning rather than realizing that conferences are held at times when parents are unable to attend, incorrect judgments are made because of those attributions.

When the problem is identified incorrectly or time is invested in solving the "wrong" problem, misdiagnosis has occurred. For example, when problems in student discipline are framed as issues of inadequate policy, school leaders often set out to develop even more detailed rules and regulations. If discipline issues are framed from a lens that focuses on relationship building, different choices are made. In this way, misdiagnosis of the problem can direct school leaders toward unproductive and potentially damaging conclusions. Simply put, better problem framing leads to better, more readily accepted and equitable problem solutions.

When more voices are included in the problem-solving and decision-making agenda, the door is opened to better problem framing as well as innovative, inclusive solutions. By adopting a participant-focused model of problem solving (Jeynes, 2012; Hamlin & Flessa, 2016), multiple perspectives on an issue can be surfaced, saving time and avoiding error. As we broadly discuss in Chapter 4, communication with families and the community fosters equity through the inclusion of multiple voices. Doing so is practicing equity-oriented and culturally responsive leadership.

Instructional and Curricular Leadership

Traditionally, instructional and curricular leadership has focused on the adoption and use of pedagogical best practices. Yet, rarely are those practices collaboratively and publicly probed for how they preserve or challenge existing disparities or differences. By aligning their leadership energies with the core business of teaching school leaders can do much to foster the conditions that promote student success.

As research (Brown, 2006; Capper & Young, 2014; Davis, 2017; McKenzie and Locke, 2009; Milner, 2011) suggests, EOL, as it relates to instructional and curricular leadership, rests on six foundational beliefs:

- All children, with the exception of those with profound disabilities, are capable of high levels of academic success.
- That "all children" is an inclusive term, suggesting that the exclusion of a child because of his or her race, gender, social class, disability, culture, language, religion, and so on is unacceptable and should not be supported.
- Teachers and school leaders hold primary responsibility for student learning, including the provision of high-quality instruction, differentiation as necessary to assure growth and progress, and that access to classroom instruction should not be withheld for reasons other than threats to student safety or well-being.
- High-quality teaching skill must be required of all teachers, and the provision of professional learning opportunities, designed to foster excellence, is the responsibility of school and district leadership.
- Student learning should be supported by consistent, coherent, and aligned curriculum, policy, and practice designed to engage students in cognitively challenging work.
- Substantial opportunities for and use of formative and summative assessments should be present to ensure that pedagogical decision making is informed by relevant and recent data regarding each student's learning.

For schools to be both excellent and equitable requires strong instructional and curricular leadership. When approached through EOL and CRL lenses, instructional and curricular leadership becomes a rich opportunity for school leaders to foster deep understandings of the ways in which each student learns and grows. In turn, they are more likely to have a positive impact on students' long-term academic and personal well-being.

Mediating Conflict and Dispute

A primary role of school leaders is to mediate conflicts and disputes. No matter how robust the effort to create a school environment that is positive and inclusive, conflict and disagreement will arise. It is unavoidable that students will misbehave and faculty members will disagree. It is also unavoidable that when conflict and disagreement occur, we bring to those instances our own values and beliefs about how these incidences should be handled and resolved. Moreover, managing conflicts related to equity and inclusion are particularly sensitive, and we often miss opportunities to experience and consider events through the eyes of others.

Leading through EOL and CRL lenses provides school leaders with a way into a courageous conversation (Singleton, 2015) and creates a context for the understanding of issues related to race, class, gender, and disability. Doing so centers school leaders' thinking on the ways in which leadership choices and decisions related to conflict and dispute promote or repress equity. Current research addressing best practices toward resolving conflicts related to student misbehavior and disobedience include restorative practices (Gregory, Clawson, Davis, & Gerewitz, 2014; Skiba, Mediratta, & Rausch, 2016), positive behavior interventions and supports (McIntosh, Kelm, & Delabra, 2015; Bornstein, 2017), attention to classroom ecology (Pryce & Fredrickson, 2013), and the development of positive and supportive classroom climate (Davis, 2017). On the faculty and staff side of the work, current research suggests a variety of approaches, including creating strong and collaborative school cultures (Deal & Peterson, 2016; Kruse & Louis, 2009), the development of deep and focused professional learning communities (Gray, Kruse, & Tarter, 2016; Stoll & Louis, 2007), distributing leadership (Spillane, 2005; Tian, Risku, & Collin, 2015), and mindful leadership practice (Brown, Ryan, & Creswell, 2007; Gates, 2015). Furthermore, this is not a fully inclusive list. There are numerous examples of efforts to confront and mitigate poor student behavior, and to enhance faculty and staff relationships as they relate to shared work.

However, additional research (Utheim, 2014; Wing, 2009) suggests that many of these practices themselves carry implicit and significant cultural assumptions. At the root of this critique is the assertion that foundational components of conflict and dispute mediation, including objectivity, impartiality, and neutrality, themselves are culturally bound and reproduce potentially damaging hierarchical power structures. For example, Positive Behavioral Interventions and Supports (PBIS) and restorative justice models emphasize the role of an impartial and neutral mediator as the facilitator of conversations concerning student misconduct. Both models follow fairly prescriptive techniques designed to further increase the objectivity of the administrator or teacher. A notable strength of these models is consistency of practice as well as attention to constructive interventions. The use of PBIS and restorative justice appears to reduce the use of exclusionary discipline practices in schools (Gregory, Clawson, Davis, & Gerewitz, 2014; Skiba, Mediratta, & Rausch, 2016). Doing so has gone far to promote a climate of inclusion and respect.

Yet, for example, many indigenous and non-Western conflict resolution models emphasize relationships over techniques, favoring the inclusion of family and community members in conflict resolution. Whereas Western approaches tend to value individualistic, time-bound, and linear solutions to problem solving and decision making as they relate to conflict management, many non-Western communities value more communal, interconnected, and cyclical approaches to mediation. We are careful here in our characterizations as we acknowledge that "many" is not all, and even within the Western world there are numerous approaches to conflict management and mediation. This is not to say that one approach is better than the other. Instead, we stress that understanding how our race, class, gender, sexual orientation, and disability status influences our approaches to mediating conflict and dispute is important.

In conclusion, leading through EOL and CRL lenses does not happen by chance. It takes thoughtful attention to the work of school leadership if traction is to be gained concerning the historical and institutional inequities present in our schools. Furthermore, purposeful and intentional leadership action is required to transform our schools into places where each student feels welcome and safe, and families and communities believe their culturally informed perspectives are valued.

CASES FOR ANALYSIS

CASE 6.1

What Are You? Defining Racial Identity

Margret "Maggie" Chapmen-Morris prided herself on being a third-generation educator in the same small town she grew up in. Her maternal grandmother had begun her 35-year career as a kindergarten teacher in a "black school" when the Harrison Schools were still segregated. Unlike many of her peers, after desegregation, she had successfully transitioned into a teaching position in a formerly "white" school. Maggie's father, Oscar Chapmen, a graduate of Harrison High, attended college and returned to Harrison as a high school teacher and football coach. He became the district's first black high school principal in the mid-1990s. By the middle 2000s he had risen to a prominent role in the district office and upon his retirement in 2016, the high school gym was renamed in his honor.

Maggie always knew she wanted to be a teacher, but also wanted to establish herself as a professional outside of the town who "knew me before I knew myself." She chose to attend college "up north" and began her teaching career in the same state where she had attended school. However, a recent divorce had left her unsettled and Maggie moved back to Harrison. She reasoned that being close to her parents would provide more stability for her two children, both under the age of 10.

Happily, she was hired for an elementary teaching position and the Harrison School District warmly welcomed her back. As she described it:

> I was excited to come home. I loved this town as a kid and I wanted to be part of it again. I had a great education and I wanted my kids to have that same sense of family and support. I also wanted to be part of the Chapmen legacy here. My family had been a part of these schools for decades and I saw it as my role to continue our work as excellent black educators in the south.

Harrison schools had comfortably integrated in the 1960s, avoiding much of the political strife that had afflicted neighboring districts. Perhaps it was because the district had been small to begin with or that the town had deep religious roots, race relations had never seemed like much of an issue in Harrison. Yet, school leaders knew that race was always an issue. They were continually attentive to data concerning graduation rates, advanced placement (AP) and honors enrollment, as well as other indicators of inequality.

Additionally, several prominent local black leaders held positions on the school board and by all accounts when an issue that related to race arose, it was addressed openly and confronted honestly. As the Black Lives Matter (BLM) movement gained national attention, the district preemptively issued a statement of support for students, faculty, and staff who wanted to march or wear BLM T-shirts in class. As athletic teams across the nation began to "take a knee" in protest of police brutality, members of Harrison teams were afforded the option of doing so without risk of censor.

Therefore, when Maggie returned to Harrison she was expecting, as she shared, "things would be easy, you know, like I was coming home and knew I'd be safe. Not that I didn't feel safe up north, but that I could breathe a little easier. I thought I knew this place." In many ways, Maggie's expectation proved itself accurate as it related to her own experience. She wasn't as prepared for how her children would be received.

Early in her marriage, Maggie and her now ex-husband had discovered that a prior medical condition would make having a biological child difficult and they decided to adopt. For Maggie, it "just made sense." She explained, "We would be able to provide a child a home" and avoid expensive and painful medical intervention. At the time of application, they had first suggested that they only wanted to adopt a black child, but later in the process had "fallen in love" with a biracial son and later adopted an Asian daughter. Consequently, the children looked nothing like each other and neither looked like Maggie.

To Maggie, each child was hers and equally loved. Yet, upon return to Harrison she found herself explaining who her children were and how she had come to be their parent. Especially troubling to her was the question, "But what are they?" When she was feeling generous, she explained the adoption process. When she was feeling less generous, she often responded, "Children." Privately, she felt that the question was intrusive and discriminatory.

Just after school began, Maggie's fourth grade daughter, Adela, came home in tears. Adela reported that the teacher had pressed her in front of the class to "explain her heritage" and that during recess several other students had teased her suggesting that Maggie had adopted her, "because no one else wanted you." Additionally, Adela reported that when she tried to take an empty seat at the lunch table, several girls told her that the chair was only for "white kids." Adela claimed that when she went to the teacher, she had been told that "she heard it incorrectly" that "those were nice girls."

Maggie was torn. What could the teacher have been thinking? Should she complain? Was she in danger of making more of the situation than it might really be? Could Adela handle this on her own? Her concerns were further complicated because the teacher was a colleague. How could she handle this without compromising her relationship with a new peer? She told Adela to head outside to play with her brother and that she would need to think about what they would do next. Unenthusiastically, she pulled out her materials to begin planning for the next day at school, wondering if there were issues in Harrison that she had ignored in her hopes to return.

Discussing the Case

- What are the issues this case raises?
- What aspects of equity and culture are at play in this case?
- How might Maggie respond to Adela?
- Should Maggie call the principal?
- What might you do if you were the principal of the school and Maggie called you?
- How might Maggie's position as a parent in this case be balanced with her new position and her family's legacy in the community?

CASE 6.2

Access Issues

Leaders at Lower Boone Schools (LBS) were proud of the work they had done concerning equity. In concert with the school board, the district had recently passed a new LGBTQ rule, including a transgender bathroom policy that they believed was a state model for inclusionary practice. Comprehensive professional learning had been developed for faculty and staff related to the new rule and it had been well received. The effort had been aided by the willingness of a local family to share the gender transition of their own daughter who had attended LBS. The family had been open about their own process and the former student had returned to share her moving story.

Similarly, LBS had implemented across-the-board policy and practice for racial and ethnic equity policies. A shift to restorative justice in the schools had lowered suspension and expulsion rates for both black and Hispanic youth, and several programs focused on increased student learning had closed historical achievement gaps among all groups in the school district. School climate and culture survey data showed an increase in items related to student well-being, school community, and belonging. Most notable was a double-digit rise in strongly agreed responses to the item, "My teacher cares about me." Comparable increases were noted in items such as, "If I have a problem I know a teacher will help me find help," "This school is a safe place for me to learn," and "I know I am a valued student in this school."

Justifiably so, the superintendent stated, "I'm proud of our efforts. We all worked hard, learned a lot of new and uncomfortable things and came out the other end stronger. I feel like our schools are good places for kids." Therefore, when a group of parents came to the school board to complain about the ability of their children to access the curriculum, he was a bit stunned.

The parents, a well-mannered and articulate group, laid out three complaints. The first related to a new district policy of flipping instructions so that students were required, for homework, to view online videos and other materials as preparation for classes. The board listened intently as the flipped classroom project had been a point of pride. Pointing to it as "cutting edge" pedagogy that provided for increased time within the school day to provide tutoring and other learning assistance to students, they noted that it had rated highly among the changes that students reported helped their learning. However, as the parents pointed out, many video links lacked closed captioning or closed captioning that was incomplete or meaningless. Part of the parents' presentation included a short clip where it was evident that the teacher had said "Invert the numerator and the denominator" and the closed caption had read "Alert the numbers." Clearly, the parents pointed out, the learning of students with hearing difficulties was compromised in this situation.

Second, the parents raised the point that the schools employed only limited interpreters for the population of deaf and hard of hearing students (DHH) in the schools. The parent group praised the schools for their inclusion policies and stressed they did not want their students pulled out of class for special programs. Yet, they did note that the absence of interpreters limited students' ability to interact with hearing peers in situations outside of the academic setting. Parents also noted that even within the academic setting, teachers often grouped DHH students together at assemblies or other events, further restricting their interactions with hearing peers.

Finally, the parent group noted that visual access to whiteboards and other supportive assistive technologies was sometimes inadequate, and that the number of bilingual (i.e., American Sign Language/English) teachers in the system was unknown. They did praise several teachers who had taken it upon themselves to "learn some sign" to better connect with their children. However, overall, they were troubled that their students' needs were often not understood, even in the presence of well-written IEP and 504 plans.

The parent group acknowledged that due to medical and technological advances such as cochlear implants and classroom sound-field or FM systems, students who might have gone to a school for the deaf in the past, were now attending public schools. Doing so provided the students and their families the opportunity to enjoy a traditional family life, as schools for the deaf are few and many DHH children needed to live on-site to receive an education. Finally, the parents also acknowledged that they had learned that their children were DHH soon after they were born. Early identification allowed the children to receive immediate intervention and experience visually language-rich environments from birth.

As one parent put it, "We worked hard so that when Kriss got to school, she'd be ready. Now that she's here and doesn't look like she needs help, she isn't getting it." Another parent added, "We get that special education is hard. We just want our kids to be treated according to the law and with dignity." A third closed by saying, "I know our kids aren't as in your face as the LGBTQ kids or some other minorities, but I think they have side-tracked your attention in the past few years. Our kids need your help too." The parents closed their presentation by asking that LBS look closely at their access practices, the flipped classroom, and online material. They noted that, "Although we are here this evening to advocate for our DHH students, we believe that if someone were to consider your services for the visually impaired, you'd find similar access issues."

The superintendent and the board thanked the group and promised to look closely at district and school policy. He shared that he was appreciative of the thoughtful presentation and that he would immediately form a committee to address the flipped curriculum materials. As soon as the parent group left, he turned to the board and asked, "What do you think?"

Discussing the Case

- What are the equity issues this case raises?
- How are issues of equity related to DHH and visually impaired students handled in your school?
- Have issues of special education inclusion been "side-tracked" by other more vocal groups?
- What should the district and school leaders do next?

- How can school leaders both address equity and access issues, and move forward on "cutting-edge" instructional initiatives like the flipped classroom?
- How can principals and others stay aware of the multiple equity issues that confront schools today?

CASE 6.3

In or Out?

By all accounts, Hunter Mellen was a popular, well-adjusted high school junior at Scatter Key High School. He maintained a 3.25 grade point average (GPA), played for the soccer team, and sang in the school choir. Scatter Key was not a large high school and most of the 400 students had known each other all of their lives. Therefore, when the daughter of his parents' close friends asked him to the junior prom, Hunter didn't hesitate to say yes. Since he hadn't planned on asking anyone himself and the school only sold tickets for couples, he had decided to skip the event. Hunter had known Kellie Lyttle since kindergarten and it seemed reasonable that they could enjoy the dance together and have a fun evening out.

Shortly after agreeing, Hunter began to realize that the invitation was not as innocent as he had first imagined. Kellie began to pressure him to offer her an elaborate and public "promposal," as well as "treat her like his girlfriend." Kellie had also enlisted her mother in the prom-planning effort. Ms. Lyttle then contacted Hunter's mother about how they might "make the evening a special memory." She also confided that "It would be so much fun to have the two of them get together." Concerned, Cathy Mellen decided that she needed to explore Hunter's level of comfort concerning the Lyttle family's expectations and his interest in making the dance an "official date."

Cathy asked that Hunter be home for dinner on Thursday night and took the afternoon off to make his favorite meal. A single parent, Cathy and Hunter often cooked together, talking amicably about sports, Hunter's classes, and television shows they both enjoyed. When they were able to eat together dinner was, for both of them, a time to connect in a low-key way, absent the usual pressure of their daily lives.

Yet, when Hunter sat down on Thursday, Cathy immediately sensed his discomfort. Guessing that Hunter "felt over his head," she immediately launched into a monologue about the ways in which he might offer the requested promposal and how perhaps he might consider planning a group dinner before the dance so that the event felt less like a date and more like "just a bunch of friends going out." As she offered more and more ideas, Hunter appeared to shrink further into his seat. Noticing that he had barely eaten anything, she said, "Do you want me to help you figure out how to get out of this? I could invent a reason you had to go see your dad or your grandparents that weekend."

At last, Hunter looked up. Sensing that she had landed on a way to engage him, she pressed further, "I'm just confused, I thought you liked Kellie just fine." Hunter hesitated, "I do." He took a deep breath. "So here's the deal. Kellie really wants it to look like she has a boyfriend to make her mother happy. She's gay and I'm supposed to keep it a secret. She thinks her mother will kill her if she finds out. She also says that if I tell on her, she'll tell everyone that I'm the one who's gay. And I didn't know any of this until after she asked me."

Cathy felt stunned. She had been friends with Vera Lyttle a long time and could easily understand Kellie's apprehension. Vera could be judgmental. She claimed to be tolerant and accepting, but was rarely willing to entertain others' ideas or opinions. Furthermore, as the mother of two boys in addition to Kellie, Vera had made it clear that she expected that she and Kellie would "grow to have the same close relationship she had with her mother." Cathy worried that discovering that Kellie was gay wouldn't align with Vera's heteronormative aspirations. She felt for Kellie. Things couldn't be easy for her right now. She understood that coming out was an intensely personal decision and that LGBTQ students had a right to privacy, regarding the confidentiality of their sexual orientation.

Yet, Cathy was concerned about Hunter's unwilling involvement in Kellie's drama. She was also disturbed that should she make good on her threat, Hunter's right to privacy was at stake here as well. She worried that Hunter might become a target for bullying at Scatter Key High. Cathy was aware of several incidences where students had been called "gay" or a "fag," and that while the bullying was limited to verbal attacks, the tone in the school was not welcoming. She feared that should Kellie lash out, Hunter would be unable to handle the harassment.

Cathy was also aware that several years ago, Scatter Key had made national news because a teacher had disclosed a student's orientation to his parents without the student's permission. Even though his parents had been supportive, the emotional toll on the student had been great. He claimed that he could not trust Scatter Key teachers to act in his best interest. Much to the relief of the schools, while his family expressed outrage at the situation, they decided not to sue the schools. They did, however, request that Scatter Key start an LGBTQ awareness club modeled after the popular Gay/Straight Alliance network. The afterschool club was founded and moderately promoted. Several meetings were held but attendance was light. After several months, the club disbanded. Cathy believed that the Scatter Key community was not interested in pressing an agenda of inclusivity for LGBTQ students.

Cathy took her own deep breath and asked Hunter, "So, maybe we need to figure out how to support Kellie and also get you out of the middle of this. What do you think?"

Discussing the Case

- What are the equity issues this case raises?
- What are the issues of import to Scatter Creek High School in this case?
- If you were the principal and Cathy Mellen approached you with her fears of potential harassment concerning her son, what would you do?
- How might Scatter Creek make the school culture more welcoming for LGBTQ students?
- What role might a school play in the larger community with regards to clarifying issues like this one?
- How might school leaders take steps to begin this work?

ACTIVITIES

The following activities will further expand your understanding concerning how to promote educational opportunity and culturally responsive practices.

ACTIVITY 6.1

Exploring Your Cultural Identity

Prior to engaging in leadership work focused on promoting educational opportunity and culturally responsive practices, it is worthwhile to step back and consider your own cultural narrative. Take a moment and reflect on the ways that your experiences inform your thinking about schools, schooling, and education. What is your background? What were the influential experiences and events that make you who you are today? What messages about culture and cultural expression do you carry with you? You may decide to do this work as a personal and private essay. If so, reflect on the questions that follow and craft three to five paragraphs that can serve to center your thinking and leadership activity going forward. Alternatively, you may want to consider how sharing your cultural autobiography with others might enhance your leadership work. What forms of communication might work best in your context? How would sharing your story change the way you lead?

Describe your family of origin—What is your primary culture? Your parents? Their parents? How many generations back can you trace your history? If you are unable to go back more than one or two generations, why is that? Are there historical or political events that impact your cultural story? If so, what are they and how do they inform your sense of self? What is your primary language, religion, race, and sexual orientation? How does your language, religion, race, and sexual orientation inform who you are? What messages have you heard about your identity as it relates to your language, religion, race, and sexual orientation? What identity are you most comfortable with and in? What identity are you least comfortable with and in?

Describe your meaningful life experiences—Where did you grow up? Where did you go to school? What are your important moments? What makes you happy? What makes you sad? What values and beliefs inform your life choices? From where did they originate? How are they related to your views of success and failure? In what ways does your definition of these ideas inform your work in schools?

Describe your experiences with others—What are your experiences with people who are different than you? Why are these experiences memorable? What assumptions did you bring to these encounters? How has your own cultural background shaped your sense of people who are not like you? What messages from your larger cultural context has informed your thinking? What have you learned from the media, broader society, or your community?

ACTIVITY 6.2

A School Equity Audit

Complete an equity audit of your school. Collect and consider data in the following categories:

- Demographic and social class of your faculty and certified staff, students, and other non-certified support personnel.
- Categories of students within your school and school system (e.g., gifted, at risk, disability, English Language Learners, bilingual).
- Achievement data (e.g., grade level data as it exists in your setting, graduation rates, drop-out and transfer rates, participation in and test results for ACT, SAT, AP and other exams) as they relate to gender, race, disability, ELL and bilingual students, and those students receiving free and reduced price lunch and other special services.
- Discipline data (e.g., classroom and school-site incidents, in-house and out-of-school suspension, and expulsion) as they relate to gender, race, disability, ELL and bilingual students, and those students receiving free and reduced lunch and other special services.

What does your data tell you? Are there patterns that stand out? How do these items compare across groups? What strengths do you find? What weaknesses do you find? What opportunities for improvement are evident? Who might engage in this work? What are concrete, specific ideas for addressing areas of challenge and need?

ACTIVITY 6.3

Visioning for Equity-Oriented and Culturally Responsive Leadership

Develop a vision for equity-oriented and culturally responsive leadership in your school or district. How would your school look and feel different? What aspects of leadership, curriculum and instruction, and teaching and learning might change? How would the community play a role? How could individually held or shared understandings about equity be changed? What professional learning would need to take place for your equity vision to be realized? Who would need to be included in those sessions? How could you make that happen? How might your equity vision be integrated with other diversity initiatives? What would be the desired outcomes of this work? How would you communicate your equity vision? Who could you enlist to support this work?

RESOURCES

Equity leadership work requires more than a commitment to aspirational goals. It requires attention to the tasks of and collaborative relationships for this work. Thankfully, there are a number of excellent national resources with a focus in this area. These include:

Teaching Tolerance: www.tolerance.org
This national non-profit organization is a project of the Southern Poverty Law Center. They offer free classroom resources, professional development, grant opportunities, and other supports to schools and school leaders engaging in this work. Emphasizing social justice, the materials address four domains of anti-bias education—identity, diversity, justice, and action. Their materials can provide a much-needed start to this work in your school or district.

National Equity Project: http://nationalequityproject.org
Driven by the core belief that educational equity is achievable, the national equity project offers coaching and consulting services designed to support school leaders in transforming their systems. They will partner with your school or district to develop listening campaigns and complete equity analysis work as well as provide webinars, residential, and non-residential institutes centered on developing equity leadership knowledge and skills.

Rethinking Schools: www.rethinkingschools.org
Rethinking Schools began as a local Milwaukee, WI, organization in 1986 with the purpose to address local problems of practice, particularly issues of race. Now a national organization with a print journal, online Web-based magazine, and blog posts, Rethinking Schools offers comprehensive print-based resources to teachers and school leaders working to promote equity and culturally responsive practices.

Readings

Finally, there have been several amazing books published recently that address these topics head on. Among our favorites are:

David, J. (2010). *Growing up black*. New York: HarperCollins.

Emdin, C. (2016). *For white folks who teach in the hood . . . and the rest of y'all too: Reality pedagogy and urban education*. Boston, MA: Beacon Press.

Goldstein, D. (2014). *The teacher wars: A history of America's most embattled profession*. New York: Random House.

Morris, M.W. (2016). *Pushout: The criminalization of black girls in schools*. New York: The New Press.

Packer, Z.Z. (2004). *Drinking coffee elsewhere: Stories*. London: Penguin Books.

REFERENCES

Adamson, F., & Darling-Hammond, L. (2012). Funding disparities and the inequitable distribution of teachers: Evaluating sources and solutions. *Education Policy Analysis Archives*, 20. http://epaa.asu.edu/ojs/article/view/1053

Bertrand, M., & Rodela, K.C. (2018). A framework for rethinking educational leadership in the margins: Implications for social justice leadership preparation. *Journal of Research on Leadership Education*, 13(1), 1–26.

Bornstein, J. (2017) Can PBIS build justice rather than merely restore order? In *The school to prison pipeline: The role of culture and discipline in school*, 4, 135–167. Available at: http://dx.doi.org/10.1108/S2051-231720160000004008

Brooks, J. S., Jean-Marie, G., Normore, A. H., & Hodgins, D. W. (2008). Distributed leadership for social justice: Exploring how influence and equity are stretched over an urban high school. *Journal of School Leadership*, 17(4), 378–408.

Brown, K.M. (2004). Leadership for social justice and equity: Weaving a transformative framework and pedagogy. *Educational Administration Quarterly*, 40(1), 77–108.

Brown, K.M. (2006). Leadership for social justice and equity: Evaluating a transformative framework and andragogy. *Educational Administration Quarterly*, 42(5), 700–745.

Brown, K.W., Ryan, R.M., & Creswell, J.D. (2007). Mindfulness: Theoretical foundations and evidence for its salutary effects. *Psychological Inquiry*, 18(4), 211–237.

Cambron-McCabe, N., & McCarthy, M.M. (2005). Educating school leaders for social justice. *Educational Policy*, 19(1), 201–222.

Capper, C.A., & Young, M.D. (2014). Ironies and limitations of educational leadership for social justice: A call to social justice educators. *Theory Into Practice*, 53(2), 158–164.

Capper, C. A., Theoharis, G., & Sebastian, J. (2006). Toward a framework for preparing leaders for social justice. *Journal of Educational Administration*, 44(3), 209–224.

Dantley, M.E., & Tillman, L.C. (2010). Social justice and moral transformative leadership. In Marshall, C. & Oliva, M. (Ed.), *Leadership for social justice: Making revolutions in education* (pp. 19–34). Boston, MA: Allyn & Bacon.

Darling-Hammond, L. (2004). The color line in American education. *Du Bois Review*, 1(2), 213–246.

Davis, J.R (2017). From discipline to dynamic pedagogy: A re-conceptualization of classroom management. *Berkeley Review of Education*, 6(2), 129–153.

Deal, T.E., & Peterson, K.D. (2016). *Shaping school culture: The heart of leadership* (3rd ed.). San Francisco, CA: Jossey-Bass.

Egalite, A.J., Kisida, B., & Winters, M.A. (2015). Representation in the classroom: The effect of own-race teachers on student achievement. *Economics of Education Review*, 45, 44–52.

Foster, L. (2005). The practice of educational leadership in African American communities of learning: Context, scope, and meaning. *Educational Administration Quarterly*, 41(4), 689–700.

Furman, G. (2012). Social justice leadership as praxis: Developing capacities through preparation programs. *Educational Administration Quarterly*, 48(2), 191–229.

Furman, G. C., & Shields, C. M. (2005). How can educational leaders promote and support social justice and democratic community in schools? In Firestone, W.A. & Riehl, C. (Eds.), *A new agenda for research in educational leadership* (pp. 119–137). New York: Teachers College Press.

Garcia, S.B., & Guerra, P.L. (2004). Deconstructing deficit thinking: Working with educators to create more equitable learning environments. *Education and Urban Society*, 36(2), 150–168.

Garvey, B., Stokes, P., & Meggison, D. (2018). *Coaching and mentoring: Theory and practice.* London: Sage.

Gates, G. (2015). *Mindfulness for educational practice: A path to resilience for challenging work.* Charlotte, NC: Information Age Publishing.

Gershenson, S., Holt, S.B., & Papageorge, N.W. (2016). Who believes in me? The effect of student–teacher demographic match on teacher expectations. *Economics of Education Review, 52,* 209–224.

Gooden, M.A. (2005). The role of an African American principal in an urban information technology high school. *Educational Administration Quarterly, 41*(4), 630–650.

Gray, D.E., Garvey, B., & Lane, D.A. (2016). *A critical introduction to coaching and mentoring: Debates, dialogues, and discourses.* London: Sage.

Gray, J., Kruse, S., & Tarter, C. J. (2016). Enabling school structures, collegial trust, and academic emphasis: Antecedents of professional learning communities. *Educational Management, Administration, & Leadership, 44*(6), 875–891.

Gregory, A., Skiba, R.J., & Noguera, P.A. (2010). The achievement gap and the discipline gap: Two sides of the same coin. *Educational Researcher, 39*(1), 59–68.

Gregory, A., Clawson. K., Davis, A., & Gerewitz, J. (2014). The promise of restorative practices to transform teacher–student relationships and achieve equity in school discipline. *Journal of Educational and Psychological Consultation, 4,* 325–353.

Hamlin, D., & Flessa, J. (2016). Parental involvement initiatives: An analysis. *Educational Policy.* Available at: http://journals.sagepub.com/doi/abs/10.1177/0895904816673739

Hernandez, F., Murakami, E.T., & Quijada Cerecer, P. (2014). A Latina principal leading for social justice: Influences of racial and gender identity. *Journal of School Leadership, 24*(4), 586–598.

Hill, J., Otten, R., & DeRoche, J. (2016). *Trends in public and private school principal demographics and qualifications.* Washington, DC: National Center for Education Statistics.

Jean-Marie, G., Normore, A. H., & Brooks, J. S. (2009). Leadership for social justice: Preparing 21st century school leaders for a new social order. *Journal of Research on Leadership Education, 4*(1), 1–31.

Jeynes, W. (2012). A meta-analysis of the efficacy of different types of parental involvement programs for urban schools. *Urban Education, 47*(4), 706–742.

Johnson, B.L., and Kruse, S.D. (2009). *Decision making for educational leaders: Under-examined dimensions and issues.* Albany, NY: SUNY.

Jones, E.E., & Harris, V.A. (1967). The attribution of attitudes. *Journal of Experimental Psychology, 3*(1), 1–24.

Kena, G., Aud, S., Johnson, F., Wang, X., Zhang, J., Rathbun, A., Wilkinson-Flicker, S., and Kristapovich, P. (2014). *The Condition of Education 2014* (NCES 2014–083). U.S. Department of Education, National Center for Education Statistics. Washington, DC.

Khalifa, M.A., Gooden, M.A., & Davis, J.E. (2016). Culturally responsive school leadership: A synthesis of the literature. *Review of Educational Research, 86*(4), 1272–1311.

Kim, J.N., & Grunig, J.E. (2011). Problem solving and communicative action: A situational theory of problem solving. *Journal of Communication, 61*(1), 120–149.

Kraft, M.A., Marinell, W.H., & Yee, S.S.W. (2016). School organizational contexts, teacher turnover, and student achievement: Evidence from panel data. *American Educational Research Journal, 53*(5), 1411–1449.

Kruse, S.D., & Louis, K.S. (2009). *Building strong school cultures: A guide to leading change.* Thousand Oaks, CA: Corwin Press.

Kruse, S.D., Rodela, K.C., & Huggins, K.S. (2018). Messy messages and making sense across complex contexts: A regional network of superintendents confronting equity. *Journal of School Leadership*, 28(1), 82–109.

Ladson-Billings, G. (2011). "Yes, but how do we do it?" Practicing culturally relevant pedagogy. In Landsman, J.G. & Lewis, C.W. (Eds.) *White teachers/diverse classrooms: Creating inclusive schools, building on Students' Diversity and Providing True Educational Equity* (pp. 33–55). Sterling, VA: Stylus Publishing.

Larson, C.L., & Murtadha, K. (2002). Leadership for social justice. *Yearbook of the National Society for the Study of Education*, 101(1), 134–161.

Marshall, C., & Oliva, M. (2010). *Leadership for social justice: Making revolutions in education* (2nd ed.). Boston, MA: Allyn & Bacon.

Martinez, M.A., Marquez, J., Cantú, Y., & Rocha, P.A. (2016). *Tenura y tenacidad: Testimonios of Latina School Leaders. Association of Mexican American Educators (AMAE) Journal*, 10(3), 11–29.

McFarland, J., Hussar, B., de Brey, C., Snyder, T., Wang, X., Wilkinson-Flicker, S., Gebrekristos, S., Zhang, J., Rathbun, A., Barmer, A., Bullock Mann, F., & Hinz, S. (2017). *The condition of education 2017*. Washington, DC: National Center for Education Statistics.

McIntosh, K., Kelm, J.L., & Delabra, A.C. (2015). In search of how principals change: A qualitative study of events that help and hinder administrator support for school-wide PBIS. *Journal of Positive Behavior Interventions*, 18(2), 100–110.

McKenzie, K.B., & Locke, L.A. (2009). Becoming a leader for equity and excellence: It starts with instruction. In Douglass Horsford, S. (Ed.) *New perspectives in educational leadership: Exploring social, political, and community contexts and meaning* (pp. 47–65). New York: Peter Lang.

McKenzie, K.B., Christman, D.E., Hernandez, F., Fierro, E., Capper, C.A., Dantley, M., & Scheurich, J.J. (2008). From the field: A proposal for educating leaders for social justice. *Educational Administration Quarterly*, 44(1), 111–138.

Milner, H.R. (2011). But good intentions are not enough: Doing what's necessary to teach for diversity. In Landsman, J.G. & Lewis, C.W. (Eds.) *White teachers/diverse classrooms: Creating inclusive schools, building on students' diversity and providing true educational equity* (pp. 56–74). Sterling, VA: Stylus Publishing.

Mullen, C.A. (2009). Re-imagining the human dimension of mentoring: A framework for research administration and the academy. *Journal of Research Administration*, 40(1), 10–31.

Murakami, E.T, Valle, F., & Méndez-Morse, S.E. (2013). Latina/o learners and academic success. *The handbook of research on educational leadership for equity and diversity*, 134–175.

Murakami, E.T., Hernandez, F., Mendez-Morse, S. & Byrne-Jimenez, M. (2016). Latina/o school principals: Identity, leadership and advocacy. *International Journal of Leadership in Education*, (19)3, 280–299.

Pedroza, A., & Mendez-Morse, S. (2016). *Dichos* as cultural influences on one Latina's leadership praxis. *National Forum of Educational Administration and Supervision Journal*, 33(2), 61–72.

Peterson, D., & Vergara, V. (2016). Thriving in school leadership: Latina/o leaders speak out. *National Forum of Educational Administration and Supervision Journal*, 34(4), 2–15.

Pryce, S., & Fredrickson, N. (2013). Bullying behavior, intentions, and classroom ecology. *Learning Environments Research*, 16(2), 183–199.

Santamaria, L.J. (2014). Critical change for the greater good: Multicultural perceptions in educational leadership toward social justice. *Educational Administration Quarterly*, 50(3), 347–391.

Singleton, G. (2015). *Courageous conversations about race: A field guide for achieving equity in schools.* Thousand Oaks, CA: Corwin Press.

Skiba, R., Mediratta, M., & Rausch, M.K. (2016). Inequality in school discipline: Research and practice to reduce disparities. New York: Palgrave Macmillan.

Spillane, J. (2005). Distributed leadership. *The Education Forum, 69*(2), 143–150.

Stoll, L., & Louis, K.S. (2007). *Professional learning communities: Divergence, detail and difficulties.* London: Swets & Zeitlinger.

Theoharis, G. (2007). Social justice educational leaders and resistance: Toward a theory of social justice leadership. *Educational Administration Quarterly, 43*(2), 221–258.

Theoharis, G. (2009). *The school leaders our children deserve: Seven keys to equity, social justice, and school reform.* New York: Teachers College Press.

Tian, M., Rosku, M., & Collin, K. (2015). A meta-analysis of distributed leadership 2002–2013: Theory development, empirical evidence and future research focus. *Educational Management Administration & Leadership, 44*(1), 146–164.

Utheim, R. (2014). Restorative justice, reintegration, and race: Reclaiming collective identity in the post-racial era. *Anthropology and Education, 45*(4), 355–372.

Valencia, R. (1997). *The evolution of deficit thinking: Educational thought and practice.* New York: Routledge Farmer.

Willie, C.V., Edwards, R., & Alves, M.J. (2002). *Student diversity, choice and school improvement.* Westport, CA: Greenwood Publishing Group.

Wing, L. (2009). Mediation and inequality reconsidered: Bringing the discussion to the table. *Conflict Resolution Quarterly, 26*(4), 383–404.

CHAPTER **7**

Improvement, Innovation, and Reform

PSEL STANDARD 10—SCHOOL IMPROVEMENT
Effective leaders act as agents of continuous improvement to promote each student's academic success and well-being.

The idea that schools should improve is not new. Beginning in 1954, the Supreme Court decision *Brown* v. *Board of Education* drew our attention to issues of equity in schooling. The launch of Sputnik, in 1957, is credited with our on-going attention to curriculum, particularly that of mathematics and science education. A more fundamental policy shift occurred in 1965 when the Elementary and Secondary Education Act (ESEA) was first passed by Congress providing more generalized federal support for schools. Notably, ESEA provided the first federal funding for special needs students (Title I) as well as funding for school library recourses (Title II), educational service centers (Title III), research and professional learning (Title IV), and grants to strengthen state departments of education (Title V).

Perhaps most salient to our discussion concerning school improvement was the 1983 report, *A Nation at Risk*, comparing the achievement of students across the United States with that of other nations and concluding that the US was sorely lacking. In many ways, *A Nation at Risk* set the stage for *No Child Left Behind* in 2001 and the *Every Student Succeeds Act* in 2015. In each, student achievement and school accountability for student growth and progress were highlighted, with the results including increased transparency and standardization of educational practice (Kingdon, 2003).

Clearly, there are other forces that have contributed to the school improvement agenda beyond those credited above. The nation's emphasis on Civil Rights in the

1960s changed the ways in which resources to schools were allocated and in turn, increased accountability for the use of those resources. Additionally, teachers' unions rose to prominence in the 1960s, and teachers became viewed less as civil servants and more as organized employees. School choice, shifts in teacher and administrator preparation, and teacher and administrator evaluation have also impacted policy and practice within education. In totality, these changes suggest that schools have moved far beyond Tyack's (1974) description of the nation's schools as "one best system." Instead, vocal, persistent, and determined attention has been on how to "fix" schools. It is within this contested terrain that school improvement efforts are positioned (Mitchell, 2011).

At its core, school improvement seeks to address three core issues (Mintrop, 2016). First, the focus is on *organizational effectiveness*. A focus on organizational effectiveness suggests that a school leader should focus attention on the coherent coordination of community, district, and school resources in ways that benefit students. Resources may include the tangible physical, financial, human, and cultural assets present within the community as well as less tangible strengths such as a school's reputation, a staff's motivation, or a principal's influence. However, it is not enough for a school leader to align the work of organizational members and then leave outcomes to chance. Effective school improvement requires follow-through and iterative determination for results to be considered lasting and reliable.

Second, school improvement requires a focus on the *facilitation of complex learning* for students and faculty alike. A focus on the facilitation of complex learning suggests that improvement efforts center around the development of core instructional competencies and builds capacity among faculty and staff to address the learning needs of students. Unlike efforts that stress fidelity to set routines and procedures, focusing on complex learning suggests that faculty, staff, and students are regarded as intellectually competent and capable. In this way, autonomy for instructional decisions is encouraged and commitments to diverse learning opportunities are fostered.

Third, effective school improvement focuses school leaders on issues of *equity*. Here too, regard for students irrespective of race, class, ethnicity, sexual orientation, immigration status, or special needs designation is required for improvement efforts to be effective. Equity leadership focuses on transforming educational policies and practices toward improved outcomes for all students. Equity leadership requires that policy, practice, and programs be aligned so that all students are provided access to high-quality learning opportunities and environments. It takes on the challenge of school improvement in multifaceted and complex ways.

In this chapter, we tackle the issues of organizational effectiveness, complex learning and equity by unpacking what they mean for school and school leaders. We argue that school improvement lies at the heart of school leadership. Our logic is simple. As long as students are not being served as well as they might, improvement is required. As we will see in the case presented below, when school leaders lose sight of improvement goals they risk losing traction toward what matters most—student learning and well-being.

KEY LEARNINGS

In this chapter, you will learn to:

- employ methods of continuous improvement to achieve school organization vision, mission, and goals, promote the core values of the school, and engage others in these processes;
- promote leadership among teachers, staff, and parents to support continuous improvement and innovation; and
- monitor continuous improvement efforts for coherence and effectiveness.

FEATURED CASE

Making and Unmaking: An Innovation Failure Analysis

The Woodlake City School District (WCSD) and high school (WHS) are typical of many districts and schools in the Midwest. A suburb of a once thriving industrial city, Woodlake, like the region, now struggles. Home to seven elementary schools, two middle schools, and one high school, WCSD's student population is relatively stable with mobility adversely affecting the black non-Hispanic and Hispanic populations more than their white non-Hispanic peers. Some 50 percent of students qualify for free and reduced price lunch. The district has worked diligently to provide educational opportunities for the 5,200 students who attend WCSD, earning an "A" in overall progress and a "B" for students with disabilities on state report cards. Yet, the district has been less effective in closing the achievement gap and meeting its annual measurable performance objectives (AYP). In each of these areas the district has scored an "F" in recent years.

Woodlake High School is home to 1,600 students and is typical of high schools across the nation. The school operates on a nine-period day with 40-minute classes, requiring four years each of English/language arts and mathematics, including algebra II, and three years each of science and social studies. A walk down any hall suggests that instructionally the lecture dominates and students report that homework is nearly universally assigned and graded.

Invention and Innovation

Yet, within this otherwise classic setting, there was a sense that school could and should be different. An interdisciplinary group of teachers including teachers of mathematics, English, science, social studies, and special education, successfully proposed a program for freshman and sophomores. Funded by a state technology grant, the program blocked out four of the nine periods of the school day, offering 100 students a learning opportunity that integrated content learning and technology through the study of thematic units. The district and building leadership enthusiastically supported this small school within a school approach.

Labeled High School 2.0 (HS2.0), pedagogy in the new program was strongly influenced by the growing national maker movement. HS2.0 embraced a makerspace philosophy of learning (Crawford, 2009, 2015). Rooted in constructivist thought and emphasizing learning through doing, educational makerspace philosophy imagines a classroom where deep learning is fostered, student ownership in learning is enhanced, and curiosity is promoted.

Focusing on real world, project-based learning, students explored biology, social stigma and shame, and the possibility of activism through the study of AIDS. They designed and built chairs using wikiseat (www.wikiseat.org) catalyst material, while reading Emerson's *The American Scholar* and *Self-Reliance,* blogged about their experience, and presented the finished products at a local art gallery. They studied American history by addressing big ideas and essential questions concerning society and historical thought. Technology replaced most textbooks. Assessment was authentic and emphasized a formative model with ample opportunities for all students to review, revise, rewrite, and retest to demonstrate they had mastered the standards that each unit addressed. The assessment approach helped provide access to complex and challenging learning to all students, including those with disabilities. Creativity in presentation, voice, and thought was encouraged. Reflection on learning was required. An external grant evaluation, showed that HS2.0 students had statistically significantly out-scored their peers in state testing. Things could not have been more positive.

External Accolades and Internal Assault

Based on their early success, the team was interested in scaling up the program and exploring what the development of a school founded on makerspace philosophy might look like. With the encouragement of building and district administration, the team sought a national planning grant to expand HS2.0 into a school of choice for WCSD students. The successful $100,000 application was to provide the teachers with money for travel to national conferences, release time for program development, additional technology and classroom resources, and to establish a Woodlake maker conference where national thinkers could gather to discuss the intersection of education and the maker movement.

Even with the planning grant secured, a district-wide budget reduction closed the popular program. The math and special education teacher returned to a team-taught intervention-focused classroom. The English and science teachers moved into instructional support positions designed promote the use of technology to enhance instruction throughout the district. The principal was promoted to a district office position. While there was some sadness that HS2.0 had closed, a sense of support and empowerment for change invigorated the team.

Almost as soon as the new work began, tensions started to arise between the teachers and administration. An assistant superintendent assigned to oversee the work immediately began to question the motives, vision, and intent that underscored the project. The team was informed that all grant-related planning would need to occur outside of the contracted school day, making it nearly impossible for the teachers to pursue collaborative work during business hours. Furthermore, it had the unintended consequence of making all the work unsupervised, a point that would become significant in later communications.

Simultaneously, a blog and Twitter feed started by the team began to draw national attention. Spearheaded by the English teacher who had been instrumental in the development of HS2.0, the public blog and Twitter feed critiqued schools and schooling as antiquated structures that were ineffective at meeting the learning needs of students today. In blog posts, they built their case:

> I became a teacher because I hated school. It wasn't that my experience was particularly bad it was just boring. I decided to re-enter the classroom and see if maybe I could go back and design the kind of learning space that I sorely wish I would have had coming up. It's been ten years, and I'm now more convinced than ever, we need to stop aiming at the test answers stored temporarily in our students' brains, and instead we should ignite the spark of curiosity and engagement that is innate in their souls.

And, on the purposes of education,

> Education should be relevant and engaging. It's something done for, not to, a person. Relevant doesn't always mean contemporary, and engaging doesn't always mean fun, but the things people do in the pursuit of learning should be compelling and meaningful to them in a real sense … In this golden age of information and communication it is required of our education system that we consider altering from a form that no longer suits its function.

Typical tweets included items stating, "Learn how to learn. Learn to love learning, no lesser motivations," "Learning should happen all the time, no more division between school and life," "Teachers: if you're not curious, find something else to do, no more coasting on when you used to learn," and "Learning isn't a behavior, it's an event. Let's not measure behavior. Let's describe and discuss the event of learning."

Many of the tweets went viral among the education innovation community. The team enjoyed attention from leaders in the maker movement and when the Woodlake maker conference was held, over a dozen national leaders eagerly attended the weekend retreat. The agenda was simple and ambitious. It contained a single item—design a makerspace school founded on the idea that the way forward in education is via networks and not bureaucracy. The two-day retreat was marked by vigorous debate and discussion cumulating in what would evolve to become the signature curriculum model for the school. It was described in the launch grant application as curriculum that begins,

> With a view of learning as a process to be provoked through engagement in experiential practice and performance, assessed descriptively, and in conversation

with the learner. Beginning with a "Catalyst" phase, students will learn how to coordinate and schedule their time, compose thoughts, ideas and arguments in writing and dialogue, transition between direct instruction and self-directed learning, identify where to ask for help and how to seek the support of others to enhance learning, use the tools, resources and technology of the school, become engaged in the makerspace community, self-assess learning and progress toward learning goals, critique arguments, product and process work, accept critique and feedback, and incorporate others' ideas into their understandings of content and product. They will learn to curate their work, present results, findings, projects and performances, and relate their learning to standards and outcomes. Following the Catalyst phase is the Project Phase where students pursue individually designed learning events that are formed, executed, critiqued, and presented to the makerspace community guided by the Common Core Standards and authentic problems relevant to Woodlake and the region . . .

Those in attendance left feeling like they had been part of something important. Publicly, it appeared as if the team had all the support it could hope for as they moved forward in developing the launch grant application. However, privately tensions mounted.

For the launch grant to be successful, the district needed to fully commit to sponsoring the school, allocating budget, space, and staffing. On each point, district leadership equivocated. The assistant superintendent would task the team to move the project forward and then withhold the very information needed for work to proceed. The team, individually and as a group, were summoned to meetings where their commitment to teaching and professionalism was criticized. They were accused of hiding their work and meeting in secret. Interestingly and simultaneously to growing internal tensions, administration publicly supported the development of a local makerspace cohort, and on more than one occasion used the work of the teachers in media releases. Understandably, the team's confusion grew.

As the launch grant submission deadline neared, district leadership posed a 76-question document for the team. Many of the questions revisited issues thought to have been resolved (e.g., utilization of the common core standards); others suggested that documents had not been read (e.g., grant budget line items), and still others were simply inappropriate at this phase of planning (e.g., field trip permission policies). Response was obligatory. Finally, district administration required that the proposal be presented to the school board in a formal public meeting. The board found the plan "invigorating" and praised the teachers for "forward-thinking work." While the teachers were pleased with the board's response, administration was not.

Yet, with a tepid letter of support, the district agreed to the submission of the completed launch grant. Letters of support from local business leaders and the thought-leaders who had attended the retreat accompanied the document. The team hoped that the strength of the plan and the strong support of national thought-leaders would overshadow the district's reticence. The funding agency evaluation team regretfully declined to fund the work going forward, citing the district's obvious lack of support as the only reason they could not extend financing.

Hard Feelings and Lost Opportunities

Rejection of the proposal hit the team hard. They felt "betrayed and puzzled" by what had occurred. In the words of one member, "I thought when we produced good work they'd come around. It was all so shortsighted." The English teacher took a year-long leave of absence to reflect on his commitment to teaching. The others returned to their classrooms vowing to "continue to do right by kids" but unable to "trust this district."

SCHOOL IMPROVEMENT ASSUMPTIONS

In keeping with the broad themes of organizational effectiveness, complex learning, and equity that underscore the purpose of and for school improvement, we now turn our discussion to thinking about how school leaders can work to achieve valued organizational outcomes. We highlight aspects of the Woodlake case to underscore the importance of focusing leadership work in coherent and aligned ways that, in turn, foster success.

An Action and Developmental Orientation Is Essential

It is generally assumed that school improvement approaches are *action and developmentally oriented*. As Anderson and Shattuck (2012) suggest, there is no single formula that assures successful school improvement. Instead, school improvement work should be considered an evolutionary process in which planning and implementation occur simultaneously and are supported by focused leadership effort. Developmental in nature, school improvement work suggests a cycle of action, informed by hard and soft data, and focused on shared values and outcomes. Smylie (2010) simplifies the continuous improvement cycle, suggesting that the basic features include:

1. Clarification of school vision and values.
2. Assessment, supported by compelling evidence, concerning progress toward attaining the school's vision and values.
3. Development of goals and objectives designed to address the gaps between where the school is and where it would like to be.
4. Articulation of strategies to achieve goals and objectives supported by plans for implementation and the identification of supportive resources.
5. Implementation of strategies.
6. Assessment of implementation processes and outcomes.
7. Feedback from implementation assessment into the development of new goals and objectives.

As we observed in the Woodlake case, this cycle of developmental action can take on many forms. Beginning with the pilot of HS2.0, the teachers worked to test how curriculum and instruction might be delivered to and received by students. Goals and objectives for the project were identified. Curriculum and assessments were developed.

Partnering with an evaluator, they studied aspects of their work, looking for both quantitative and qualitative evidence of success. Discovering that test scores rose and students were engaged in their learning fostered teachers' confidence in their choices and provided assurance to school leaders and parents that the program was educationally sound. Finally, new goals were developed to expand the program beyond the pilot stage.

The School Must Be the Unit of Change

The second assumption is that in school improvement the *school is the unit of change* (Fullan, 2007; Smylie, 2010). Irrespective of the forces that motivate improvement efforts, ultimately schools must implement instructional and curricular change if results are to occur. Yet, as the Woodlake case illustrates, the scope of an improvement's impact matters. Often, small-scale and limited change efforts lack a robust footprint, potentially fostering the very inequities they were created to mitigate. When programs designed to support broad school improvement fail to scale up, equity goals are compromised and organizational effectiveness can be eroded. Sadly, improvement failure is a common educational outcome across the nation (Bryk, Gomez, Grunow, & LeMahieu, 2015). Often, schools move from one initiative to another, seeking a silver bullet that will solve the problems a school faces, yet never gaining traction or results.

If we are to break the all too common cycle of failed school reform, broad and deep interpretations of how the school currently functions must be taken into account prior to and as part of the innovation effort. Work should be directed toward remedying a specific, clearly acknowledged, and accepted schoolwide problem. Likewise, when remedies are identified, school leaders and teachers alike need to probe adoption practices, inquiring as to the circumstances *under which* the innovation has proved effective and *for whom* the innovation is most effective. In this way, innovations can be adopted and implemented in ways that align with vision and mission, and a system can be developed to monitor intended and unexpected outcomes. Change ideas can then be refined based on shared evidence and deeper thinking about meaningful improvement can be promoted among the full faculty and staff.

Attention to School Culture Is Necessary

As Leithwood and Louis (2012) assert, it is almost impossible to make significant changes in education without changing the culture of the school organization. The third assumption of school improvement suggests that an emphasis on *school culture* must be an integral part of the change effort (Deal & Peterson, 2016). As we observed in the Woodlake case, ultimately entrenched and intractable cultural practices within the school and district undermined the implementation of the makerspace school. Moreover, the program was designed as a critique of and a response to the existing traditional and well-established school culture. Absent a far-reaching conversation about the ways in which the project challenged the existing culture and how responses to those challenges would be handled prior to implementation, the potential for long-term success was all but guaranteed to fail.

Multi-Level Perspectives Are Needed

The fourth school improvement assumption suggests that *multi-level perspectives* are required for success (Kruse & Louis, 2009; Murphy, 2016). This is to suggest that improving schools requires making changes at various levels of the organization, including attention to the school level (e.g., vision, curriculum), the classroom level (e.g., instruction and assessment), and the individual level (e.g., reflection on practice). The call for a multi-level perspective is, in many ways, paradoxical. It requires that leaders of change efforts balance supporting those aspects of the school that are thriving with those areas where improvement and innovation is required. Leaders must do both and do both well.

Balancing support for that which is currently working with those aspects of the school program that involve change, requires leaders to make explicit the core values that underscore practice. When values are clearly understood and explicitly shared throughout the school community, they can serve in foundational ways to support strong practice. Thus, when evidence supports that practices are working to support student learning and well-being, it makes sense to all that maintaining them is good for students. Where evidence is less clear, the identification of shared values can aid in the establishment of mission, vision, and goals that can better move the school toward improvement.

As we noted in Chapter 2, for most schools and districts the focus of vision and mission should center on student learning, progress, achievement, and student well-being. Certainly, other goals can be indicated or implied. However, a focus on school improvement suggests that student learning must be the primary feature of the vision and mission, and secondary intentions are employed in service to the vision. In this way, school, classroom, and individual level reforms can be aligned and coherent, supporting coordinated efforts to achieve shared goals.

Both Bottom-Up and Top-Down Approaches Matter

Tightly linked to the assumption that a multi-level perspective is needed, is the assumption that school improvement strategies should include *bottom-up and top-down approaches*. It is thought that centralization (i.e., administratively coordinated effort) of overall strategy, policy, and operational planning allows for alignment and consistency across efforts. However, classroom, grade-level, or departmental decision-making includes teachers and parents in improvement efforts. Decentralizing how strategies might be employed broadens the scope of input, involvement, and impact resulting in greater acceptance of innovation (Murphy, 2016). Consequently, a reciprocal relationship between centralization and decentralization is crucial for striking a balance between pressure and support for change.

Research into school improvement, especially that of failed efforts (Anderson & Shattuck, 2012; Leithwood & Louis, 2012; Mintrop, 2016), has long suggested that when schools adopt too many or too few projects or projects that lack a complementary focus, success can be undermined. The adoption of too many projects dilutes the energy of faculty and staff to implement innovation with fidelity and care. The adoption of too few projects results in failure because not enough effort and energy are focused on needed change. When programs are unaligned or incoherent, efforts realized in one area may be undercut in others or initial gains lost when later efforts fail to capitalize on early success. As such, balancing those initiatives that come from the top with those that emerge within classrooms, grade level teams, and departments is paramount for long-term growth and progress.

Woodlake serves as an interesting case for examining how a balance of bottom-up and top-down approaches matters. Clearly, the teachers involved in the project were motivated to do good work. They believed in the project, based decisions on sound educational theory, consulted with experts in the field, and employed a rigorous evaluation model to examine results. Within the team, their work was well paced, aligned, and coherent. Yet, a failure to develop affiliation with district goals, practice, and policy ultimately destabilized the work to the point that the teachers felt betrayed and deceived.

Moreover, leadership for school improvement must attend to more than the implementation of a cycle of improvement. School improvement work is hard work. Change itself is hard. Yet, when school leaders are explicit about core improvement issues—organizational effectiveness, complex learning, and equity—and intentionally focus action toward addressing them, success is more likely. When principals, teacher leaders, and influential parents acknowledge that school improvement must adopt an action and developmental orientation, focus on the school as the unit of change, acknowledge and address school culture, employ multi-level perspectives and balance top-down with bottom-up efforts, success is enhanced. Yet, at the core school improvement is about the work of classroom teachers.

HIGH-IMPACT PRACTICES

The literature suggests that leadership attention should be paid to six areas of the school. These include instruction, curriculum, professional learning, school climate and culture, parental involvement, and performance and goal accountability. We acknowledge that these are mutually reinforcing yet, for purposes of clarity, examine each separately.

Effective Classroom Instruction

Darling-Hammond (2000, 2004) has long suggested that the kinds of changes required in school achievement are not a mystery. Instead, she argues that school improvement efforts should place high-quality instruction at the center of improvement design. At a minimum, it is expected that high-quality instruction be standards-based, employ strategies that have been empirically proven to enhance student learning, be differentiated and culturally responsive, and take place in a classroom that facilitates learning. Contributing factors include the effective use of time, formative and summative feedback about learning, well-planned and intentional use of grouping, and parent and caregiver involvement in relationships beneficial to the student.

The role of leadership as Mitchell and Sackney (2015) suggest is to develop the conditions under which instructional practice can be motivated toward the goal of effective student learning. Mitchell and Sackney (2015) suggest that school leaders bear primary responsibility for four categories of activity—regulating, coordinating, expanding, and protecting practice. When leaders regulate practice they hold teachers accountable, through well-crafted evaluation practices, for providing rich classroom experiences. As leaders coordinate practice, they ensure that individual effort is aligned with organizational goals and work across the school. When practice is expanded, the inclusion of new practices is encouraged, keeping classroom activities fresh, interesting, and responsive. Finally, as leaders work to protect practice—buffering teachers from distractions and interruptions—they send the message that commitment to the work of instruction matters and that high-quality instruction is valued within the school.

Challenging, Rigorous Curriculum

As we noted at the start of this chapter, a commitment to complex learning suggests that students are regarded as intellectually competent and capable (Mintrop, 2016). A rigorous curriculum ensures student learning by guaranteeing that subject matter is taught in academically, intellectually, and personally challenging ways, and a balance of procedural and conceptual knowledge is present (Newmann, Carmichael Tanka, & King, 2015). When students are challenged by rigorous curriculum, they are provided learning experiences that motivate them to learn more and learn it more deeply. It is not that schoolwork is simply hard. Challenge is different than difficulty. Challenge implies that curriculum and student learning is scaffolded in ways that require students to apply what they know and evaluate their thinking along the way. When students master challenging work, they experience a sense of accomplishment. Work that is simply hard may result in frustration, disengagement, and discouragement.

Collective Professional Learning Opportunities for Teachers

Schools motivated by an improvement agenda exhibit a culture of collaborative learning among their teachers. Additionally, they are led and structured in ways that facilitate and institutionalize this group-learning dynamic toward the realization of desired educational outcomes (Johnson & Kruse, 2009). As the work of school improvement becomes organized in ways that develop a supportive and engaging work environment, teachers are better able to concentrate on improving pedagogy alongside other features of the school. Whereas all high-quality professional learning is characterized by a focus on student learning and collaborative professional inquiry and reflection, professional learning that lacks a collective focus is less likely to impact school change in lasting ways (Kruse & Louis, 2009; Kruse & Johnson, 2017). Moreover, when effective collective learning is focused on reinventing practice and shared professional growth, school-wide improvement is increasingly possible because attentions are focused on learning designed to impact the many rather than the few (Murphy, 2015).

Supportive Learning Climate and Culture

Learning-focused leaders are aware that school climate and culture can support or detract from the learning environment. Climate, our perceptions about how we feel in the school, and culture, our commonly held expectations for being and acting within the school, both influence the way in which those who work and learn within the school experience it. A sense of connectedness or belonging to the school has the potential to enhance student learning outcomes. Likewise, when faculty and staff feel committed to the school, they are more likely to engage in work that feels risky or hard (Deal & Peterson, 2016). Neither children nor adults want to come and spend time in a place that does not feel welcoming. Climate is about feeling. Yet, feeling good about the school is a necessary but not sufficient condition for improvement. Culture change requires that our beliefs about what we do and how we do it change. Culture change is harder but ultimately necessary if school improvement goals are to be realized.

Sustained and Meaningful Parental Involvement

As we stress in Chapter 4, research into parental involvement is evolving quickly. As a cornerstone of school improvement, collaboration efforts with parents have greater potential to impact student achievement and well-being than those that work to merely inform parents of school expectation and outcomes (Ishimaru, 2017). Inasmuch as school improvement focuses on change regarding what leaders do and innovation involving how they do it, the reconsideration of how parents and caregivers are included in the school bears consideration. As school leaders and teachers employ reciprocal, collective, and relational strategies with increasing efficacy, collective capacity is enhanced, resulting in better learning and well-being outcomes for students (Hong, 2011).

Shared Performance and Goal Accountability

Strong individual performance is not enough for school improvement efforts to have lasting traction. For school improvement efforts to robustly impact student learning, they must be embraced and employed schoolwide. Furthermore, clear measures are needed to evaluate performance and to hold teachers and others accountable for attainment. Across the globe, reliable measures of and for performance remain contested (Anderson, Heinesen, & Pedersen, 2016). Yet, even within this contested terrain, there is general agreement that some form of teacher evaluation is necessary, as is some requirement for assessing student performance. As Gabriel and Woulfin (2017) note, effective teacher evaluation need not be an unproductive, standardized practice. Done well, it promotes teacher growth and schoolwide student achievement. Yet, as Hallinger, Heck, and Murphy (2014) suggest, policy language supporting teacher evaluation is, at this juncture, stronger than the empirical evidence for its efficacy. Similarly, the worth of student testing is equally disputed (Koretz, 2009). Nonetheless, absent a focus on a collective responsibly for school performance, it is unlikely that growth and improvement will be sustained (Leithwood & Louis, 2012; Murphy, 2015, 2016).

In conclusion, researchers, practitioners, and the public alike have called for school improvement to be a primary leadership task. Yet, as we have noted, change is difficult and visioning large-scale comprehensive change can be overwhelming. When conceived of as a continuous improvement effort, where small wins build to produce considerable and impressive results, school improvement may well seem less daunting. The challenge for school leaders is to balance improvement work in ways that do not lose sight of the core purposes for doing the work, while simultaneously advancing the work and honoring the individuals engaged in these efforts. We acknowledge doing so is hard. Yet, the costs of not doing this work are far more consequential.

CASES FOR ANALYSIS

CASE 7.1

Is Change Improvement?

Teachers at Sunny Crest Elementary prided themselves on being "ahead of the instructional curve." Opportunities to attend professional development were abundant, as were resources to develop new curriculum, units, and lessons. The schedule was designed to provide time for daily PLC team meetings. A hive of activity, Sunny Crest strived to create a personalized learning environment for the 450 students in attendance.

Most recently, the staff decided that focusing their attentions on mathematics instruction could provide an opportunity to better coordinate and align their efforts and energies. A full staff professional development, led by a regional math coordinator, was held in early October and teachers prepared to revise their approach to teaching the math curriculum. Driven by the CCSS standards, they focused on promoting mathematical discourse and worked to plan curriculum that would be rigorous and relevant for students.

The staff brainstormed ideas for including discussion that focused on academic language in each lesson and created posters with questions designed to prompt mathematical dialogue. Almost as soon as the effort began, math classes were transformed across the school. Discussion flourished and small groups of students could be observed appearing to discuss strategy, compare answers, and defend solutions. The principal praised teachers and students alike for their commitment to "leading edge learning."

A "marvelous mathematicians" club was formed and students eagerly participated in the after-school math lab and problem-solving activities. In a building survey of student engagement, over 65 percent of students responded that they strongly agreed to the item "I am good at math." An additional 58 percent responded that they strongly agreed to the item "I like math."

Yet, during parent–teacher conferences several parents questioned the depth of their children's mathematical knowledge and reasoning. Parents pressed teachers asking how they knew that the changes were resulting in improved learning. Several noted that their child seemed to think all answers were reasonable and made sense simply because they drew a supporting picture or said they were right. Several others suggested that their children seemed unable to handle basic computation and they felt unable to help with homework. Still others brought in work that demonstrated errors in computation and reasoning yet, had still been scored well.

The principal stood firmly behind the curricular changes and defended the new practices. She publically stated that she knew "Change was hard but necessary." She added, "Our choices were based on what we know is best practice." The parents questioned her logic. They confronted her, asking, "Is change improvement?" She stumbled before responding, "Of course."

Discussing the Case

- What were the core issues of school improvement that Sunny Crest sought to address?
- What assumptions were employed at the school?
- What high-impact practices were evident at Sunny Crest?
- Why might the principal at this school be so invested in being "ahead of the instructional curve?" What might "leading-edge learning" mean in the context of school improvement work?
- Does school improvement require more than changed practice?
- How might Sunny Crest refocus its efforts toward meaningful improvement efforts?
- Is change improvement?
- How would you know when change does result in improvement? What kind of evidence is required?

CASE 7.2

Fast and Furious

Midvalle Middle School could be called a typical urban middle school. Over 75 percent of Midvalle's 1,250 students qualify for free and reduced price lunch. Nearly 30 percent of students are chronically absent and an even greater number are habitually late each morning. Test scores lag behind national averages and significant disparities surface when data are disaggregated for gender, race, and English language proficiency. Yet, Midvalle also differs from many urban middle schools. The school's population is mostly stable. Turnover is low and once a student enrolls in Midvalle, they are likely to remain. The surrounding community, although poor, is showing signs of rebirth and the employment rate is rising.

A close-knit, collaborative staff, Midvalle teachers are committed to their students. Willing to implement new programs and practices, the staff works hard to offer the most effective classroom instruction they can. As Delanie Grant claims, "We do the best we know how, the very best." Tamera Shay echoes her words, adding, "We work hard, we meet, we talk, we try to meet our kids where they need us. Ain't no slackers here."

A New Principal

Principal Morris Stein had been a well-regarded principal in a neighboring district for over ten years. Looking for a change, he applied for the Midvalle position with the hope that he could "make a meaningful contribution" to the school and the lives of the students who attended. As soon as he secured the position, he began frequenting local business, introducing himself and striking up short conversations with anyone willing to chat. He instituted an open-door policy and spent considerable time walking the halls of Midvalle, talking with students and teachers alike. He became known for ending conversations with the question, "If you could change one thing about Midvalle what would it be?"

Therefore, it surprised no one when Stein announced his intent to craft a new school improvement plan for Midvalle. He scheduled several voluntary meetings, but encouraged faculty meetings and, in keeping with his commitment to transparency and openness, he distributed an extensive list of "areas of opportunity." Virtually every subject area was represented, as were student study habits, note taking and writing skill, parental and community involvement, after-school programs, and school attendance, tardy, discipline, and homework policies. The message was clear, Stein expected Midvalle to change.

Yet, the comprehensiveness of the list confused many of the faculty. Teachers agreed that attendance and lateness were an issue. However, the list also contained items for which data was less evident. As one teacher noted, "It seemed a little haphazard. Like if someone said it, it got added. Kinda like it's my impression. So, it must be true." Another added, "But probably there is some truth in all of it. I know I do reading well, but my math isn't so hot." Consensus suggested that broad change was probably needed and as a parent stated, "We should get started because we have everyone's attention."

Doing the Work

Stein took advantage of the momentum that the list had produced. He formed faculty "theme teams" and asked that each team set forth an improvement goal and make recommendations for potential responses related to their assigned theme. Some themes were straightforward—for example, teachers were asked to examine the attendance and tardy polices. Others, such as the theme team for student engagement, were less clear.

Shortly after the work began, Stein set forth what he called a "grand challenge." He publically stated that within one year the school would be "radically transformed" and that Midvalle would be a "model" for urban schooling. To his credit, he called upon the community to support these efforts and was able to obtain a modest amount of funding to support the purchase of new curricular materials and some professional development. However, the big push was to work fast and decisively. In Stein's words, "Better to attempt something grand and fail, than not to attempt anything at all." When pressed, he would share that "We can fix any problems later."

Clearly, there was an air of excitement and industry at Midvalle. Teachers and parents were involved and engaged, meetings were held, progress toward planning was documented, and a shared sense of purpose appeared to emerge. Yet, as one teacher shared, "We're not quite certain, I mean, we're all running. I'm just not sure we're all running in the same direction."

Discussing the Case

- What were the core issues of school improvement that Stein sought to address?
- What assumptions were employed in his thinking?
- What high-impact practices were evident at Midvalle?
- What was Stein trying to improve?
- What assets are already present within the Midvalle community?
- What barriers to improvement might exist?
- What must faculty and staff learn for improvement efforts to be effective?
- Where are creativity and innovation required?
- How would Stein know what was attempted was working?

CASE 7.3

Let's Try This Again

Technology High School (THS) began as a small-scale magnet school in the Echo School District (ESD). Starting with just 150 freshman students, nine teachers, and two principals, the school was designed to add a class of students each year. After four years THS was expected to enroll just over 600 students and employ a staff of over three dozen. As the name implied, THS focused instructional and curricular attention toward the use of technology as a teaching tool.

In its first and second years, THS teachers worked diligently to incorporate project-based learning (PBL) into the curriculum. Utilizing technology as the primary delivery feature of the curriculum as well as a primary learning tool for students, THS sought to "prepare students for a world that is far different from when we were in school." Promoting the school as a place where "effective, meaningful, and enjoyable" learning occurs, the Echo School District (ESD) endorsed PBL as an approach that would allow "students to gain knowledge and skills by working for an extended period of time to investigate and respond to an engaging and complex question, problem, or challenge."

Acknowledging that projects have long been part of schoolwork, promotional materials suggested that historically projects had served as the "dessert" course following a long meal of more traditional coverage of content. ESD claimed that at Technology High projects would be used differently, making them the "main course" of student learning. Assessment focused on formative feedback with attention to guiding students to "complex understandings" and "deep awareness of the role of knowledge and reflection" in learning. Grades, when assigned, were summative and purposefully holistic, reflecting mastery of, rather than progress toward, a standard of learning.

Early on, teachers found the pace of PBL to be challenging. The pressure of designing projects to engage student interest and pairing interest with standards and content knowledge stretched teachers' creativity and resourcefulness. Teachers worried that even as they strived to create units that employed PBL in comprehensive ways, kids weren't really "eating their intellectual vegetables" and that it was far too easy to "load up on carbs" rather than really get a "balanced meal."

As the eleventh and twelfth grades were added, teachers began to worry that projects weren't scaling up in challenge or difficultly, and that student learning was becoming stagnant. Furthermore, as they matriculated, many of the initial freshmen were opting out of attending THS, choosing instead to enroll in a state-sponsored program that allowed them to take classes at community colleges that counted earned credit toward both high school graduation and an Associate of Arts degree. Some returned to more traditional high schools within the district. The decrease in upper level students further exacerbated THS problems. Class size in upper level courses shrank and collaborative learning, a hallmark of the PBL process, became difficult. In many cases, teachers felt that they needed to offer "independent studies" for high-performing students if they were to remain at THS.

The school's growing internal problems became the feature of faculty meeting agenda. They had expected growing pains as they scaled up, but had never considered that students would leave. Clearly, the data suggested that something in the model was not working. Yet, other data—test scores, attendance, national recognition, and community support—suggested that the school was achieving its goals. Increasingly, the staff struggled to make sense of how to respond to the pressures of maintaining the model, and maintaining rigor and enrollment. Furthermore, with enrollment lagging, ESD had no choice but to note that the school was becoming a budgetary burden to the district. Teachers began to wonder if THS might close or be repurposed.

In a bold move, the principal decided that it was time to confront the concerns the school faced in a public way. She called for a community meeting, inviting faculty and staff, current and former students, upper administration, parents, area business leaders, and the school board. Embracing and modeling the PBL focus of THS, she posed the central question, "How can THS survive?" She suggested that discussion include placing all aspects of the school "on the table," prompting the group to explore what the school might change and how they could "try this again," hoping for pioneering solutions to "start over" and mitigate the problems THS faced.

Discussing the Case

- What were the core issues of school improvement that THS was designed to address?
- What assumptions were employed in the development of the school?
- What high-impact practices were present in the THS model?
- When does starting over make sense?
- How can leaders start over, retaining the best parts of innovation and reform and jettisoning the rest?
- How can starting over be explained to parents and the public?
- Where might you choose to focus your energy if you were a leader in this school?
- What might you let go?
- How would you build support for those efforts?

ACTIVITIES

The following activities will further expand your understanding of school improvement and apply those ideas to your own school and practice.

ACTIVITY 7.1

Revisiting Woodlake

Leadership is unavoidably contextual. The context of the Woodlake case included school and district meetings, classroom practice, local and national grant agencies, and social media spaces like the blog and Twitter. Consider the following questions:

- How can innovation and reform be addressed in the school setting and in contexts beyond the school?
- How can context limit or foster discussion and action?
- What contexts provide safe spaces for innovation?
- How can school leaders create contexts that foster creativity and focus on innovations to schools and schooling that push current limits?

A turning point in this case occurred when the principal that had championed High School 2.0 moved to another position and a different district level leader stepped in to manage the process. This shift changed the way the innovation was viewed within the administration, suggesting salient questions about school improvement. These include:

- What is the role of early support in innovation?
- How can innovative efforts outlast the initial founders or supporters?
- When does an innovation idea or practice become sustainable?
- What organizational factors might have been lacking to support the effort?
- What factors might have been present but underutilized?

ACTIVITY 7.2

School Improvement Challenges

Successful school improvement is a process of identifying challenges within the school and continuously seeking to find ways to mitigate them in the future. Challenges can arise in any number of places in the school. They can be found within curricular and instructional programs, in the ways in which parents are included in school activities, or in the ways in which teachers and others are held accountable for student performance, growth, and

continued . . .

achievement. Each school differs. Context matters. Perceptions matter. How might leaders:

- Link actions to outcomes?
- Allocate time for the work of school improvement?
- Keep turnover in check?
- Minimize resistance?

ACTIVITY 7.3

Assessing Your School

Reflect on the school improvement lessons discussed in this chapter. In the table below, note the areas you believe require development in your school. What does this data tell you about the state of school improvement where you work? Where are your energies currently invested? What is underemphasized? Where could an individual address the work? Where is the support of a small (or large) team needed?

	Considerable Development Needed	Some Development Needed	Minor Development Needed	Individual Work Required	Team Work Required
Effective classroom instruction					
High-quality rigorous curriculum					
Professional learning opportunities for teachers					
Supportive learning, climate, and culture					
Sustained and meaningful parental involvement					
Shared performance and goal accountability					
Learning-centered leadership					

RESOURCES

We began the chapter by suggesting that there are many high-quality resources for school improvement work. Here, we offer resources to support your efforts.

AdvancEd: www.advanc-ed.org
AdvancEd offers a network of improvement supports including but not limited to accreditation support, diagnostic review, professional learning, technology support, and research summaries. Joining the network provides schools and school leaders access to a community of thousands of educators across the globe working to address similar concerns.

AIR—American Institutes for Research: www.air.org
AIR links schools and school leaders to cutting-edge research in the areas of early childhood, P12 Education and Social Development, higher education and career readiness, and families, communities, and social systems. AIR sponsors access to blogs written in easily understood prose and produces summaries of high-quality current research in numerous topics relevant to the school improvement agenda.

School Improvement Network: http://schoolimprovement.com
The School Improvement Network hosts webinars, face-to-face professional learning opportunities, and offers online resources to support classroom instruction, assessment and evaluation efforts, differentiated instruction, data use, classroom management, and diversity and equity training.

SUBJECT-SPECIFIC ORGANIZATIONS

There are a variety of subject-specific organizations you may find useful to your school improvement efforts. Each offers comprehensive links to national standards and thoughtful attention to best practices in teaching. Many sponsor yearly conferences where teachers can network with other committed educators.

American Council of the Teaching of Foreign Languages: www.actfl.org

Association for Career and Technical Education: www.acteonline.org

Association for Health, Physical Education, Recreation, & Dance: http://aahperd.org

Council for Exceptional Children: www.cec.sped.org

National Art Education Association: www.arteducators.org

National Association for Bilingual Education: http://nabe.org

National Association for the Education of Young Children: www.naeyc.org

National Association of Music Teachers: www.mtna.org

continued . . .

National Association of Special Education Teachers: www.naset.org

National Council for the Social Studies: www.socialstudies.org

National Council of Teachers of English: www2.ncte.org

National Council of Teachers of Mathematics: www.nctm.org

REFERENCES

Andersen, L.B., Heinesen, E., & Pedersen, L.H. (2016). Individual performance: From common source bias to institutionalized assessment. *Journal of Public Administration Research and Theory, 26*(1), 63–78.

Anderson, T., & Shattuck, J. (2012). Design-based research: A decade of progress in education research? *Educational Researcher, 41*(1), 16–25.

Bryk, A.S., Gomez. L., Grunow, A., & LeMahieu, P. (2015). *Learning to improve: How America's schools can get better at getting better*. Boston, MA: Harvard Education Publishing.

Crawford, M.B. (2009). *Shop class as soul craft: An inquiry into the value of work*. New York: Penguin Press.

Crawford, M.B. (2015). *The world beyond your head: On becoming an individual in an age of distraction*. New York: Farrar, Straus & Giroux.

Darling-Hammond, L. (2000). Teacher quality and student achievement: A review of state policy evidence. *Education Policy Analysis Archives, 8*(1). Retrieved from: http://epaa.asu.edu/epaa/v8nl

Darling-Hammond, L. (2004). Standards, accountability, and school reform. *Teachers College Record, 106*(6), 1047–1085.

Deal, T. E., & Peterson, K. D. (2016). *Shaping school culture: The heart of leadership* (3rd ed.). San Francisco, CA: Jossey-Bass.

Emerson, R.W. (1837). *The American scholar*. An oration delivered before the Phi Beta Kappa Society, at Cambridge, MA, August 31, 1837.

Emerson, R.W. (1841). *Self-Reliance*. Retrieved from https://archive.vcu.edu/english/engweb/transcendentalism/authors/emerson/essays/selfreliance.html.

Fullan, M. (2007). *The new meaning of educational change* (4th ed.). New York: Teachers College Press.

Gabriel, R., & Woulfin, S. (2017). *Making teacher evaluation work: A guide for literacy teachers and leaders*. Portsmouth, NH: Heinemann.

Hallinger, P., Heck, R.H., & Murphy, J. (2014). Teacher evaluation and school improvement: An analysis of the evidence. *Educational Assessment, Evaluation and Accountability, 26*(1) 5–28.

Hong, S. (2011). *A cord of three strands: A new approach to parent engagement in schools*. Boston, MA: Harvard Education Press.

Ishimaru, A.M. (2017). From family engagement to equitable collaboration. *Educational Policy*. 1–36. DOI: 10.1177/0895904817691841

Johnson, B., & Kruse, S. D. (2009). *Decision-making for educational leaders: Under-examined dimensions and issues.* Albany, NY: SUNY.

Kingdon, J. W. (2003). *Agendas, alternatives, and public policies* (2nd ed.). New York: Longman.

Koretz, D. (2009). *Measuring up: What educational testing really tells us.* Cambridge, MA: Harvard University Press.

Kruse, S.D., & Johnson, B.L. (2017). Tempering the normative demands of PLCs with the organizational realities of life in schools: Exploring the cognitive dilemmas faced by educational leaders. *Educational Management Administration & Leadership*, 45(4), 588–604.

Kruse, S.D., & Louis, K.S. (2009). *Building strong school cultures: A guide to leading change.* Thousand Oaks, CA: Corwin Press.

Leithwood, K. & Louis, K.S. (2012). *Linking leadership to student learning.* San Francisco, CA: Jossey-Bass.

Mintrop, R. (2016). *Design-based school improvement: A practical guide for education leaders.* Cambridge, MA: Harvard Education Press.

Mitchell, C., & Sackney, L. (2015). School improvement in high-capacity schools: Educational leadership and living-systems ontology. *Educational Management, Administration, & Leadership*, 44(5), 852–868.

Mitchell, D.E. (2011). Historical and theoretical context. In Mitchell, D.E., Crowson, R.L., & Shipps, D. (Eds.). *Shaping education policy: Power and process* (pp. 1–23). New York: Routledge.

Murphy, J. (2015). Creating communities of professionalism: Addressing cultural and structural barriers. *Journal of Educational Administration*, 53(2), 154–176.

Murphy, J. (2016). *Leading school improvement: A framework for action.* West Palm Beach, FL: Learning Sciences International.

Newmann, F., Carmichael Tanaka, D.L., & King, M.B. (2015). *Authentic intellectual work: Improving teaching for rigorous learning.* Thousand Oaks, CA: Corwin.

Smylie, M.A. (2010). *Continuous school improvement.* Thousand Oaks, CA: Corwin.

Tyack, D. (1974). *The one best system: A history of American urban education.* Boston, MA: Harvard University Press.

CHAPTER **8**

Ways Forward and Lessons Learned

That leadership differs from management has been a longstanding trope. As the adage states, "Leadership is doing the right things. Management is doing things right." In the movies, leaders take charge. Managers handle the day-to-day labor. Clearly, management tasks like budgeting, scheduling, ensuring safety, and organizing resources are less alluring than those attributed to leadership (e.g., visioning, advocating, deciding, and mentoring to name a few), but without strong management a school cannot be well organized. A principal cannot change the system if trust has not been built. Similarly, she cannot creatively problem solve if collaboration is not present. Nor can she promote inclusion and dignity unless sustained support for those efforts already exists. Therefore, we assert that leadership and management cannot be viewed as separate, distinct constructs. Instead, we argue that they need to be viewed as complimentary, mutually informing, and able to be done regularly by principals.

Yet, such work can be overwhelming. In this chapter three themes will be examined for thinking about leadership and management in broad and applied ways. The first focuses on intensifying leadership. By intensifying leadership, we mean securing the assistance, talents, and skills of a wide variety of people to support school vision and goals. The second theme concerns clarifying the means and ends of activities and actions. Here the focus is on the ways in which staying attentive to the purposes for doing what you are doing matters. Finally, the importance of communal endeavor to success will be addressed. Our aim is to help school leaders learn to balance their work and strategically include others in the effort so that goals and objectives can be met and the school can be a happy and healthy place in which to learn and work.

A note on format, instead of our usual feature case and cases for discussion, after a discussion of our key themes, this chapter offers two longer cases for analysis. We are hoping that as you consider these, you take into consideration all the broad themes of this text.

KEY LEARNINGS

In this chapter, you will learn to:

- empower and motivate teachers and staff to the highest levels of professional practice, continuous learning, and improvement;
- foster continuous improvement of individual and collective instructional capacity to achieve outcomes envisioned for each student;
- tend to your own professional learning and effectiveness through reflection, study, and improvement, while maintaining a healthy work–life balance.

FEATURED CASE

Intensifying Leadership

It has been well acknowledged that, in today's context, successful school leadership requires more than the actions of a single person (DiPaola & Tschannnen-Moran, 2003; Kruse & Louis, 2009; Mayrowetz, Murphy, Louis, & Smylie, 2007). No matter how well motivated or educated, the task of running a school is too hard to do alone. Additionally, if leaders try to handle the work all by themselves not only do they run the risk of burning out, they open themselves up to the criticism that they are not transparent or collaborative. Building on the legacy of the work in instructional leadership (Day, Gu, & Sammons, 2016; Hallinger, 2005), shared leadership (Leithwood & Mascall, 2008; Urick, 2016), distributed leadership (Bush, 2013; Tian, Risku, & Collin, 2016), and servant leadership (Greenleaf, 1977; Block, 1993; Parris & Peachey, 2013), *intensified leadership* highlights the roles that others play in school success. Intensified leadership suggests that by increasing the number of people engaged in meaningful leadership roles, the goals of the school are more likely to be achieved (Kruse & Louis, 2009).

We argue that by intensifying leadership, leaders deliberately broaden the involvement of others (e.g., teachers, staff, parents, community, and, as appropriate, students) in the work of school leadership. Intensified leadership assumes that multiple voices are engaged in agenda setting, finding and solving problems, and choosing activities and tasks designed to resolve the issues facing the schools. In this way, a personal connection to the work of the school can be established and made clear (Block, 2008; Kruse, 2009). Moreover, understanding of processes and practices is enhanced because people can see why they are participating in shared work and feel a connection to its success.

Intensified leadership both acknowledges and celebrates the fact that expertise is distributed among many members of the school community and that those members care deeply about the school. As a result, individual and collective knowledge can be pooled and better outcomes can be achieved. As shared understanding and effort is built by intensifying leadership, members are empowered and motivated to contribute to shared goals. In turn, collective responsibility is deepened as interactions between and among school community members are strengthened.

Yet, intensifying leadership is not simple. It requires that school leaders willingly and openly engage others in the identification of meaningful work and support them in its pursuit. For some, meaningful work will include attention to the internal life of the school, including foci on pedagogical practice, school culture, and improvement. For others, meaningful work may be more external in focus to include engaging in community involvement and outreach, or partnerships and collaborations. In any case, the intensification of leadership entails more than the creation of teams charged with specific tasks and activities. Intensification suggests that while small groups might address an aspect of an effort, once completed, those efforts are integrated into the broader community's work and focus on a shared school goal. In this way, leadership work becomes purposefully synergistic.

Purposeful synergy suggests that the integration of effort is not left to chance. Work done toward, for example, including parents in decisions about the school, should be widely known and understood. Synergy suggests that as initiatives are undertaken, the ways in which they support other work is considered. Similarly, the potential for inconsistencies may also surface. As difference is uncovered, decisions can be made and communicated concerning the reasons why diverse approaches might be needed. Transparency is enhanced, whereas in the past less clearly understood patterns of activity may have contributed to mistrust.

Simply put, it is impossible to see how things are connected if an effort has not been made to draw coherent connections between and among decisions, practices, or processes. When we cannot find coherence, it is easy to ignore requests, attend meetings but not pay attention, or simply go through the motions of an activity. Practicing intensified leadership boosts a principal's ability to help others understand and make meaning out of daily efforts. In turn, as understanding and meaning are developed, teachers, parents, and others become increasingly motivated to participate, especially as they understand the purpose of doing the work.

Furthermore, as synergy grows through the intensification of leadership efforts, the school's ability to effectively respond to multiple challenges is also enhanced. As members work toward communal goals, in ways that matter to them, more can be accomplished by the group effort. Yet, intensifying leadership also requires humility (Schein, 2013). It requires that leaders learn to say "we" rather than "I" and to listen more than they speak. It requires that leaders ask questions they have not already formulated an answer to and listen to the answer. Asking, and then listening, empowers others. Done repeatedly, it suggests that as a leader you are open to learning and are able to interact for the good of the school community.

CLARIFYING MEANS AND ENDS OF ACTIVITIES AND ACTIONS

As leadership is intensified, it becomes important that the reason for doing the work is clear. Yet, all too often, in education and in other fields, the purpose for what we are doing becomes confused with the doing itself. We assume that by doing something—the means—we are achieving what that thing was intended to do—the ends. In many ways, this logic makes sense, in the same way that a student attends classes as a means to achieve the goal of earning a degree. Similarly, schools adopt curricula as a means to realize the goal of educating students.

When we use the word "means," it implies that we are looking toward a set of actions or activities designed to produce an intended result. Simply put, "ends" are those results. An end is what we want to achieve by putting in place the means to get there. Put formally, we can test if something is an end (B) or a means (A) in the following way. Something is a means to an end:

1. If A must be in place for B to occur.
2. If A is necessary for B to occur, even if it is not fully sufficient on its own to assure the attainment of B.
3. B most likely will not occur without some intervention and A is a likely way to get there.

Straightforward logic suggests a simple "if A then B" assumption. It supposes that the relationship between A and B is related in some fashion and that the presence of A is necessary for B to occur. Yet, in many instances a causal relationship is not always evident, nor does it acknowledge that any goal may well take multiple efforts—means—to attain results. In our example of the class-taking student above, A is represented by coursework and B by the degree.

Yet, attaining a degree is unlikely to be the sole end of school attendance. Rather, degrees are attained for other purposes—future employment, curiosity, and personal reward, to name a few. In this case, the degree is both a means and an end. Similarly, course attendance is not the only means by which a student comes educated. At the very least, students must do the reading, complete labs, reflect on what is learned, and ultimately apply what they have learned in new situations for coursework to be of value. Clearly, at least in modern educational systems and structures, coursework is part of a continuum of events designed to create educated people. In this way, human activity can be seen as continuous and our actions as part of an ongoing stream of events where ends are, in fact, endless (Evans, 2000; Whitford, 2002). Attaining our ultimate goals requires we do not confuse our means and ends.

Rational planning models suggest that we can plan for the outcomes or ends we wish to attain by determining which means are needed to attain them along the way

(Cohen, 2007; Dinkelman, 2003). When our choices are straightforward, we can create clear linkages between point A and point B. Rational planning would suggest that decisions can be made in the following manner:

1. Analyze the situation at hand.
2. Determine what outcomes or ends are desired.
3. Identify what activities or means are required to attain identified outcomes.
4. Select the action or actions most likely to attain the desired outcome.

As we discussed in Chapter 7, no choice is perfectly rational nor do decision makers have at hand all the data or time needed to make a fully rational decision. However, it is possible to be relatively systematic in reviewing potential alternatives and predicting possible consequences.

Yet, rational planning often breaks down when purposes and motivations for activities are forgotten. All too often in schools, interventions are chosen for implementation because someone believes they will provide the means to address a problem. Take, for example, the presence of a professional learning community (PLC) in a school. PLCs have become ubiquitous as a means to better coordinate teachers' work. Make no mistake, when done well, the PLC can produce its intended results (Feger & Arruda, 2008; Huggins, Scheurich, & Morgan, 2011). Yet, in many places they have failed to produce their intended results (Kruse & Johnson, 2017; Stoll & Louis, 2007).

When we visit schools, we often hear that a staff has "done" PLCs. Inevitably, what follows is the lament that "it didn't work for us." When pressed, the story often unfolds that the faculty and staff got so wrapped up in "doing" PLCs that they lost sight of the reason why they adopted them in the first place. Organizing faculty and staff into teams, setting an agenda for those teams, and supporting their work can be difficult. Yet, in the cases where the initiative has faltered, most often, leaders exhausted their time, energy, and social capital introducing the effort and then failed to sustain the work. When faced with challenges, many chose to abandon or water down the practice, rather than redirect their energies to the goals of the PLC. It is as if the development of the PLC became the end, rather than the means for the structure to attain the school's goals.

What gets lost when the purpose for adopting the new pedagogy or creating a PLC is forgotten is the meaning, a shared and clear purpose, for doing the work. Absent a purpose for a PLC, the daily or weekly meetings are without grounding. Simply meeting, putting in the time, becomes the end. When means get confused with ends, little gets accomplished. Goals and purposes are not realized because they get lost along the way, confused with the thing that was chosen to help them get there.

IMPORTANCE OF COMMUNAL ACTION FOR SUCCESS

So, what is a leader to do? The key to intensifying leadership and to solving the means/ends dilemma is to focus on communal action. Communal action is more than the coordination of effort, or cooperation. When people coordinate effort they each develop their own plans and provide those to the team. When team members cooperate, there may be some discussion of outcomes and activities but, in the end, the focus is on individual endeavors and goals rather than a collective strategy. Communal action suggests that attention is focused on collective activity and shared goals. Ideas are shared and decisions made with the intent of enhancing the collective whole, and the outcome often leads to new ways of thinking (Argyris, 1992; Weick, 2002).

However, communal action is not easy to initiate or maintain. A focus on communal endeavor often fails when it is viewed as an activity (i.e., an end in itself) rather than as a tool to attain shared, common purposes and goals. Furthermore, leading, managing, and participating in group efforts creates a layer of added communication and interaction. Getting teams to work together, to critically discuss practice, and to grow as professionals, is more difficult. In teams, teachers with distinct knowledge and skills may work alongside each other on common goals, but do not engage in critical discussion and debate. To experience the full potential of communal action, professional critical discussion that challenges thinking and practice is a must for goals to be fully realized.

Yet, in a profession that remains highly individualized (Little, 1990), communal work does not come naturally. Doing this work well requires attention to the development of new knowledge and skills designed to foster overall improved practice. We share the following five leadership habits as strategies to develop communal actions within your school.

Celebrate Individual Strengths in a Collaborative Context

Commitment to communal work forms from an intentional acknowledgment of the individuals who are working together (Louis, 2006; Mayrowetz et al., 2007). Everyone brings to the work a unique set of knowledge, skills, and experiences. In many ways, the foundation for intensified leadership is built as we learn, together, what we all bring to the work. By publicly sharing and celebrating viewpoints, talents, and skills, we are better able to draw on those resources when they are needed. Just as intensifying leadership requires that we bring many voices into the conversation and the work, strengthening communal effort relies on our ability to hear what those voices have to offer.

Voice the Language of Commitment and Purpose

Communal action fails when group members do not pull their weight, are not accountable, or purposefully work at odds to shared goals (Murphy, 2013). As leaders work to develop communal action, it is important that the vision, purposes and intended outcomes for the work are made clear. Early on, it may become apparent that some groups are struggling and need additional support or assistance. There should be clearly communicated "rules of engagement" to encourage participants to share who they are and what they hope to accomplish as a group. In education, we have long accepted that schools will have "pockets of excellence" (Jenlink, 2008;

Smylie, 2010). However, it has also been well established that doing so will not produce equitable outcomes for students (Bush, 2013; Day, Gu, & Sammons, 2016). Leaders must voice and communicate clear expectations for professionalism as part of communal work.

View Conflict as Growth and Opportunity

Closely linked to the habit of voice is the notion that conflict, when handled well, can produce personal and professional growth (Field, Tobin, & Reese-Weber, 2014). No one likes conflict and, frankly, there is too much work that needs to be done to spend much time on drama. Yet, when handled well (Abrams, 2009, 2016; Schein, 2013) rather than left to fester, both the individual and the collective stands to gain.

Organize Opportunities for Inquiry and Critical Thinking

A school leader we know well likes to set aside a meeting every month or so to ask the question "What's about to go wrong?" Occasionally, he phrases it differently, asking "What's bothering you?" but the intention is clear. The meeting is a safe space for teachers and staff to come together and raise concerns. What makes this practice work so well and why it does not simply devolve into a gripe session, is that at the end of each meeting, the group outlines what might be done to address the concern. In this phase of the meeting, those in attendance are prompted to begin their ideas with the words, "What if . . .". By creating spaces where questioning is encouraged, problems tend not to fester, and creativity is enhanced. Because the process flows naturally in this school, where communal work is well established, the meetings act as a way to further enrich the school's already strong culture.

Plan for Reflection and Mindfulness

Throughout this volume, we have noted that the task of school leadership is challenging. Yet, self-care and the maintenance of a healthy work–life balance matters if one is to have a happy, productive career. The development of reflectivity and mindful practice creates a venue for leaders to explore multiple ways of understanding and seeing the school around them. It opens the door for more nuanced understandings of how schools operate and provides a venue for testing hypotheses and reflective thought. In this sense, reflective, mindful practice serves an important sensitizing function. When collectively employed, mindful praxis, as evidenced in reflectivity in action, and establishes an on-the-ground, real-time orientation to communal learning, further enhancing the knowledge and skill set available for members to draw from and, in turn, contribute to (Hoy, 2003; Langer, 2009).

Reflectivity and mindful practice can be attended to in any number of ways. Work by Weick and colleagues (Vogus & Sutcliffe, 2012; Weick & Sutcliffe, 2001; Weick, Sutcliffe, & Obstfeld, 1999) outlines five defining features of mindful organizations. First, mindful organizations exhibit a healthy preoccupation with failure. Our example of the school leader's monthly inquiry sessions demonstrates how a preoccupation with failure can encourage members to reflect on their work in meaningful ways to avoid future difficulties. Second, mindful organizations are characterized by a reluctance to simplify interpretations of what is happening in the organization. As members work to understand each other and value the ways in which members see the work of the school, they can deepen their shared understanding of how the school functions and, in turn, how it serves students and their families. By encouraging deep and complex interpretations of events and issues, mindful practice is enhanced, leading to positive outcomes.

Third, mindful organizations are further distinguished by a heightened sensitivity to the link between organizational processes and outcome. When leadership attention is paid not only to what happens in the school, but also to what happens because of the activity undertaken, we are able to learn about what is effective and what is less successful. Leaders can then do more of the former and less of the latter, resulting in an economy of effort and greater success. Fourth, members of mindful organizations tend to be resilient to change, accepting of inevitable failure, and tenacious in their ability to learn from said failures. This defining commitment promotes a robust culture of communal learning where not succeeding is viewed as an opportunity for growth and change. Finally, mindful organizations embrace approaches to problem solving that defer to expertise rather than formal authority. Mindful organizations not only promote communal approaches to learning, but also flatten coordinating structures. In this way, individuals are celebrated for what they bring to the effort no matter their position in the school.

While our discussion of reflection and mindfulness has focused on what leaders can do at an organizational level, we would note that all of these practices work well at the individual level as well. When issues and concerns can be seen as opportunities for learning and growth, we can be less worried and attention can be turned to resolving that which vexes us. Similarly, when we are able to plan for setbacks and disappointments, we are more resilient when they arise. Mindful work is challenging and imperfect, yet allows participants to grow as professionals who are reflective and contemplative of their work, which can be both gratifying and rewarding.

CASES FOR ANALYSIS

CASE 8.1

Million Dollar Scholars

With the arrival of Shaylen Whitter as principal in 2005, Rossman High School established a school goal to develop a college-going culture among its student body. Prior to Whitter's tenure, RHS had a 77 pecent graduation rate and moderate post-secondary enrollment. Historical data is unclear as to exactly how many students went on to college because, as one teacher stated, "We didn't see that as our job. Keeping track like that, it just didn't matter."

Now, the large, urban, and Midwestern school prides itself on its 97 percent on-time graduation rate. Thanks to community sponsorship, graduating seniors are now able to take the ACT free of charge. As a result, the class averages on the ACT have steadily grown. The 2016 class average was 21.3, besting the 2015 class by almost a full point. As students receive college admissions letters, they are encouraged to bring them in and post a copy on the "big board" for everyone to see. Additionally, prizes are awarded for acceptances to competitive schools, the Ivy Leagues, admission to multiple schools, and overall scholarship offers.

College Bound

Clearly, there is much good to say about Rossman High's focus on college. Overall academic achievement has improved throughout the school, a source of pride for the community. Many of Rossman's graduates are the first in their families to attend college and for many, acceptance to multiple schools is a source of great pride. Additionally, the school's focus on scholarship applications as well as acceptance has made it possible for many students to afford to attend college. However, there are those within the school who object to the focus on numbers. As Toma King, a biology teacher says,

> I'm not sure how it happened, but there's become kind of a competition to be the kid with the most acceptances, the most money. Maybe it began when we first announced how much each student had been promised as part of the graduation ceremony. I don't know, but I do know kids are chasing the wrong things.

Whitter defends the focus on cumulative acceptances as "inspirational" and credits the focus on aggregate scholarship awards "helping my kids see what they're really worth." Her goal is to see a full quarter of the senior class be a "million-dollar scholar," adding, "When a kid, who doesn't come from much, sees that colleges are willing to give them a million dollars, they see that they're worth something, something special."

Disappointment and Misunderstandings

Whitter works hard to acknowledge her million-dollar scholars, a program she initiated in 2013. When a student reaches a million dollars in overall scholarship pledges, Whitter visits the student in their home room with a large ceremonial check and commemorative T-shirt welcoming the student "into the club." By all accounts, it is a club that students want to join. As Senior Charlene Ross notes, "It's a big goal to accomplish, like I didn't think I could do it but when I did, it just made me like being a senior even more." Ross applied to over 60 schools to attain her status, doing so by searching the Internet for schools with no application fees and soliciting financial assistance for those that required a fee. Her only regret came when she had to choose where she was planning on attending school in the fall. She shared,

> I really wanted to go to the state university. They gave me some money but not a full ride. I thought I could use some of my other money to go there for free. But

then I learned you only get it if you go to them. Like, it really wasn't mine to begin with. Other kids don't get that either, like they thought the money was theirs no matter what. It was kind of like, disappointing.

Toma King reinforces that Ross' confusion is not an isolated event,

The kids get super caught up in getting the money. How scholarships work isn't really explained. They also don't get a lot of guidance to understand which school might be best for them. They really don't know much about the schools they're applying to because there's too many. Then they have to choose and they don't have a clue what to do.

Char Ross's parents agree: "We're not stupid, we tried to tell her that the money wasn't really hers but she was getting so much attention for getting it, she was even on TV. She just wasn't listening." When asked where Char planned to go to school in the fall, tellingly, her father replied, "One of the ones that gave her the full ride, right? Which was it?"

Guidance counselors have also questioned the program's focus. Citing data that suggests that, on average, a WHS senior applies to three-dozen schools, counselors assert,

We aren't doing a good job at this any more. We can't even think about offering real guidance. What's sad is when kids have to accept somewhere, to make a decision. We often have to tell them to settle for where they got the most money. Often, it's a place they've never visited—they don't even know where it is sometimes. They just know they got in and can afford it. And they should be happy about it. I mean, a whole bunch of them aren't even sure what they want to study once they get there. They're being set up.

Increasing Tensions

Whitter defends the attention she pays to the million-dollar scholar program by pointing to numerous students who, in past years, have used their scholarship money well and thrived at their chosen school. Reaching for her tablet, she pulls up the Facebook page she hosts for prior scholars. The page is filled with pictures of former students in residence halls, at football games, and studying hard in the library. Almost uniformly, the posts paint a picture of engaged, happy students enjoying their college years. She says, "I'm waiting for next year, when I start getting graduation announcements." However, not all students have thrived. A "handful," Whitter suggests, did not "fit" once they got to college. She defends RHS stating that, "To my knowledge no one has struggled academically." Yet, she admits, "several didn't fit socially, culturally" and still others, "couldn't handle being away from home."

King, along with a group of six other teachers, believes that the outcomes are less rosy than Whitter suggests, and that many students attend their first year and don't return to college for "any number of reasons." He agrees that students are "for the most part academically ready. They just have little in the way of emotional or social support to succeed once they get there." Currently, his team has mounted a campaign demanding that the school do better. They have publically called for an end to the program and are asking that instead, resources go to assisting students "to craft thoughtful applications to no more than a dozen carefully chosen schools." His team also suggests that time and energy that is currently being used "making big checks and T-shirts" go into mentoring for college-bound students who "should know what it's going to be like when they get there."

Whitter and her supporters counter suggesting that the million-dollar scholar has put RHS "on the map" and to pull back on the program would "jeopardize" future students' success. Further complicating the matter is a small but insistent parent group that supports the program but worries that "some kids get disappointed, they don't get as much money, or they don't want to play the game." One parent of a recently graduated student who chose to enter the military felt that "Other options for kids aren't valued. It's college or nothing here. My daughter's choice deserved to be celebrated. It was kind of insulting that she didn't get any recognition."

Still another parent noted,

My kid only really wanted to go to one school. My husband wanted him there also. He could play football. He's lucky that way. So that's the only place he applied. Got in. Got some money, we were happy, but the high school, it was like he was a big loser. How is it losing to get to do something you want, at a place you want to do it? Lots of principals would have been happy for him—not Whitter, not here.

Whitter claims, "When you set one goal, others suffer." However, she believes, "Whatever the downside, what we're doing is right. The kids buy in, our test scores show it, the program results show it. Until someone tells me different, I'm keeping the pressure on to create more million dollar scholars."

Discussing the Case

- What are the core issues in this case?
- On which literature might you draw to explain the issues as you have identified them?
- Who are the key players and what are their values?
- How might intensified leadership and collective effort be used to mitigate this situation?
- In what ways were means and ends confused in this case?
- What do you think of the focus on college enrollment? Is college appropriate for all students? Who decides?
- What do you think about the focus on multiple admissions and overall scholarship dollars as measures of success?
- Of the arguments for the program, which are most compelling?
- Of the arguments against the program, which are most compelling?
- Can middle ground be found? What might it look like?
- If you were Whitter, what would you do next?

- If you were King, what would you do next?
- If you were the parent of a student at RHS, how might you see this program?

CASE 8.2

Grading and Reporting

Anthony Kesselmann, Ed.D. was proud to have been chosen as the first principal of the new Swallow's Bay Intermediate School. The interview process was extensive. Comprising three interviews and a final community forum, the process had stretched over five months. On more than one occasion he had left the interview venue believing that his no-nonsense approach to discipline and school governance was not aligned with the district's more laid-back vibe. Kesslemann knew how he wanted a school to run. He knew what he believed in and how he expected students to behave. He reasoned that if he was not a good fit for the district, he would not be happy in the position. He explained, "I like where I'm at now. This job would be a nice step for me. If I get it, that's great; if not, another one will come along."

When in late April, the call came to offer him the position he was surprised. Concerned about fit, he probed the superintendent about his sense that his style might be more assertive than that of other administrators in the district. He openly worried that he wouldn't fit in, suggesting, "I don't want friction with you or other principals. I also don't want to change how I work." More than once as he was negotiating the terms of his contract, Kesslemann asked the superintendent, "Are you sure?" The superintendent assured him that it was exactly his style that had secured him the offer. Parents and community members had loved his take-charge attitude and confidence. Teachers had given him high marks as well. One anonymous written comment had said, "I get the sense you'd know exactly what he wanted of you, there wouldn't be any gray areas. Some teachers might not like that, but I think it would be great to work for someone so clear."

As part of the planning process for Swallow's Bay, about half of the faculty had been chosen over a year ago. Fifteen lead teachers had been part of the interview process and had provided ongoing feedback into building and classroom design. Swallow's Bay Intermediate had been designed to be the district's third comprehensive fourth through eighth grade school, offering a full range of core courses, and electives. As in all of the district's intermediate schools, foreign language, honors and advanced courses would be offered, as well as a comprehensive fine arts program.

First Steps

Kesselmann began work in his new role in early June. A first order of business would be to complete hiring for the school. As part of his negotiation, he had insisted that he should be able to look outside the district for teachers and support staff to achieve the "right mix of talent and skill." Kesselmann was hoping that by mixing in "new blood" with the founding teacher group, he might be able to balance insider knowledge with fresh ideas and thinking. He invited several teachers from the original team of lead teachers for the interview process, demonstrating his plan of having these teacher leaders active in school governance in the new school.

At the first lead teacher meeting, a veteran fourth grade teacher, Shirley Oliver, began discussion by addressing Kesselmann as Anthony. He quickly interrupted her, "It's Dr. Kesselmann." The room fell silent. Surely, he was joking. The superintendent, the only other member of the leadership team to hold a doctorate, went by his first name. The teachers looked nervously at each other waiting for the tension to abate. Finally, Kesselmann broke the silence himself stating, "I worked hard for that degree, it's a sign of professional respect to use the title, please do so. Ms. Oliver, you were saying . . ." Shaken, Oliver completed her thought. The meeting ended quickly with little discussion about interview items and responsibilities.

In late July, Kesselmann hosted a staff and faculty barbeque at his home. It was the first time that the full faculty had been assembled and he wanted a low-pressure way for everyone to meet. Word had traveled concerning Kesselmann's preference for the use of his formal title. At the event, most of the faculty chose not to address him by name at all. Oliver explained, "It was a barbeque, like informal, right? Who wants to be corrected? But, who wants to risk it?" The evening passed without incident, leading the teachers to hope that school would open without further tensions.

School Opens

As was district tradition, the new school would open its doors in August and additional contracted time would be provided for teachers to move in and begin their collaborative work. The district maintenance staff had been hard at work since mid-June unpacking desks, books, and computers so that the building would be ready. On the official first day back, Kesselmann visited each teacher, welcoming each to the building with a small plant to symbolize "our new growth together." He also left behind a new faculty handbook and a collection of school notecards. He explained, "Email can be so cold. It's efficient but . . . I find a handwritten note goes a long way with parents." Many teachers thought the effort was nice. However, others vowed to keep their eye on Kesselmann, wondering if his message might be less welcoming than it first appeared.

Just after Labor Say, Swallow's Bay Intermediate School opened with much fanfare. The building sparkled and its newness impressed. Kesselmann greeted the buses that first morning and each subsequent morning. Often, he could be seen walking the halls. He regularly popped into classrooms, working to learn each of the over 600 students by name. The teaching staff seemed to settle in and students and their families seemed happy to be attending Swallow's Bay. Early tensions seemed to dissipate. Although many of the teachers found Kesselmann's insistence on formality odd, they had to agree he was a hard worker and seemed devoted to the school.

Mid-terms?

The October faculty meeting began with a discussion about setting school traditions. Discussion had been lively and everyone seemed excited to be thinking about how Swallow's Bay was growing into a real community. Just as the meeting was drawing to a close, Kesselmann announced, "Don't forget your mid-term grades are due to me by November 1." The faculty stopped short. Mid-term grades? Finally, Matt Duncan, a sixth-grade math teacher asked for the bewildered group, "We're turning mid-terms in? When was that decided?" Kesselmann looked up and answered quickly, "It's in the handbook I distributed. I assumed you'd read it."

"Read it? I'm not even sure I know where I put it," was Duncan's retort. Kesselmann looked startled and after a moment replied, "I suggest you find it. I've outlined a very specific process. You know that I believe in regular and informative communication about student learning."

Back in their classrooms, the teachers quickly discovered that, in fact, the handbook did outline a process for mid-term grade reports to be submitted for every student earning a C or below. Included in the report was to be the grade, a breakdown of all assignments and points earned, a summary of student learning needs linked to grade level standards, a plan for remediation, and an opportunity for parent conferences to discuss how they might support their child's progress. Many teachers breathed a sigh of relief. Yes, it was extra work, but not all that unexpected or different than what they were doing anyway.

However, the math team was troubled. They prided themselves on mastery teaching. Students in their classes earned either an A, B, or an IP (in progress). The opportunity to revise and resubmit work was a hallmark of their philosophy of student success. Believing that intermediate math set the stage for upper level mathematics success, they wanted all of their students to have a solid foundation of understanding. In their minds, anything less than mastery of the basics was unacceptable. Their gradebooks were posted online so that students could share progress reports with their parents, a requirement and expectation. Furthermore, they believed that Kesselmann knew about their philosophy and practice concerning formative assessment. They had explained it to him early in the year and he had seemed supportive. Confident that their practices fit "the spirit" of the policy, they decided not to submit any mid-term reports since they didn't have any students receiving a C or lower.

About a week later, Kesselmann appeared at the classroom door of the team's lead teacher. He began the conversation by asking, "Mr. Duncan, I failed to receive any mid-term reports from the math program. Surely, all the students can't be getting As and Bs?" Duncan responded, "No, you're correct, some of them have IPs and they're working toward mastery. We shared our policy with you. We thought you'd agreed."

In the moment, Kesselmann felt some relief, he had entered the room thinking he was being challenged and he didn't want a battle. His immediate thought was he would be able to reframe this as a misunderstanding, "Oh, then that's the list I'll need. I guess I wasn't clear enough in the handbook." Duncan smiled, "No, you were clear, it's just that an IP is not a C. An IP is a formative assessment that says a student needs more time. A C is a summative grade saying the student hasn't mastered the material at more than an adequate level. That's simply not good enough for us."

Squaring Off

Kesselmann understood the logic behind Duncan's claims. He had read the research and knew there was support for his approach. Furthermore, he was impressed that the math department worked closely together. He knew that they had completed an extensive assessment at the start of the year and students had been placed in an instructional group according to educational need. Kesselmann also knew that parents seemed excited by the team's approach. He had heard positive comments from parents of kids who "had a second chance" and those who "got to skip ahead and weren't bored any more."

Yet, he was concerned that an entire unit was operating completely differently than the rest of the school. Also, he worried about the school's test scores. He wondered, "How could I lead data management efforts regarding student achievement absent any data?" After much thought, he decided to take the matter to the lead teacher team. An email alerted the team about the next meeting:

To: Lead Teacher Team

From: Dr. Kesselmann

Re: Grading and assessment policies

Thank you all for your response to my mid-term grade requests. I appreciate your coordination of this effort and realize that my request might have been communicated more clearly. I know many of you did extra work to make the deadline and I cannot thank you enough for that work. As you are aware, I care deeply about the academic success of students at Swallow's Bay. I have found that regular collection of student grades and information about student progress and growth allows for better instructional and curricular decision making. I have learned that not all faculty here view this issue as I do. I would like to have a conversation about our philosophy. I think we need to meet as soon as possible to begin this discussion. My administrative assistant, Ms. Bell, will be in touch regarding meeting time and place. Please make it a priority to attend.

Doughnuts And Discussion

Kesselmann had arranged for doughnuts, coffee, and fresh fruit, hoping that he could set a welcoming tone for the team. He also began with an apology of sorts,

I wish we were having this meeting under different circumstances. I thought as part of the hiring process I had made clear my interest in data use to inform student learning decisions. I guess my message wasn't as clear as I thought it was. I also know this isn't only about the mid-terms policy. I think we need to talk.

The teachers looked around the room uncertain about where to start. Finally, Oliver broke the ice, "Thanks for the doughnuts, Doc." She waited for Kesselmann to smile. Thankfully, he did. Emboldened she continued,

I know opening this place hasn't been easy. I want to thank you for all the work you've done. But you know, we're good and we got these jobs because of that.

I know you didn't hire us like you hired the others. That you don't know us really well. But, you could trust us a bit more.

She paused.

Kesselmann sat for a moment, he then took an audible deep breath and began,

Many of you know I worried about fit when I took this job. I'm a hard charger because I want what's best for the kids. You know, I talked with my wife, Ana, about this meeting. She says that if I'm going to be successful here, I'm going to need to talk less, manage less, and stop trying so hard.

The room fell silent. He continued,

When I started in administration, I believed that it was my job to lead. To set the direction, to make people do what's right. I still think there's some truth to that. I also see what Ana says is also true. So, I guess the question is how can we do this together?

Discussing the Case

- What are the core issues in this case?
- On which literature might you draw to explain the issues as you have identified them?
- Who are the key players and what are their values?
- Where are the real conflicts here?
- If you were Kesselmann, what would you do next?
- If you were the lead teacher team, what would you do next?
- How might this situation be mitigated?
- What would a best outcome look like?
- How might it be achieved?
- How might you, as a new principal, guard against this kind of issue?

ACTIVITIES

ACTIVITY 8.1

Thinking About Your School: A Summary Plan for Action

This activity is an extension of Activity 1.1 from Chapter 1. Reread and reconsider the case you wrote about your school. How would you change your understanding of any of the following issues? How might you frame your thinking now? On what new thinking are you drawing?

continued . . .

- Who are the key decision makers in your organization?
- What are the key issues the leadership is facing?
- Where are the points of disagreement and pressure?
- What do you know about those issues?
- Where do you need to learn more?
- How might others tell that same story?
- How should you respond?
- What are your next steps?
- How might you evaluate your progress?

ACTIVITY 8.2

Welcome Back

Plan a welcome back event for your faculty and staff. What would your agenda look like? Who will attend? How will you build in activities to strengthen culture, communication, and community? Who will you invite to help plan the day? Who will help you handle the events and activities during the day's events? How will you assure participation? What core message(s) will you be sending? What would you hope would be the outcome of this work? Are there roles for students, families, or community members? If so, what would those roles entail? How can you use this day to intensify leadership within your school?

ACTIVITY 8.3

One Last Inventory

In this activity, think about your school in broad and general terms, assessing the state of current activity in the leadership areas that have been addressed. After completing the inventory, the following questions can be used to plan the next steps:

- What areas need immediate attention?
- Who should you include in planning efforts? What roles would they hold?
- What resources are needed to gain traction in this area?
- When is the best time to begin this work and how long should it take to complete?
- What would a best outcome look like?
- What would an outcome you can live with look like?

continued . . .

- What barriers are present that might impede this work?
- Who can you count on to champion this effort?
- Where is maintenance exactly where you need to be?
- What aspects of your school are ready for revitalization?

At this juncture, leadership efforts are focused on . . .			
	Revitalization	Maintenance	Establishing
Mission, Vision, and Core Values (PSEL Standard 1)	The current mission, vision, and values statements need to reflect new, shared directions. Most, if not all of the goals have been met and objectives achieved. It is time to rethink the good work that has been done and be sure that everyone is on board with where the school is heading in the future.	Mission, vision, and core values guide the day-to-day work of the school. Faculty, staff, families, and community members agree that the goals and objectives are still relevant and continued work is needed for the school to attain its goals.	The school lacks a mission, vision, or shared understanding of core values. Work needs to be completed to establish guiding principles, shared directions, valued futures, and identification of goals and objectives to achieve communal outcomes.
Instruction, Curriculum, and Assessment (PSEL Standard 4)	Instruction, curriculum, and assessment supports student learning. The school is achieving goals and objectives. Yet, there is a sense that more could be done to capitalize on the foundation that has been laid. Now is the time to think about new programs, practices, and policies. What is the next step for growth? How can you ignite thinking to take the school to the next level?	Instruction, curriculum, and assessment practices are coherent and aligned. Ongoing data is collected to inform teaching and learning decisions. Best practices can be observed in classrooms across the building. Students and parents are clear about learning goals and progress. Ongoing work is focused on maintaining high-quality practice.	Instruction, curriculum, and assessment efforts lack solid alignment across the school. Some areas may excel but others lag. Work needs to be done to develop communal understandings concerning what practices best serve all students. Focus needs to be on additional professional learning to support teachers and their students.

continued . . .

At this juncture, leadership efforts are focused on . . .			
	Revitalization	Maintenance	Establishing
School Community Involvement and Engagement (PSEL Standard 8)	The school, community, and families work well together toward shared goals and outcomes. Participation is at record levels and outcomes address students' academic and personal well-being. Now is the time to think big— what partnerships might be further developed? Who could be included that is not currently part of your effort?	Work needs to be done to fine tune the relationships that are already in place and productive. Reaching out to include new partners may be the focus this year or reaching out to include current partners in deeper, more aligned ways to support student learning and well-being has potential to solidify current work in new ways.	School community engagement needs attention. While some parents participate, others do not. Uneven participation hampers the school's efforts to enhance student learning and well-being. Setting a goal for even one additional project has the potential to provide big gains.
School Culture, Climate, and Internal Community (PSEL Standard 7)	Teachers, staff, and leadership are clear about the ways things get done in the school. Shared values are clear yet, it is possible to push the edges even further. What new shared foci might be developed? How might the faculty and staff become even more committed to shared values and norms of professional practice?	Members of the school community work in coherent and aligned ways. Core values are understood and shared. When disagreement arises, it is productive and serves to further reinforce who we are and the ways we do things.	Strong cultures exist in some pockets of the school but not others. Coherent understandings about who we are need to be developed, as does clarity concerning what we value and who we are.
Equity and Inclusion (PSEL Standard 3)	A focus on equity informs decisions making. Faculty and staff share a common commitment to and definition of equity and work together as a team to enhance opportunities for all	Discussions concerning equity are honest and open. As a team teachers, staff, and leadership continue to make practices, policies, and procedures fair to and for all students. There may	Equity is still a hard topic for whole staff discussion. It may be too charged, too political, or too difficult to approach for any number of contextual reasons. Focus needs to be on working toward

continued . . .

At this juncture, leadership efforts are focused on . . .

	Revitalization	Maintenance	Establishing
	students. Are there new projects that might be developed? Might your equity agenda be a more central part of the school's work with others in the broader community?	be work to still complete but most members are committed to working on these goals.	small wins so that a larger agenda can be set.
Ongoing Innovation, Improvement, and Reform (PSEL Standard 10)	The school has been good enough for quite a long time. Members are satisfied with where they are but know it is possible to break out and become more. What might a new vision include? What could motivate others to become engaged with new work? How might students and families benefit from those efforts?	Data is used to develop goals and objectives for communal work. Clarity about goals and the activities needed to meet those goals exists. It is a matter of getting the work done so that results can be achieved.	Improvement efforts have stagnated. Members are uncertain how ambitious goals might be met or their role in meeting them. Focus needs to be on re-centering faculty and staff around the purposes of their work and the ways their effort contributes to the greater whole.

RESOURCES

Here are resources designed to inspire and strengthen your leadership muscle. As has been noted throughout this volume, leadership is not a spectator activity, nor is it for the timid. Yet, it is possible to lead and to lead well even in challenging times. Offered here are some recommendations designed to support your work.

TED Talks: www.ted.com

As you are probably aware, TED talks are short (18 minutes or less) speeches that focus attention on topics of controversy, interest, and significance. They are designed so that a clear message is delivered. TED talks are long enough to be serious and short enough to hold people's attention. Happily, they fit easily into a meeting or a lunchbreak. TED includes considerable research-based offerings and plenty of inspirational presentations. The Web page is

continued . . .

updated often and it is also quite readily searched (look for leadership or education as key words). Additionally, in many cases, a reading list is offered to support your future learning.

Here are a few leadership favorites:

- Adam Grant: *Are you a giver or a taker*—This TED talk summarizes the key themes from his 2013 book *Give and take: Why helping others drives our success*, and focuses on the power of promoting a culture of generosity in the workplace. The talk offers a great introduction into thinking about how work can be structured in ways that support others and sustain ourselves as a result of that effort. www.ted.com/talks/adam_grant_are_you_a_giver_or_a_taker
- Adam Galinsky: *How to speak up for yourself*—This talk also summarizes recent writing, in this case, Galinsky and Schweitzer's 2015 book *Friend & foe: When to cooperate, when to compete and how to succeed at both*. Focusing on how to hold professional dialogue and conversation, this talk examines the ways in which power is developed, trust is built and repaired, and how to diffuse workplace conflict and bias. www.ted.com/talks/adam_galinsky_how_to_speak_up_for_yourself
- Julia Galef: *Why you think you're right—even when you're wrong*—Galef, the founder of the non-profit Center for Applied Rationality (http://rationality.org) and host of the podcast Rationally Speaking (http://rationallyspeaking.org), explores the motivations behind why we believe what we believe. Galef offers suggestions for working with others who get dug in and how to avoid those traps ourselves. www.ted.com/talks/julia_galef_why_you_think_you_re_right_even_if_you_re_wrong
- Tom Wujec: *Got a wicked problem? First let me tell you how to make toast*—Wujec offers a great leadership exercise in this TED talk about drawing toast. He offers insights into what he has learned from doing this exercise with thousands of people and the ways in which how these drawings tell us about how people solve problems and think about communication. This talk offers a great back to school faculty and staff activity to set the stage for decision making work. (See also www.drawtoast.com where you can also sign up for his newsletter.) www.ted.com/talks/tom_wujec_got_a_wicked_problem_first_tell_me_how_you_make_toast
- Dan Ariely: *What makes us feel good about our work?*—Ariely, author of *Predictably irrational: The hidden forces that shape our decisions and Payoff: The hidden logic that shapes our motivations*, explores why people persist and make meaning from the work they choose to do. His thinking offers insights into how leadership can motivate those around them to engage with hard tasks and respond to challenge and difficulty. www.ted.com/talks/dan_ariely_what_makes_us_feel_good_about_our_work

continued . . .

99U: http://99u.com

TED is not alone in the online short talk world. Several other sites exist and among them 99U is one of the best. 99U focuses on "empowering the creative community" and like TED, offers conferences to connect creatives (e.g., graphic designers and architects) to like-minded individuals. Unlike TED talks that offer multiple topics and themes, 99U focuses solely on five categories—careers, collaboration, the creative process, productivity, and psychology. The talks tend to be a bit longer than TED talks, but they are equally engaging and thought-provoking. The weekly featured video is worth checking out. Among our favorites are:

- Heidi Grant Halvorson: *Why no one understands you (and what to do about it)*—Grant Halvorson focuses on misunderstanding in the 24-minute piece. The co-author of *Focus: Using different ways of seeing the world for success and influence*, Grant Halvorson offers insights into the obstacles that derail us as we work toward goals we value as well as things we can do to get our point across when it matters. http://99u.com/videos/51854/heidi-grant-halvorson-why-no-one-understands-you-and-what-to-do-about-it
- Kristy Tillman: *Inviting yourself to the table*—Technically, this talk is about career choices and changes, but it has import for leaders who are trying to foster change. Tillman, who works for the Society of Grownups (yes, it really does exist—www.societyofgrownups.com), a financial literacy concern that focuses on ways to take advantage of the opportunities that present themselves in the workplace and how we can make our own opportunities. Society of Grownups also has great financial education resources for students. http://99u.com/videos/53998/kristy-tillman-inviting-yourself-to-the-table

Readings

We wouldn't be good academics if we didn't leave you with a few readings worth looking into.

- *Design-based school improvement: A practical guide for education leaders.* Written by Rick Mintrop, this excellent volume takes a design development approach to thinking about school improvement work. Design thinking has long been popular in fields outside of education. Mintrop's case-based volume brings the best of those ideas and applies them to issues such as identifying practical problems, assessing evidence of outcomes, accounting for variability in implementation and results, and establishing a foundation for broader understanding of the problem and proposed solutions.
- *Coherence: The right drivers in action for schools, districts, and systems.* Veteran education author Michael Fullan pairs with Joanne Quinn in the

continued . . .

excellent volume designed to motivate leaders to action. The team focuses on developing focused direction, collaborative cultures, deep learning, and accountability as drivers for success. We have discussed many of these themes in this text and we recommend Fullan and Quinn for additional clarity into these ideas.

- *Hard conversations unpacked: The who's, the why's, and the what-ifs.* A follow-up to *Having hard conversations*, this book delves into the ways in which communication can get messy and how to handle difficult conversations in schools with skill and ease. Jennifer Abrams explores how organizational dynamics, communicative clarity, and internal politics impact leaders' work. Abrams also addresses how to be a better recipient of feedback and offers possible responses for use during tough times. Unlike more general texts on communication, Abrams uses school examples and research from school settings in her discussion, making the text particularly school and district leader friendly.

REFERENCES

Abrams, J. (2009). *Having hard conversations*. Thousand Oaks, CA: Corwin.

Abrams, J. (2016). *Hard conversations unpacked: The who's, the why's, and the what-ifs.* Thousand Oaks, CA: Corwin.

Argyris, C. (1992). *On organizational learning*. Boston, MA: Blackwell.

Ariely, D. (2009). *Predictably irrational: The hidden forces that shape our decisions*. New York: HarperCollins.

Ariely, D. (2016). *Payoff: The hidden logic that shapes our motivations*. New York: Simon & Schuster.

Block, P. (1993). *Stewardship: Choosing service over self-interest*. San Francisco, CA: Berrett-Koehler.

Block, P. (2008). *Community: The structure of belonging*. San Francisco, CA: Berrett-Koehler.

Bush, T. (2013). Distributed leadership: The model of choice in the 21st century. *Educational Management Administration & Leadership, 41*(5), 543–544.

Cohen, M.D. (2007). Reading Dewey: Reflections on the study of routine. *Organization Studies, 28*(5), 773–786.

Day, C., Gu, Q., & Sammons, P. (2016). The impact of leadership on student outcomes: How successful school leaders use transformational and instructional strategies to make a difference. *Educational Administration Quarterly, 52*(2), 221–258.

Dinkelman, T. (2003). Self-study in teacher education: A means and ends tool for promoting reflective teaching. *Journal of Teacher Education, 54*(1), 6–18.

DiPaola, M., & Tschannen-Moran, M. (2003). The principalship at a crossroads: A study of the conditions and concerns of principals. *NASSP Bulletin, 87*(634), 43–61.

Evans, K.G. (2000). Reclaiming John Dewey: Democracy, inquiry, pragmatism, and public management. *Administration & Society, 32*(3), 308–328.

Feger, S., & Arruda, E. (2008). *Professional learning communities: Key themes from the literature.* Providence, RI: The Education Alliance.

Field, R.D., Tobin, R.M., & Reese-Weber, M. (2014). Agreeableness, social self-efficacy, and conflict resolution strategies. *Journal of Individual Differences, 35*(2), 95–102.

Fullan, M., & Quinn, J. (2016). *Coherence: The right drivers in action for schools, districts, and systems.* Thousand Oaks, CA: Corwin Press.

Galinsky, A., & Schweitzer, M. (2015). *Friend & foe: When to cooperate, when to compete and how to succeed at both.* New York: Crown Random House.

Grant, A., (2013). *Give and take: Why helping others drives our success.* New York: Penguin Books.

Grant Halvorson, H., & Higgins, E.T. (2014). *Focus: Using different ways of seeing the world for success and influence.* New York: Penguin Books.

Greenleaf, R.K. (1977). *Servant leadership: A journey into the nature of legitimate power and greatness.* New York: Paulist Press.

Hallinger, P. (2005). Instructional leadership and the school principal: A passing fancy that refuses to fade away. *Leadership and Policy in Schools, 4,* 221–239.

Hoy, W.K. (2003). An analysis of enabling and mindful school structures: Some theoretical, research and practical considerations. *Journal of Educational Administration, 41*(1), 87–108.

Huggins, K.S., Scheurich, J.J., & Morgan, J.R. (2011). Professional learning communities as a leadership strategy to drive math success in an urban high school serving diverse, low-income students: A case study. *Journal of Education for Students Placed at Risk, 16*(2), 67–88.

Jenlink, P.M. (2008). Reconceptualizing curriculum studies in educational leadership as bricolage. *Journal of Curriculum & Pedagogy, 5*(2), 35–58.

Kruse, S.D. (2009). *Working smart: Problem-solving strategies for school leaders.* New York: Rowman & Littlefield.

Kruse, S.D., & Johnson, B.L. (2017). Tempering the normative demands of PLCs with the organizational realities of life in schools: Exploring the cognitive dilemmas faced by educational leaders. *Educational Management Administration & Leadership, 45*(4) 588–604.

Kruse, S.D., & Louis, K.S. (2009). *Building strong school cultures: A guide to leading change.* Thousand Oaks, CA: Corwin Press.

Langer, E. (2009). *Mindfulness.* Jackson, TN: Perseus Books.

Leithwood, K., & Mascall, B. (2008). Collective leadership effects on student achievement. *Educational Administration Quarterly, 44*(4), 529–561.

Little, J.W. (1990). The persistence of privacy: Autonomy and initiative in teachers' professional relations. *Teachers College Record, 91*(4), 509–536.

Louis, K. S. (2006). Changing the culture of schools: Professional community, organizational learning, and trust. *Journal of School Leadership, 16*(5), 477–489.

Mayrowetz, D., Murphy, J., Louis, K.S., & Smylie, M. (2007). Distributed leadership as work redesign: Retrofitting the job characteristics model. *Educational Policy and Leadership, 6*(1), 69–103.

Mintrop, R. (2016). *Design-based school improvement: A practical guide for education leaders.* Cambridge, MA: Harvard Education Press.

Murphy, J. (2013). *The architecture of school improvement: Lessons learned.* Thousand Oaks, CA: Corwin Press.

Parris, D.L., & Peachey, J.W. (2013). A systematic literature review of servant leadership theory in organizational contexts. *Journal of Business Ethics, 113*(3), 377–393.

Schein, E. (2013). *Humble inquiry: The gentle art of asking instead of telling*. San Francisco, CA: Berrett-Koehler.

Smylie, M.A. (2010). *Continuous school improvement*. Thousand Oaks, CA: Corwin.

Stoll, L., & Louis, K.S. (2007). *Professional learning communities: Divergence, detail and difficulties*. London: Swets & Zeitlinger.

Tian, M., Risku, M., & Collin, K. (2017). A meta-analysis of distributed leadership from 2001 to 2013: Theory development, empirical evidence, and future research focus. *Educational Management, Administration, & Leadership*, 44(1), 146–164.

Urick, A. (2016). Examining US principal perception of multiple leadership styles used to practice shared instructional leadership. *Journal of Educational Administration*, 54(2), 152–172.

Vogus, T., & Sutcliffe, K. (2012). Organizational mindfulness and mindful organization: A reconciliation and path forward. *Academy of Management Learning and Education*, 11(4), 722–735.

Weick, K.E., (2002). Puzzles in organizational learning: An exercise in disciplined imagination. *British Journal of Management*, 13(2), 7–15.

Weick, K.E., & Sutcliffe, K. (2001). *Managing the unexpected: Assuring high performance in an age of complexity*. San Francisco, CA: Jossey-Bass.

Weick, K.E., Sutcliffe, K., & Obstfeld, D. (1999). Organizing for high reliability: Processes of collective mindfulness. In Sutton, R.S., & Staw, B.M. (Eds.). *Research in organizational behavior* (pp. 81–124). Stanford, CA: Jai Press.

Whitford, J. (2002). Pragmatism and the untenable dualism of means and ends: Why rational choice theory does not deserve paradigmatic privilege. *Theory and Society*, 31, 325–363.

Index

Note: The Index uses US spelling. Page numbers in **bold** refer to Tables.

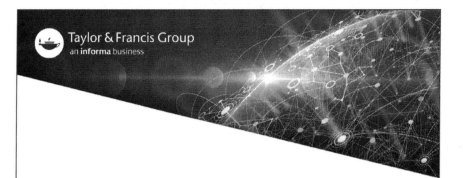

Made in the USA
Columbia, SC
23 October 2022

69882678R00120